Adorno's Poetics of Critique

Continuum Studies in Continental Philosophy
Series Editor: James Fieser, University of Tennessee at Martin, USA

Continuum Studies in Continental Philosophy is a major monograph series
from Continuum. The series features first-class scholarly research
monographs across the field of Continental philosophy. Each work makes
a major contribution to the field of philosophical research.

Adorno's Poetics of Critique

Steven Helmling

continuum

Continuum International Publishing Group
The Tower Building   80 Maiden Lane
11 York Road   Suite 704
London SE1 7NX   New York NY 10038

www.continuumbooks.com

British Library Cataloguing-in-Publication Data
A catalogue record for this book is available from the British Library.

ISBN-10: HB: 0-8264-4688-4
ISBN-13: HB: 978-0-8264-4688-6

Library of Congress Cataloging-in-Publication Data
Helmling, Steven, 1947–
    Adorno's poetics of critique / Steven Helmling.
      p. cm.
    Includes bibliographical references.
    ISBN 978-0-8264-4688-6
1. Adorno, Theodor W., 1903–1969. 2. Critical theory. I. Title.

B3199.A34H45 2009
193—dc22

                      2008034120

Typeset by Newgen Imaging Systems Pvt Ltd, Chennai, India
Printed and bound in the UK by the MPG Books Group

For
EYAL AMIRAN

Contents

Acknowledgments

The author is grateful to Columbia University Press for permission to quote Theodor W. Adorno, *Notes on Literature*, two volumes (trans. Shierry Weber Nicholsen. New York: Columbia UP, 1992); to MIT Press for permission to quote from T. W. Adorno, *Prisms* (trans. Samuel and Shierry Weber, 1981); to Stanford University Press for permission to quote from T. W. Adorno, *Beethoven: The Philosophy of Music* (ed. Rolf Tiedemann; trans. Edmund Jephcott, 1998); and to Verso, for permission to quote from Max Horkheimer and T. W. Adorno, *Dialectic of Enlightenment* (trans. John Cumming. New York: Continuum, 1988).

Earlier versions of some sections of this book have appeared as follows:

'How to Read Adorno on How to Read Hegel'. *Postmodern Culture*, v. 17. n. 2 (January 2007). http://muse.jhu.edu/journals/pmc/v017/17.2helmling.html

'Adorno's Taboo—and Its Transgression'. *Transgression and Taboo: Critical Essays*, ed. Vartan Messier and Nandita Batra (Mayaguez, PR: College English Association/ Caribbean Chapter Publications, 2005), 79–94.

'"Immanent Critique" and "Dialectical Mimesis" in Adorno and Horkheimer's *Dialectic of Enlightenment*'. *Boundary 2*, v. 32, n. 3 (Fall 2005), 97–117. http://boundary2. dukejournals.org/cgi/reprint/32/3/97.pdf

'"During Auschwitz": Adorno, Hegel, and the Unhappy Consciousness of Critique'. *Postmodern Culture*, v. 15, n. 2 (May 2005). http://muse.jhu.edu/journals/ postmodern_culture/v015/15.2helmling.html

'Constellation and Critique: Adorno's "Constellation", Benjamin's "Dialectical Image"'. *Postmodern Culture*, v. 14, n. 1 (September 2003). http://www3.iath. virginia.edu/pmc/text-only/issue.903/14.1helmling.txt

A Note on References, Translations, and Translation

All references are in the text; for a key to the abbreviations used for Adorno's works, and full bibliographical citations for other authors and titles, see the 'Works Cited'.

I've (mostly) assumed a German-less reader who encounters Adorno in translation. All of Adorno's major texts, and many minor ones too, have been translated, some of them more than once—though the magnum opus most deserving and most in need of retranslation, *Negative Dialectics*, remains as yet available only in a version (E. B. Ashton's of 1973) that all agree is inadequate (see, e.g., Fredric Jameson's comment in *Late Marxism* ix–x). When more than one translation was available, I've opted for the newer one over the earlier, with one minor and one major exception. This project was near completion when Robert Hullot-Kentor's retranslation of *Philosophie der neuen Musik* appeared in 2006, displacing the Mitchell and Blomster version of 1973 (for full bibliographic details, see Adorno's 'Works Cited', keyed '*PMM*' and '*PNM*'). I have adopted the Hullot-Kentor version except for one passage, for reasons explained in the text. At the other end of the process, when I *started* the writing that became this book, John Cumming's 1972 translation was the only English version of *Dialectic of Enlightenment* extant.* In 2002, Stanford University Press published a new translation by Edmund Jephcott, and I adopted the newer version. (Again, see Adorno's 'Works Cited', keys 'Cumming' and 'Jephcott'.) But I found that particular figures of speech and the like that I wanted to discuss survived into Cumming's English better than into Jephcott's. I found myself citing both, and explaining my preference for the Cumming—it was often a useful way to sharpen a point, and a few such passages remain—but eventually I just reverted to Cumming. Apart from particular word-choices and fidelity to the text's figuration, Cumming's text sounds to my 'reading ear' more energetic and (fruitfully) 'difficult' than Jephcott's—in short, I agree with Fredric Jameson that Cumming's *Dialectic of Enlightenment* 'has a stronger German accent' than other

---

* Robert Hullot-Kentor translates and introduces 'Excursus I' of *Dialectic of Enlightenment* as 'Odysseus or Myth and Enlightenment', in *New German Critique* 56 (Spring–Summer 1992): 101–42.

translations of Adorno (*Late Marxism* ix; note, though, that Jameson was writing a decade before Jephcott's translation appeared).

Cumming is inconsistent in capitalizing 'Enlightenment', and so am I. Insofar as there's a 'rule', I capitalize 'Enlightenment' when the referent is the eighteenth-century intellectual ferment associated with Voltaire, Hume, Kant, etc.; I make it small-e 'enlightenment' when the meaning is rather the more general idea of the intellectual progress of humankind. For Adorno, this isn't an ambiguity to be neatly resolved, but a symptomatic 'equivocation' to be critically exploited—to highlight, for (one) example, how bourgeois society universalized, i.e., de-historicized, a self-consciously self-historicizing intellectual movement (the one indeed that inaugurated 'historicizing' as such), Enlightenment itself. A 'rule' for capitalizing 'enlightenment', then, would contravene Adorno's strategic 'equivocation'. But this is a problem, the German-less reader should be advised, only in English, because German usage capitalizes all nouns, '*Aufklärung*' (enlightenment) of course included, thus preserving the equivocation that English typographical convention would resolve.

The German-less reader might welcome a few further tips: one of Adorno's most potent scare-words, 'domination', is '*Herrschaft*' in German—as in Hegel's '*Herrschaft und Knechtschaft*', the rubric for what English-speakers usually call the 'master/slave' motif from the *Phenomenology*. Both translators of the *Phenomenology*, A. V. Miller and J. B. Baillie, render '*Herrschaft und Knechtschaft*' as 'Lordship and Bondage', and the two antagonists as 'lord' and 'bondsman'; Baillie sometimes translates '*Herr*' as 'master'. The point: in German, Adorno's '*Herrschaft*' and such cognates as '*herrschen*', '*beherrschen*', '*Beherrschung*', etc., echo Hegel in a way that the English 'domination' misses.

Translations of Adorno render '*der Begriff*' as 'the concept'; translations of Hegel (both Miller and Baillie at least) render it as 'the Notion'—which connotes, to my American ear, a dime-store trinket; more substantively I want readers to keep the Hegelian resonances of Adorno's vocabulary in mind; so when I quote Hegel adverting to 'the Notion', I insert 'the concept' in brackets. (Observe, again, the capitalization problem.) Relatedly, an important word (sc. concept) in Hegel and Adorno both is 'speculative', which connotes 'dialectical', 'self-conscious', and 'conceptualizing' in distinction from 'reflective', which (usually, but not always) connotes literal-mindedness, naive mistaking of perception for fact, of words for things, of ideas for reality, etc. The English 'speculative' often renders the German '*spekulativ*', but often enough the German is '*begreifend*' (the present participle of '*begreifen*', to conceive) in which the cognate with '*Begriff*' is visible (Cf. '*begreiflich*', '*begreifbar*', etc.).

Introduction:
Adorno's Poetics of Critique

. . . I at any rate think it the task of philosophical discourse to attempt as far as possible to express as discourse—in other words, through the form in which it is presented—something of the content it wishes to convey. It is an essential feature of philosophy that form and content cannot be separated from each other . . .

—*Adorno* (PMP *23*)

Form and Content

This book is about how Adorno writes, and why, and with what effects. Everyone agrees that Adorno's writing is 'difficult', and that the difficulty is deliberate; but most commentary then goes on to set the difficulty of the writing aside in order to facilitate your access to Adorno's difficult arguments and positions.[1] I want to do the reverse: to foreground the deliberate difficulty of Adorno's prose, to *read* it, to inquire into its meanings and its motivations, to ask what Adorno's arguments and positions look like when considered not as a content for which the writing is a mere vehicle, but rather as consubstantial with the writing, *produced* by it, ineluctably conditioned by the twists and turns and turmoils of a self-consciously and motivatedly agitated prose—a prose that foregrounds its signifiers in multifarious ways, which Adorno usually evoked (as in the epigraph above) in the word 'form'.

Like many modern problems, the relation of form and content has a long pedigree. Adorno is modernist in aligning with Aristotle and Hegel, as against Plato and Kant, in the view that form and content are immanent rather than transcendent to each other: that every content dictates or generates or emanates its own distinctive form, and complementarily that form itself carries meaning, even makes (or breaks) meaning, such that form becomes a kind or an aspect or a level or a moment—indeed, an *agent*—of content. As often happens with such philosophical positions or positings, we may hesitate whether to take them descriptively or prescriptively—or, to put it in a vocabulary Adorno never used, constatively or performatively. Adorno's writings about language deconstruct (another anachronism) the opposition of constative to performative (in Adorno's terminology, of 'representation' to 'negation') in a way to sublate the former entirely into the latter. But more immediately, on every page, the high affective voltages of Adorno's writing, whatever other polemical objects they cathect, always obey, and often enough explicitly urge, the imperative, binding on both art *and* philosophy, to achieve a productive, meaning-making tension (not an organic unity, harmony, or identity) between form and content.

Primary among the aims of this book is to foreground how insistently and how self-consciously Adorno prescribes such a poetics of critique, proposing not only *what* critique should do, but *how*—it being understood that the question of *how* is where theory realizes itself in, or as, or to the extent of, its tension with practice. Specifically, of writing practice: not by precept only, but also by example, Adorno urges a kind of writing that goes by many aliases: philosophy, theory, critique, among others. In Adorno's oftenest-read and most explicit manifesto on these questions, the alias is the titular 'Essay as Form', which, Adorno advises,

> works emphatically at the form of its presentation. Consciousness of the non-identity of presentation and subject matter forces presentation to unremitting efforts. In this alone the essay resembles art (*NL1* 18).

NB: *resembles* art: does not *become* art: again, the non-identity, the tension, is the point. The 'essay' resembles art 'in this alone' (that is, in a certain self-consciousness as to form): in Adorno's poetics or aesthetics of critique, an art-like semblance ('*das Künstähnliche*' [*GS11* 26]) is a constant and emphatic provocation.

It is that provocation—that performative contradiction—that I foreground throughout this book. But let's be clear that there is no question here of 'aestheticizing' Adorno, if that would mean reducing his work to a kind of critical poetry, to be admired for its verbal brilliance, but discountable as 'pseudo-statement', with no validity as truth-claim. 'Philosophy', Adorno advises, 'is neither a science nor the "cogitative poetry" to which positivists would degrade it in a stupid oxymoron' (*ND* 109). Just such a reduction of the aesthetic has been the usual empiricist, positivist, scientific, 'dialectic of enlightenment' way of keeping art in its place—and not only art: religion, philosophy, and other such 'humane' or 'unscientific' discourses (sc. 'language games') as well. Adorno regarded this 'enlightened' compact as utterly ideological, and his combat against it was career-long. *Aesthetic Theory*, his magnum opus on the problem, left unfinished at his death but clearly meant as capstone to his oeuvre, can be summarized as a ringing vindication of the truth-claim of the aesthetic. Which gives point to Michael Cahn's suggestion that its title should be understood on the model of the phrase 'critical theory' (Cahn 42): *Aesthetic Theory* is not merely a theory (and a critique) *of* 'the aesthetic', it is also a theorizing critique that aspires to *be* 'aesthetic'—aesthetic in all the enlarged senses whose 'truth content' (*Wahrheitsgehalt*) Adorno pushes for so passionately in the book itself.

Adorno's aesthetic theory is every bit as critical as anything else in his critical theory.

Adorno's bid to rehabilitate the aesthetic has been a central theme in the revival of interest that has brought his reputation back, in the last generation, from its nadir following the May '68 events at Frankfurt, when Adorno as rector of the university called in police to remove student demonstrators. But even Adorno's admirers can't quite conclude that Adorno has laid the question of 'the ideology of the aesthetic' entirely to rest. Adorno's onetime protégé, Jürgen Habermas, judged Adorno's practice in *Dialectic of Enlightenment* and elsewhere more a lapse into that ideology than a critique of it (*Philosophical Discourse of Modernity* 106–30); in this he was seconded by Albrecht Wellmer and others. Lambert Zuidervaart's extensive study of *Aesthetic Theory* is more dispassionate, but generally finds Adorno's claims for the political force (sc. 'truth') of art more asserted than proven; Peter Bürger's limited defense of Adorno's aesthetics is similarly grudging. Terry Eagleton's chapter on Adorno in *The Ideology of the Aesthetic* doesn't even consider exempting Adorno from the book's *donnée* that the aesthetic as such simply *is* ideology. Granted, the ideology-problem has constructed itself in such a way that virtually by definition, 'ideological closure' can *not* be breached; and commentators on Adorno's aesthetic theory can't help making it sound like a failure even when they are sympathetic to it. Eagleton isn't wrong when he says that Adorno has a 'compact with failure' (349); on the contrary, Adorno's construction of the problem indicts the very notion that critique in a bad time might aspire to anything that could be called 'success'. Adorno's model of 'immanent critique' spurns any aim to get *outside* 'ideological closure'; rather the task is to find or invent the needful 'truth(s)' that conditions inside the prison-house of ideology are all but consciously constructed to rule out. For Adorno, getting *outside* those conditions would put you out of touch with just the truth the prison-house needs. As if getting outside it were even possible!—or desirable, for where else to seek the truth of the prison-house than inside the prison-house? Where else to engage the adversary than where the adversary lives? For Adorno, the failure to overcome ideology is part of the 'objective' situation critique must enact—indeed, must suffer.

Which is only to say that for Adorno critique, too, is bound to the ethos of the 'broken promise' (Stendhal's *promesse de bonheur*) that he prescribes for art; Adorno's oft-noted *Bilderverbot* on utopia is likewise meant to enforce critique's renunciation of any premature consolation ('imaginary solution to a real contradiction')—e.g., in Adorno's own day, the assurance, 'official' on the left, that history must end in the 'inevitable' triumph of Socialism. Jameson, Jay, Nicholsen, Bernstein, Hullot-Kentor—all have written more sympathetically and with more generosity to Adorno's hopes than most, but neither they, nor I, nor anyone else can offer a better solution to Adorno's problem than Adorno did, because Adorno's point is that the problem can *not* be 'solved'—and that very impossibility is the condition, the 'truth', of everything that art, and critique too, must labor to evoke. Hence Adorno's most ardent defenders can seem to agree with his most incisive detractors that his gambit amounts to declaring defeat and refusing to move on. Adorno's account of the aesthetic persists as problematic not because Adorno failed to 'solve' the problem, but because he so brilliantly dramatized—amplified, complexified, agitated, accomplished—its problematization.

It's this power of problematization—the performative contradiction of Adorno's 'compact with failure'—that I want to foreground in this study, and as textual effect of his writing every bit as much as a thetic or theoretic commitment. Adorno's writing is 'difficult' very much in the modernist way, as enactment of the 'difficulty' of the political, philosophical, aesthetic (etc.) problems it engages. But to a degree unusual even in 'difficult' modernism, Adorno makes things harder by keeping his writing practice in tension, even in antagonism (or 'negative dialectic') with, his argued theory or positions. ('Consciousness of the non-identity of presentation and subject matter forces presentation to unremitting efforts' [*NL1* 18].) Hence at least my own frequent experience, after consulting helpful expositions of Adorno's 'thought' or 'ideas', only to undergo renewed bewilderment on return to Adorno's own text. Habermas, Wellmer, Zuidervaart, and many others have judged Adorno's *theory* of the aesthetic; Jameson, Jay, Nicholsen, and Hullot-Kentor have, more sympathetically, acceded to Adorno's insistence that the writing of critique must perform, must enact or test, what it argues; but in all of these critics, the interest and energy of discussion flow in the direction of Adorno's argued positions—as if *what* Adorno is saying were, 'in the last analysis', the point of the exercise. My procedure here is the reverse: each chapter surveys Adorno's thinking about some crux or array of problems, then moves to a detailed reading of a text that sets the relevant tensions and contradictions into conflicted interaction. The aim is not to discount Adorno's 'theory' in favor of his (writing) 'practice', but rather to foreground how the writing conditions, produces, qualifies, volatilizes received and reified concepts and arguments; and attempts to resist in advance their relapse into reification, into fixed, stable, portable take-aways of the type that so quickly become shortcuts to an ersatz already-thought, rather than relays, stimuli, events in and provocations to an unfinished, unfinishable activity of thinking.

Adorno's writing is a constant polemic against the 'administered world' of his period, whether manifested in liberal capitalism, statist fascism, or (dubiously) revolutionary Comintern communism. The scope and complexity of these and their concomitant problems is vast, and might seem to dwarf the question of how critique should be written. But for Adorno, it is the urgency of those vast catastrophes that makes the writing of critique itself so urgent. 'Criticism', he insists, 'has power only to the extent to which every successful or unsuccessful sentence has something to do with the fate of humankind' (*NL2* 307). Hence the emphasis on how (to adapt Gertrude Stein) the writing of critique should be written. A virtually constant subtext of Adorno's polemic is about how works of spirit—art or philosophy—should be done or made. How things should be done or made is a question of poetics (Greek *poeisis*, 'making'), and hence the title of this book. Calling it the 'Aesthetics of Critique' would have bidden defiance, in Adorno's own spirit, to all who would enforce against Adorno the charge of lapsing into 'the ideology of the aesthetic'; but obviously, I have opted for 'Poetics of Critique' instead, and want to say a few words about why.

Aesthetics and Poetics

The most immediate liability of 'the aesthetic'—just the word—is that in English, at least, it has long connoted 'the beautiful'. When Kant invoked 'the sublime' in the Third Critique, it was to delineate the limit of the beautiful: to illuminate the beautiful by contrast with its other, with what the beautiful was not. Adorno disparaged the rhetoric of the sublime ('the twaddle of culture religion', he called it [*AT* 198]), but he scorned the beautiful—Brecht's 'culinary'—even more. His own rhetoric of 'shock', 'horror', and 'ugliness' is fundamental to his aesthetic theory (*AT* 244–6, 319–24, 45–50), and equally to his critical theory: it is, after all, an ugly and shocking world out there—and of course more so in Adorno's period than in ours.

Not that 'poetics' has any better purchase than 'aesthetics' on such crypto-sublimities; moreover, to the extent that the etymology of 'making' implies contrivance and 'effect', 'poetics' might connote instrumental mastery (*Herrschaft*) of just the sort Adorno's modernist shock aims to disrupt and disown. But 'poetics' suggests much better than 'aesthetics' Adorno's hands-on sense of the writing—writing as a labor, an activity, a practice—of critique. In Lukácsean terms, 'aesthetic' connotes (Kantian) contemplation; 'poetics' suggests (Hegelian) work—an activity at once action and passion, as in Hegel's 'labor and suffering of the negative'. (Recall Hegel's aside on labor as 'desire held in check' [*Phenomenology* 118]—a condition definitive of the slave, not the master.) The emphasis on 'labor' accords with Adorno's preoccupation with questions of 'production' rather than 'reception', it being understood that in Adorno, 'production' implies not the artist/author/critic as culture-hero 'master', but rather the process by which a never-concluded struggle between an opposing (critical) self overmatched in agon with the cultural predicament at large generates evidences of its working-through in works of art and critique. If Adorno's febrile tone often, in effect, reinscribes the culture-hero atmospherics nominally under ban, that is another symptom, effect, or performative contradiction of the conflicted and agitated textuality I mean to highlight in this study.

But my most substantive reasons for preferring 'poetics' to 'aesthetics' are hinted in the speech-act terminology I've already borrowed from J. L. Austin's *How to Do Things With Words*: for Adorno, critique is 'performative', an attempt at intervention in the cultural situation, not 'constative' in the sense of aspiring to an accurate or adequate 'representation' of a state of affairs presumed to be given in advance, external and prior to the critic or the critique. This, most simply, is what Adorno means by 'immanent' as opposed to 'external' or 'transcendent' critique. Austin's donnish sangfroid, as different as can be from Adorno's heat, has perhaps narcotized the implication of his title, that what matters is how to '*do* things', not merely 'represent' (or 'constate') them, with words. Such a sense of language as transitive, transformative, performative, projects language (and critique, and its making, its poetics: the writing) as a kind of action, makes it 'symbolic action' in a sense that needn't belittlingly mean *merely* (or 'nothing but') symbolic. Adorno's 'compact with failure' (Eagleton 349) or 'will to powerlessness' (Niethammer 138–42) manifests in Adorno's insistence on arts's (and critique's) refusal of 'domination', which is to say of power itself—an ethos that my talk here of transitivity and symbolic action aims, 'dialectically', to contravene: another performative contradiction transmitting its conflicted energies to Adorno's difficult and agitated writing. I intend 'poetics of critique' to evoke Adorno's theory-and-practice of critique as deed, as action, as 'negation': critical writing as something *done* as well as *made*. Hence Adorno's constant insistence that in critique, the writing matters, on the premise that the language, the verbal embodiment, in which critique achieves its expression—its 'form', as in the epigraph above—is the measure and the authentication of its critical, performative effectivity. Which is to say that the formula, 'How critique should be done or made', implies also, 'What critique should (try to) do or make or make happen'. The ambition of Adorno's performative critique involves not only how critique should be performed, but what functions critique itself might perform, what social work or symbolic action it might do, what dereifications its critical negations might attempt.

If 'aesthetics' is to 'poetics' (roughly) as 'theory' is to 'practice', then 'Poetics of Critique' puts the emphasis where I want it, on Adorno's practice, *not* (again) in opposition to his theory, but as its enactment: its test, its interrogation, its realization. The proof of that pudding will be in the reading: close readings, as specific and detailed as I can make them, of 'difficult' passages from Adorno's most potent and effective text, the *Dialectic of Enlightenment* that he co-authored with Max Horkheimer in American exile during the darkest days of World War Two. Each of my chapters recurs to *Dialectic of Enlightenment* because in that book Adorno most resourcefully (and critically) *performs* the aesthetic theory most commentary considers as merely argued. And it does so, as I've suggested, in a thoroughly modernist way. I don't shrink from putting it that, as a piece of writing, *Dialectic of Enlightenment* is not only Adorno's most devious, 'difficult', and challenging text, but a modernist masterpiece that demands, and repays, the kind of attention we usually reserve for Joyce or Proust or Musil. Uniquely among Adorno's works *Dialectic of Enlightenment* enacts, in its 'form' as much as or more than in its mere arguments, Adorno's very modernist conviction that human reality is inescapably mediated by mind and language, which entails (for Adorno as for Hegel) that philosophy and its expression are not two separable things, but one seething, conflicted, pulsing 'dialectical' process or activity, or labor, or suffering, enacted but not exhausted, driven but never completed, in the tension between them. In this tension 'the ancient quarrel of philosophy and literature' (Plato) is rejoined, the separation of the critical from the aesthetic discourses undone, philosophy and literature forced once again into productive if conflicted—productive *because* conflicted—collision with each other. In Adorno's writing, and in *Dialectic of Enlightenment* most of all, the writing, word-by-word, is meaning-making, and form forges for itself a power, an 'agency of form' (*NL2* 114), very much in the way of the great modernist literary masters. 'Form' is a crucial category for Adorno, and for modernism—on the premise that the first thing an artwork 'makes' is its own form:

> . . . a work of art [or, we'll add, of critique] only properly comes to grips with its material in the moment when it engages with the internal contradictions of the latter, and these contradictions then translate themselves inevitably into the problem of form [artistic or philosophical] itself. If we fail to encounter such difficulties, then—at least in the sense of the sole and highest criterion—it is surely not worth starting at all (*AMC* 83–4).

Which of course poses challenges for the reader, who must learn to attend not merely to the particular matter or 'content' in view at the current moment of reading, but also to its often contradictory relation to, its tonal or other dissonances from, what preceded it: its place, or its revolt against its place, in the trajectory of the whole as it has developed so far. You read ruptures and clashes as much as continuities: you find meaning in gestures of form (or de-forming), of composition (or decomposition), in rhythms and dynamics and tempo, as much as in the argued 'theses'—which is to say that in Adorno, form and gesture, provocation and challenge, themselves become (part of) the content. Adorno requires you to read with an awareness that forms and genres have a history, in relation to which the form of the text you are reading mobilizes a 'sedimented content' (*NL2* 128) that acts to stir meaning-making tensions with the foreground content itself. ('Only in this confrontation with tradition of which style is a record can art express suffering' [Cumming 130–1].)

Adorno's headlong, dauntless prose, wide-ranging as it is, defying all difficulties and pushing always further, energetically enacts what Adorno calls 'the kinetic force of the concept' (*PMM* 26), to produce a text that can feel frantic, an agitated, flailing, ideational running-in-place meant to answer—'dialectics at a standstill'—to the horrors of an awful century. Adorno's evocation of an 'administered world' of conflicted, self-interfering energies often manifests as instability of connotation in vocabulary. Among the things a novice reader of Adorno must get the hang of is that certain supercharged words—'philosophy', 'theory', 'science', 'enlightenment', 'concept', 'mimesis'—can change their valences according to context, somewhat on the model of Freud's 'antithetical words'. Thus 'philosophy' might mean philosophy as Adorno wants it to be: 'unrelenting theory' (Cumming 42) in opposition to all naturalizing and reifying mystification; on the other hand, it might mean philosophy as it too often has been, ideological handmaiden to positivism and the natural sciences. And both meanings might be mobilized in the same paragraph, even the same sentence, so as to dramatize the conflict between these potentials experientially, in the very writing, and reading, moment-by-moment, of the text. As Adorno explains in 'The Essay as Form':

> The essay [i.e., a writing practice like Adorno's own] uses equivocations not out of sloppiness, nor in ignorance of the scientific ban on them, but to make it clear—something the critique of equivocation, which merely separates meanings, seldom succeeds in doing—that when a word covers different things they are not completely different; the unity of the word calls to mind a unity, however hidden, in the object itself (*NL1* 22).

'However hidden' the contradictions, Adorno's writing 'uses equivocations' to expose them to critical scrutiny, bringing antithetical meanings into dialectical friction—even though, or especially because, the 'objectivity of contradiction' (*ND* 151) in our social and cultural condition has contaminated dialectic itself, which thereby becomes hyper-cathected among Adorno's antithetical words. ('Hypostatized dialectics becomes undialectical' [*PDGS* 26]—the theme of *Dialectic of Enlightenment* in four words.) But the difficulty of the writing of *Dialectic of Enlightenment* raises this performativity of 'equivocation' to another level, as these words begin not merely to oscillate under the pulsions of the conflicting charges they bear, but to perform as something like *actants* in a seething drama—'dialectics at a standstill', but of a turbulent, not (à la Benjamin) a static sort, churning ceaselessly within the parameters indicated by the double-, triple-, multiple-entendres of the book's very title. (*Dialectic of Enlightenment*: the peculiar, historically specific ironies by which the late-eighteenth-century Enlightenment cancelled its own radical potential. Or: enlightenment as an ideological 'identity thinking' going back to Plato and beyond. Or: dialectic as a 'labor of the concept' that enlightened bourgeois modernity, in the name of common sense, has shirked, and must resume. Or: 'dialectic' as the tradition of revolutionary critique misconstrued it, subordinated it to exigencies of power, and at last turned it, reified it, into an ideology . . .)

Adorno mobilizes 'equivocation', in short, as a function or motivation of 'performative contradiction' a seeming expository failure that in fact registers the contradictory character of 'the matter at hand' better than expository clarity could ever do. Adorno regarded the law of non-contradiction as an ideology sacrificing the tangled and unhappy 'truth' to the idols of clarity and consistency: it's his premise that contradiction comes closer than consistency ever can to the crux and the pain of whatever questions and problems are at stake. Again, performative contradiction—a presentational device compelled, justified, motivated by, and as a theoretical commitment—enacts Adorno's insistence that the theory of practice should be indissociable from the practice of theory. The insistently wrought tension of that non-identity, of critical theory with writerly practice, is this book's focus, with the (quite immodest) aim of enlarging—enlivening, empassioning, *changing*—the way we read Adorno.

'The need to lend a voice to suffering', writes Adorno, 'is the condition of all truth' (*ND* 17–18). Adorno lived through an exorbitantly traumatic historical era, replete with horrors, quite as if modernity meant, perversely, to trump the unhappy consciousness of all preceding history. 'Unhappy consciousness' was the normative affect of critique and the arts throughout Adorno's period, but Adorno is unique among critics in his commitment, and in his power, to make that unhappiness not only a central theme or problem, but also a palpable 'textual effect' or affect, a felt pathos, in the critical labor of his writing. Yet Western philosophy or enlightenment has always conditioned its quest for truth upon its dispassion. Hence the first chapter of this book, 'Cathecting Philosophy', develops the theme sketched above, of Adorno's rehabilitation of the aesthetic (of *affect* itself) as 'truth', setting his effort in relation to the assessment and the place of feeling in the critical/philosophical traditions he recognizes as his own. Adorno consistently dissents from the Enlightenment-and-after compact according to which the aesthetic is granted its expressive (affective) license only on condition that it renounces any claim to be a 'truth discourse', along with its corollary that the earnest of philosophy's (sc. critique's) truth-claim—a necessary though not a sufficient condition—must be its refusal (i.e., its 'mastery' or 'domination') of affect. For Adorno,

> The moment called cathexis in psychology, thought's affective investment in the object, is not extrinsic to thought, not merely psychological, but rather the condition of its truth. Where cathexis atrophies, intelligence becomes stultified (*CM* 109).

And likewise for Adorno, at stake in the truth claim of art is the complementary restitution of affect and pathos ('cathexis') to philosophy (a.k.a. critique). The point is to demonstrate how much more than critique as usual Adorno would oblige critique, obliges himself as critic, to suffer, and perform, in the writing.

Accordingly this book starts with affect—with 'The Unhappy Consciousness of Critique'—to emphasize that the difficulty of Adorno's writing is difficulty of feeling fully as much as of thought, analysis, political insight, 'theory', or any other such nominally more cognitive concern usually thought of as critique's proper domain. It should go without saying that affect here connotes not Adorno's own individual emotional states, nor the emotions his prose might arouse in a reader, but rather Adorno's textualization of an objective, trans-individual, lived-and-felt—or *not*-felt: numbed, traumatized—historical situation. Thus this first chapter is concerned to elicit a problematic of affect in the philosophical tradition Adorno regarded as his own, starting with Hegel, who first named, diagnosed, and prescribed for 'unhappy consciousness' as the recurring problem of our historical species-being. Hegel is also notably (as Derrida says) 'the first thinker of writing' (*Grammatology* 26)—a conjunction that suggests a convergence of critical poetics with cultural therapeutics very much to the point of Adorno's project; moreover, Hegel writes of 'unhappy consciousness' in tones many have faulted as inappropriately or unrealistically—i.e., ideologically— 'optimistic': a performative contradiction fertile for many figures after Hegel (Kierkegaard, Marx, Nietzsche, Weber, Freud, Heidegger, Lacan, and of course Adorno himself) in ways the chapter develops. The discussion concludes with detailed readings of the opening of *Dialectic of Enlightenment* (1944), in which Horkheimer and Adorno link the critical and political difficulties of the World War Two crisis to the affective difficulties (numbing, *ataraxia*) of this culture-wide trauma in a way to motivate, in classically modernist terms, the expressive difficulty of *Dialectic of Enlightenment* as a written text.

The second chapter of the book, 'Rewriting the Dialectic', considers Adorno's own thematization of the writing (sc. 'poetics') of critique more directly, first by way of a reading of Adorno's 'Skoteinos, or How to Read Hegel'—Adorno's revealing meditation on the strengths and weaknesses, as writer, of his most potent philosophical precursor. It was Hegel, after all, who first put philosophy's *written*-ness on the agenda; and for our purposes, the primary subtext of 'How to Read Hegel' is, How Adorno wants us to read Adorno: otherwise put, How Adorno means to rewrite Hegel—to write more knowingly than Hegel, more philosophically, with greater critical effect, which turns out to mean, with a more acute self-consciousness of the 'poetics of critique'. Adorno's indictment, in 'Skoteinos', of Hegel's 'sovereignly indifferent attitude toward language' (*HTS* 109), sheds light on the ways, throughout his career, Adorno rewrites some of the larger themes or motifs of the Hegelian legacy—dialectic, concept, negation et al.—in a fashion to project them as prescriptions not only for critical thinking, but also for critical writing. Adorno's rewriting of Hegel also evinces a recurrent premise of this book, that Adorno's poetics of critique is very specifically *modernist*: first of all in the motive to 'make it new'—the 'it' here being what Adorno regarded as the corrupted Hegelian (and Marxist) vocabularies and practices of critique, which had long been stale even before the advent of Stalin and the Comintern, when they became orthodoxies, and thereby ideological. But modernist also in the stress on the poetics of the writing—the *how* as well as the *what*—and the concomitant apprehension that the imperatives entailed upon critique are as much moral (affective) as technical. In Adorno's writing practice, such Hegelian properties as dialectic, concept, and negation are reconceived by the light of such modernist devices as 'juxtaposition without copula', suspensions or attenuations of narrative, and the defamiliarizations operable in 'foregrounding the signifier'. And Adorno is modernist perhaps most of all in being, also, a *critic* of modernism: in particular its residues of Romantic anti-intellectualism and its naive nostalgia (or quest) for 'immediate [i.e., un-mediated] experience'.

Dialectic, concept, and negation are Hegelian/Marxian properties in, so to speak, the public domain; the next chapter of the book, 'Writing it New', considers some other terms that are virtually signatures of Adorno and the Frankfurt School, most centrally 'constellation' and 'immanent critique'; also in the mix I place Benjamin's 'dialectical image' and Adorno's conflicted mobilization of the motif of 'mimesis'. (A whole philology premised on the 'use-is-meaning' maxim would be required to exhaust the conflicted thesaurus of meanings Adorno makes the word 'mimesis' bear.) Adorno's deployment of these terms—the way he twists them in the writing, exposing unconscious contradictions, subverting received (ideological) meanings—is especially self-conscious, theorizing his own practice, practicing his own theory, in a fashion to render the theory/practice distinction quite nugatory. Adorno's poetics of critique prescribes 'constellation' and 'immanent critique' as theoretical program, but also as devices for writing practice—a practice so insistent and self-referential as to recall the Russian formalist rubric of 'baring the device': theorizing the practice, practicing the theory as indissociable impulses everywhere agitating his prose. Adorno's defamiliarizations, whether of stale Marxist vocabulary like 'dialectic' and 'mediation', or by way of new formulae such as 'immanent critique', are (again) self-consciously modernist—and heretically so by the lights of the old guard represented (at its best) by Lukács. If I make much of the contentions between Adorno and Lukács, it's because Lukács's misprisions of Adorno can sometimes be more illuminating than Adorno's retorts as a guide, *per negativo*, to the critical purposes Adorno hoped for from these devices, and the extent to which he regarded the efficacy of critique as conditioned on its power as writing.

The final chapter, 'Narrative and Its Discontents', attempts to make explicit a theme or problem mostly subtextual in Adorno's many exchanges with Lukács over modernism and realism, namely the question of the place of *narrative* in a Hegelian-Marxian (i.e., historicizing) critical practice. To begin with, such devices as constellation or dialectical *image*, like such modernist analogues as Pound's 'ideogram', cubist 'collage', and Joyce's 'epiphany', tend to displace interest and effect away from narrative continuity to a stilled or stalled, as if a-temporal stasis marked by its very discontinuity from the temporality from which it finds itself extruded. Experiments in reconceiving history, temporality, and 'story' itself in non- or even anti-narrative ways are of course a salient feature of modernism—Joyce's 800-page novel recounting the events of a day in which nothing happens (and T. S. Eliot's theorization of Joyce's technique in '*Ulysses*, Order and Myth'), Proust's trolling through an achronological panorama of memories (and Benjamin's Freudianization of Proustian *mémoire involontaire*), Freud's figuration of the unconscious as a perpetual now (a sort of *Jetztzeit* in reverse) in which there persists, as in Rome's archaeological penti-mento, the jumbled strata of a long and conflicted past.

In critique, from Nietzsche to Benjamin, Adorno and beyond, the attenuation of narrative is motivated by the increasing distrust of the historicism that pre-vailed in philosophy after Hegel. Philosophy since Plato had concerned itself with the unchanging, with what is outside of, invulnerable and transcendent to, time and contingency—which is to say, with what is outside of history. Hegel's radical step was to philosophize history and/or historicize philosophy by mak-ing the work of philosophy (sc. theory, critique) historical, and *narrative,* an affair of (providential) story-telling. Marx, notwithstanding his boasts about turning Hegel upside-down, follows Hegel's lead in mounting his arguments historically, and within the coordinates of a narratively conceived historical framework, the long march from Asiatic despotism through feudalism, the rise of the bourgeoisie and capitalism, with time's arrow poised for launch into the as yet unrealized socialist future. Likewise Lukács: his brief for realism (the nineteenth-century novel) against an 'ideology of modernism' which discounts narrative in favor of subjective effects, has everything to do with Lukács's own commitment, as a critic in the (then-) mainstream of Marxist historicism, to historical argument and explanation in the form of historical narrative. Adorno's apostasy from narrative (Benjamin's, too) means to indict narrative itself as an ideology sustaining modernity's 'master narratives' whether left (revolution), liberal (progress), or right (the fascist apocalyptic of the 'final solution'). But more: when Adorno and Lukács contend over what kind of fiction to prefer—Mann, or Beckett?—a subtext is the question of what representational and expressive means are valid in critique as well. This chapter motivates this impulse in Adorno from his own writing, and in relation to precursors like Benjamin ('Theses on the Philosophy of History'), Nietzsche ('Use and Abuse of History', *The Genealogy of Morals*) and even Marx himself in the uncharacteristic opening section of the *Eighteenth Brumaire.* I bring all this to bear on readings of passages from *Dialectic of Enlightenment* in which Adorno's 'dialectics at a standstill' is both argued as critical theme and enacted as textual effect in the quasi- (or *faux-*) narrative of a story the West has been telling itself so obsessively in terms of progress and revolution as to have repressed, blinded itself to, the miserable realities—regress and devolution—of our actual historical condition.

The chapter goes on to consider Adorno's 'philosophy of music', in search of further models for or intimations of his poetics of critique. Because music is an ineluctably *temporal* art, Adorno's writings about it, career-long, make a good barometer of his theories-and-practices with regard to narrative. Adorno is almost always a harsh critic of the common tendency to understand music's temporality as narrative. As I've suggested, imagistic devices like 'the [dialecti-cal] image' encode both a protest and a re-enactment of modernity's failed or stalled project; but the temporality of music seemingly stands for Adorno all the more contradictorily—but for that very reason, all the more productively—as figure or vehicle for the condition of 'dialectics at a standstill'. For Adorno, music's non-narrative temporality bears the potential for protesting and confronting this culture-wide paralysis—and to that extent, intimates strategies and ambitions for the 'composition' of critique as well. Nevertheless, Adorno late in his career finds his way to a renewed hospitality to narrative. His *Mahler* (1961) celebrates Mahler's symphonic oeuvre as itself a narrative, a narrative Adorno re-tells, narrates in the form of a story. This 'return of the [narrative] repressed' in late Adorno signals a return of another 'repressed' in Adorno's work, 'Utopia' itself, Stendhal's 'promise of happiness' nominally under ban except in the form of art's (and critique's) '*broken promise*'. Adorno writes that Mahler, at least sometimes, actually 'keeps the promise' (*MMP* 43)—an unabashedly utopian avowal, linked, in Adorno's account, to a 'philosophy of the history of music' in which a (narratively conceived) 'philosophy of the history of the novel' is implicated. Thus, in one of his shortest and most passionate books, does late Adorno propose a sketch of his lifelong, never-realized project of a philosophy of music—and proposes it, moreover, narratively, as a 'philosophy of (the history of) music'.

Giving Horkheimer His Due

I've said that this study's demonstration-text will be *Dialectic of Enlightenment* because I think it Adorno's most potent, most interestingly complicated or most 'modernist' piece of writing. My reasons for thinking so will emerge fully only in the course of this study, but a couple of other things that need saying here will begin to focus the theme. To trace the movement and flux—the 'dialectic'—of *Dialectic of Enlightenment* would ideally take a paragraph-by-paragraph commentary: obviously not a feasible option. I have chosen to focus on the book's first, introductory chapter, 'The Concept of Enlightenment'. In February 1943, shortly after the completion of this 'first long section of the joint book with Max . . . the one about myth and enlightenment', Adorno characterized it as the section that 'is in fact supposed to represent our whole philosophy' (*LHP* 125). Nevertheless, it seems that this, the program-chapter for the whole, is the least-read, least-discussed chapter of *Dialectic of Enlightenment*. In America, the book is best known by way of its most-anthologized chapter, 'The Culture Industry', followed by the 'Anti-Semitism' chapter, and (distantly) the 'Excursus' on Odysseus and the Sirens. 'Excursus II: Juliette or Enlightenment and Morality', seems to have been scanted, even during the vogue for Lacan's '*Kant avec Sade*'. But least-read of all, apparently, is the chapter that interests me most: the chapter that poses the problematic from which the other sections are 'excurses'.

Perhaps what deters others from 'The Concept of Enlightenment' is just what attracts me to it, namely (again) its difficulty—for the special interest of

'The Concept of Enlightenment' for this study is that it's the chapter that most self-consciously thematizes the difficulty, as writing, of *Dialectic of Enlightenment.* I resolved to write about 'The Concept of Enlightenment' because I found so much of it baffling, and some things in it almost perversely at odds with how I expected a Marxist and 'dialectical' argument to operate. Commentators generally ignored these problems; the few exceptions deplored them as lapses from proper 'critical' procedure—most prominently, Jürgen Habermas in *The Philosophical Discourse of Modernity* (106–30). Habermas had been Adorno's pro-tégé, and it was little comfort that his critique of *Dialectic of Enlightenment* evinced an exasperation not unlike my own—as if in disbelief that his old mentor could have made *these* mistakes. Habermas protested what he thrice called Horkhe-imer and Adorno's 'performative contradiction' (*Philosophical Discourse* 119, 127, 185) in proposing a critique that undercut the very grounds of critique. Yet just this—enlightenment's self-neutralization—was the central theme of the *Dialectic of Enlightenment,* the very meaning, indeed, of its fraught and cryp-tic title. Might the performative contradiction Habermas thought so vitiating be read, rather, as the strategic motivation, the dialectical or mimetic ruse, that enables, even powers, Horkheimer and Adorno's 'immanent critique' of enlightenment? To test that premise became the ambition of my project, and remains the aim of the finished book.

A problem, though: since my project's focus was Adorno, what to do with *Dialectic of Enlightenment*'s co-author, Max Horkheimer? I had initially hoped to bracket the authorship problem, if only to avoid repetition of the cumbersome locution, 'Horkheimer and Adorno'; more substantively, I've never doubted that *Dialectic of Enlightenment,* or what's most brilliant about it, was Adorno's doing—an assumption evident, if tacitly, in virtually all commentary on *Dialectic of Enlightenment,* 'as if' Adorno were its primary author. Although Horkheimer's name appears first on the title page, it's patent that the book carries itself more in Adorno's intellectual style than in Horkheimer's. The sheer energy of the writing, the provocations of argument, the audacities of allusion and expres-sion (as against the more expositorily utilitarian prose of Horkheimer); the 'constellations' of historical disjuncta conjoined in deliberately and perversely anti-historical ways (as elsewhere in Adorno, whereas Horkheimer's writings much more conventionally, and more hopefully, stage their arguments as before-and-after narratives of historical change); the Hegelian rather than Freudian habitus, i.e., the adventures of *Geist* projected rather on a philosophi-cal than a psychological plane (as Horkheimer usually does, in a manner somewhere between Marcuse and Fromm)—all these features of *Dialectic of Enlightenment* (not to mention, on the level sheerly of typography, the lengths of the paragraphs!) say 'Adorno'. Think Horkheimer's 1947 *Eclipse of Reason* as his single-handed version of *Dialectic of Enlightenment* (even allowing that he wrote it in English, not his native tongue), and the terms of the very titles— 'eclipse' versus 'dialectic', 'reason' versus 'enlightenment') suggest the difference in voltage between Adorno's intellectual and expressive resources and Horkheimer's. There is, to be sure, an audience issue—*Eclipse of Reason* was addressed, in English, to the exiled Horkheimer's American hosts and sponsors (it was initially a lecture series at Columbia), whereas *Dialectic of Enlightenment* was written in German as an in-house Frankfurt School working paper—but the essays Horkheimer gathered in *Critical Theory* don't give me any reason to change my assessment.[2]

I intend no derogation of Horkheimer here; I, at least, would have preferred that Horkheimer, and not Fromm, had been mid-century, middle-class, middle-brow America's exemplar of 'Freud-and-Marx' (no question of Horkheimer's displacing Reich's claim to that slot among the mid-century hipsters); and I'd be pleased if Horkheimer's 'Revolt of Nature' were anthologized in freshman readers (or graduate student readers, for that matter). Granted Adorno's more charismatic and mesmerizing performativity as intellect and as writer, the very straightforwardness of Horkheimer's writing and thinking can lend an invigorating lucidity to his evocation of what the principled unhappy consciousness of Adorno's conceptual, verbal, and affective difficulty can at times occlude, namely the hope, the prospect, the promise of the utopian. But in the special case of *Dialectic of Enlightenment*, giving Horkheimer his due encompasses a good deal more. For what makes *Dialectic of Enlightenment* a special case even among Adorno's own writings—what enables the proto-Beckettian narrative non-narrativity I mean to foreground here—is precisely the armature, however attenuated in the writing, of historical narrative (from Homer to Kant, de Sade and Nietzsche, to Hitler and Hollywood) upon which the book projects its non-narrative constellations, and tests them against their historical/ideological constraints. For, as I've said above, philosophico-historical narratives (like Lukács's) were Horkheimer's penchant, in contrast to Adorno's genius (like Benjamin's) for the non- or a- or anti-narrative constellation, encoding in Benjamin the refusal of historicism, in Adorno the critique of 'progress' and its ideologies. If constellation and dialectical image suggest some of the devices of modernism (Eisenstein's montage and the like), Horkheimer's narrativity, his urge to connect narrative dots in chains of cause-and-effect, to explain everything, to make the case for progress by telling a progressive story, rather evoke the nineteenth-century realist novel. (Thought experiment: without Adorno, would Horkheimer ever have found himself party to a decades-long 'debate' with Lukács?—for truth to tell, Horkheimer's *Eclipse of Reason* has more in common with Lukács's *Destruction of Reason* than with any writing of Adorno's.)

My point here is precisely *not* that Horkheimer's share in *Dialectic of Enlightenment* is negligible, a mere piety honored by Adorno for the sake of a friendship. If *Dialectic of Enlightenment* is such a crucial text in Adorno's oeuvre, it is because in it, Adorno's non- or anti-narrative critique engaged in a negotiation, indeed, a dialectic, with Horkheimer's more traditionally narrative style of historicizing argument and explanation; the result is a text that not merely eschews (represses?)

narrative in Adorno's usual way, but more conflictedly enacts in a paradoxically narrative or pseudo-narrative form—there's the performative contradiction— the failure of narrative: not only the specific failure of the Enlightenment grand narrative to fulfill itself, to arrive at its desired progressive *telos* of human free- dom, but the failure of narrativity itself as a vehicle of intellectual inquiry and critique; the failure, moreover, of narrativity to understand or even *recognize* its own failure—which is to say, the devolution of narrative itself into an ideology, a false consciousness, and the more insidiously for its working at the level of *form* rather than *content.* In *Dialectic of Enlightenment,* all this is enacted as mime- sis and diagnosis of the progressive tradition, and of one of its most visionary founding texts, Hegel's *Phenomenology,* to evoke, with all the gestures, genre-cues, and code-prompts of narrative an agitated deadlock of progress and regress, a reification of the very principle ('officially', the engine) of historical movement and progress, the dialectic itself. The present point being that without Horkhe- imer, Adorno would never have engaged these themes in this way: would never have written anything comparable in complexity and brilliance to *Dialectic of Enlightenment.* To that (large) extent I take at face value the declaration in the book's 1969 'Preface':

> No outsider will find it easy to discern how far we [Horkheimer *and* Adorno] are both responsible for every sentence. We jointly dictated lengthy sections; and the vital principle of the *Dialectic* is the tension between the two intellec- tual temperaments conjoined in it (Cumming ix).

It is precisely in the ambiguously compromised narrativity of the book that 'the tension between the two intellectual temperaments' of Horkheimer and Adorno operates most productively, not merely to argue but more conflictedly to enact and interrogate the 'objective contradictoriness' (*ND* 151) of the self- understanding (and -misunderstanding) of what Adorno elsewhere calls 'that antagonistic unity of standstill and movement that defines the most universal bourgeois concept of progress' (*CM* 160). The feature that sets *Dialectic of Enlightenment* so far apart from the rest of Adorno's oeuvre is its enactment of that 'antagonistic unity' in the form of a seeming-narrative: it tells a story, indeed, re-tells a disastrously familiarized story, the meta-narrative that, for phi- losophers of Horkheimer and Adorno's Hegelian/Marxist tradition, amounts virtually to an origin myth, the story Hegel tells in the *Phenomenology of Spirit.* Many readers before me have observed that Horkheimer and Adorno's story reverses the valences of Hegel's, to explain how, where Hegel's theodicy had been, the Hitler/Stalin nightmare had come to be. In *Dialectic of Enlightenment,* instead of the *Phenomenology's* uplifting arc from primitive bodily sensation to the triumphant climax (itself a whole new beginning) of 'absolute knowledge', we behold catastrophe, a devolution into barbarisms more lethal than any our species-being has ever before suffered. Instead of progress, regress; instead of 'substance become subject' in an 'all are free' world, the abject-object 'administered subject' of modern 'domination'; instead of 'absolute knowledge', the 'mass deception' announced in the subtitle of the 'Culture Industry' chapter. Horkheimer and Adorno contrive to tell this 'story' so as to enact the failures of the revolutionary and/or progressive tradition—not only Hegel's story, but the adaptations of that story set forth in Marx-and-after—as a failure of narrative itself, a failure indissociable from that of dialectic, the *deus ex machina* meant, in socialist orthodoxy, to guarantee a triumphal finale to the master narrative of Marxism. To present this perversely counter-intuitive effect, this defamiliarizing performative contradiction—this non-narrative narrativity of *Dialectic of Enlightenment*—is this study's culminating aim.

Chapter 1

Cathecting Philosophy

As was already pointed out in the Dialectic of Enlightenment, *strict positivism crosses over into the feeblemindedness of the artistically insensible, the successfully castrated. The narrow-minded wisdom that sorts out feeling from knowing and rubs its hands together when it finds the two balanced is—as trivialities sometimes are—the caricature of a situation that over the centuries of the division of labor has inscribed this division in subjectivity. Yet feeling and understanding are not absolutely different in the human disposition and remain dependent even in their dividedness. The forms of reaction that are subsumed under the concept of feeling become futile enclaves of sentimentality as soon as they seal themselves off from their relation to thought and turn a blind eye to truth; thought, however, approaches tautology when it shrinks from the sublimation of the mimetic comportment. The fatal separation of the two came about historically and is revocable. . . . Ultimately, aesthetic comportment is to be defined as the capacity to shudder, as if goose bumps were the first aesthetic image. What later came to be called subjectivity, freeing itself from the blind anxiety of the shudder, is at the same time the shudder's own development; life in the subject is nothing but what shudders, the reaction to the total spell that transcends the spell. Consciousness without shudder is reified consciousness. That shudder which subjectivity stirs without yet being subjectivity is the act of being touched by the other. Aesthetic comportment assimilates itself to that other rather than subordinating it. Such a constitutive relation of the subject to objectivity in aesthetic comportment joins eros and knowledge.*

—Adorno (AT *331*)

The capacity for fear and for happiness are the same, the unrestricted openness to experience amounting to self-abandonment in which the vanquished rediscovers himself. What would happiness be that was not measured by the immeasurable grief at what is?

—Adorno (MM *200*)

The 'Unhappy Consciousness' of Critique

The 1944 'Introduction' to *Dialectic of Enlightenment* announces the book's indictment against 'enlightenment', that it has abdicated '*der Arbeit des Begriffs*' (*GS3* 14). The German phrase—a Hegelian chestnut—is Englished as 'the labor of conceptualization' in John Cumming's 1972 translation (Cumming xiv), and, more recently by Edmund Jephcott in 2002, as 'the work of concepts' (Jephcott xvii). Together the two translations suggest, as neither can by itself, the stretch of the German, which suggests both the work that concepts do, and the labor that making ourselves conscious of the problematics of the concept— 'thinking about thought' (Cumming 25), 'to "think thinking"' (Jephcott 19)— imposes on us. 'The concept' is a ubiquitous theme in Adorno, as we'll see; for now suffice it to say that in Adorno the concept evokes (à la Hegel) the mind's engagement at once with the world *and* with its own self-consciousness in this engagement; for Adorno, this self-consciousness of thought, this 'labor of the concept', is an imperative from first to last. I want to start this book with the premise that for Adorno, complementary to the 'labor of the concept' is an imperative I will call 'the work of affects' or 'the labor of affectualization'. Horkheimer and Adorno thematize this labor in their 'excursus' on Odysseus and the Sirens as founding myth of the ethic Adorno consistently denounces as '*ataraxia*'—a culture-wide affective repression, which grounds the instrumental 'domination of [external] nature' in an internalized, instrumentalizing domination of affect itself. To undo this, critique must incur an affective labor along with its other burdens. 'The need to lend a voice to suffering', writes Adorno, 'is the condition of all truth' (*ND* 17–18), a premise that rejoins affect and concept, feeling and thinking, to enact Adorno's dialectical protest against the separation of these categories—these domains of experience—in Western culture. For Adorno, 'the labor of the concept' itself involves laboring to uncover, focus, articulate, and express its chronically repressed or distorted, fetishized or reified affective elements. If affect must be completed, 'rescued', even redeemed, by being concretized in the labor of, in the Hegelian formula, 'apprehending it as thought', then likewise, thought—the labor of the concept, of thinking about thinking—must suffer the ordeal through which alone thinking may once again be apprehended as feeling. Adorno urges that to 'think thinking' obliges us to think our feeling, to feel our thinking—and (what our traumatic history has perhaps most inhibited in us) to feel our feeling as well.

Let me rehearse here a caveat sketched in the 'Introduction': in this discussion, feeling and affect (etc.) mean not Adorno's own emotions, but rather that trans-individual condition, 'objective' in the Hegelian sense, in which subject and object are not two poles of an antithesis, but rather two phases of a function whose textualization Adorno will enact in his work of writing, understanding such labor, again, performatively, as a mimesis or *methexis* rather than a 'representation' of what cannot in any case be represented; the analogy with Lacan's Real, which 'resists symbolization absolutely', can serve as reminder of Lacan's (quite Hegelian) premise that individual psychology, the subject, affect in general, crossed and fissured by collectively projected meanings and desires, are 'effects of the signifier', constituted in and by language in the first place. Hence Adorno's axiom that our experience of subjectivity is itself a principle constituent of our objective historical situation. Of course Adorno had individual emotions, and I reserve the right to speak of them when it's useful; but it's Adorno's writing, not his psychology, that I seek to illuminate here. And if 'affect' needs certification as an acknowledged Adorno-problematic, and needs it framed in more familiar philosophical terms, it would be as instantiation or 'concretization' of what Adorno designated as the 'non-conceptual', the asymmetrical 'other' of philosophy, akin to Kant's *Ding an sich* as much as to the Lacanian Real, that philosophy (in Adorno's view) too often rules out of discussion, thus—'dialectic of Enlightenment'—neutralizing itself as an agent in the developing human story.

This chapter, then, explores Adorno's textualizations of this 'labor of affectualization', both as theorized in his arguments and as performed in his writing practice. A touchstone throughout will be Adorno's chief model and counter- or cautionary example, the 'optimistic' authorial carriage of Hegel, whose utopian promise Adorno's 'unhappy [critical] consciousness' reinscribes under the rubric of the '*broken* promise'. I hope to enlarge our sense of the function or 'effect' of 'style' (to call it that) in critical projects like Hegel's and Adorno's, with reference to others (Marx, Nietzsche, Weber, Freud, Heidegger . . .) in relation to the questions that Adorno's critical-aesthetic 'labor of the affects' seems to me to raise for a reading of *Dialectic of Enlightenment*. The chapter closes with detailed readings of that book's 1944 'Introduction', in which the deliberate 'difficulty' of the text is thematized as motivated by the difficulties, both intellectual and emotional, of its historical problem and occasion (enlightenment's traumatic devolution into the barbarism of World War Two), and of the book's first chapter, which enacts the program (both critical and affective) for which the 'Introduction' serves as manifesto. The larger aim is to describe, evoke, and, in ways other commentators on Adorno seem to me to have missed, to account for the sheer power and voltage of Adorno's work, in which thinking and writing—and feeling—seethe, and in their agitation impel each other to levels of force quite unlike anything to be found in the work of anyone else.

Aesthesis and *Anaesthesis*

Adorno's will to 'rescue' repressed affect finds a sort of limit-case in a 1959 lecture in which Adorno speaks feelingly of 'the emotional force of Kant's *Critique of Pure Reason*' (*KCPR* 30). Most readers will raise eyebrows at this characterization, which Adorno will surely have meant as a provocation and a protest. It was apropos Kant, after all, that Terry Eagleton joked that in the tradition of philosophical aesthetics, 'the aesthetic might more accurately be described as an anaesthetic' (Eagleton 196)—and indeed, if indictment of Kant is the premium, Adorno himself can elsewhere characterize Kant's aesthetics as 'a castrated hedonism, desire without desire' (*AT* 11). Adorno's Kant seems proleptic of that 'heroism of modern life' (the black-suited bourgeoisie assisting in stoic dispassion, 'not breaking up its lines to weep', nor even presuming to expect a speaking role, at the funeral of its own passional energies) to which Baudelaire paid the back-handed compliment of an uncharacteristically muted mockery. Kant's 'emotional force', that is to say, partakes of that struggle *against* emotion and feeling that *Dialectic of Enlightenment* traces back to the episode of the Sirens in the *Odyssey*. Eagleton's 'anaesthetic' notwithstanding, for Adorno Kant's 'emotional force' lies in the ineradicable felt force of the agon itself, the drive for 'domination' of emotion and affect, given that the reified norm, in Adorno's indignant indictment, typically cedes the victory to numbness not only in advance, but in principle.

Obviously Adorno's project is heavily invested in an ambition to undo this anaesthesis or (Adorno's usual protest-word) '*ataraxia*'—i.e., to redeem the numbness programmatized in modern, bourgeois, enlightenment projects, whether aesthetic or scientific; or, if 'redeem' seems too Messianic, to 'rescue' (Adorno's own word: '*Rettung*') for 'critical' and 'conceptual' purposes the affective force normatively repressed in our culture's *chorismos* of thought and feeling. This is an ambition emphatically *not* to be realized by simply heightening a mere 'effect', lending to the substance of an argument the atmospherics of a mood, much less the adrenaline-jolts of a moralized *ressentiment*. Adorno evokes the 'emotional force of Kant's *Critique of Pure Reason*' to prepare the broader stipulation a page later that 'the same, the identical theses may have completely different meanings within the general parameters, the general emotional thrust of a given philosophy' (*KCPR* 31). The affect of an argument, then, isn't some merely epiphenomenal froth upon a putatively substantive content or theses that might better be considered dispassionately. No, Adorno here states explicitly that the content, the 'theses', bear different meanings according to the argument's 'emotional thrust': the affective cathexes of the text thereby become determinative, even constitutive, of the text's meanings. Moreover, the programmatic dispassion of critique generically stands revealed and indicted as an ideology, an imaginary conquest of fear, another instance of that 'anaesthesis' or '*ataraxia*' that *Dialectic of Enlightenment* laments as an impoverishing entailment of bourgeois 'coldness' (*MM* 26), from Homeric epic to tough-guy existentialism and beyond.

Adorno protests the analytic disjunction or (his code-word) *chorismos* (Greek = 'separation') of sciences, knowledges, discourses. He aims to rejoin these discourses dialectically in configurations or constellations whose transgression against positivist habits of categorization is much of their heteroclite, fish-and-fowl, apples-and-oranges point. For modern purposes, the milestone of enlightened *chorismos* is Kant, whose intervention in the 'contest of faculties' was meant to produce a ceasefire and disengagement between the combatants—in Kant's time, philosophy and theology. Kant's covert motive was that philosophy should displace theology as arbiter among the disciplines; but his overt proposal was that the warring faculties agree to disagree: they were separate discourses, exercising discriminable kinds of 'Reason' on different, non-overlapping, problems. The outcome was not what Kant had hoped for: while philosophy and religion were engrossed in their 'contest', the real power was passing to the empirical sciences and their new, and (Adorno thought) fatally narrow canons of truth and fact. This disaster—how Enlightenment thinking neutralized its own radical potential—is what Adorno meant by 'the dialectic of enlightenment'. The 'contest of faculties' was protracted and often covert, but the outcome was increasingly clear. For the losers (philosophy, religion, art), the defeat was supposed to be made more palatable by a sequestration that allowed each a client-reign in its own proper, scrupulously circumscribed domain. This Enlightenment regime tolerates aesthetic discourses as specialized disciplines on condition that they renounce their claim to 'truth'; by the same token, the truth-discourses of science offer as condition (almost as guarantee) of their truth-value their principled refusal of any affective voltage. Implicit in this compact is that affect as such is without truth-value: is, indeed, an obstacle to truth. Adorno assails these ideological premises constantly, and he ended his career, in *Aesthetic Theory*, with his most sustained effort to valorize art's claim to 'truth'—in part by stipulating the conditions under which art achieves truth, in part by so reconfiguring the question that, under Adorno's spell, one puzzles to remember how art can ever have seemed *not* 'true'.[1]

Aesthetic Theory labors to redeem the aesthetic by undoing the *chorismos* of thought and feeling that has deprived art of the philosophical (sc. critical) effectivity Adorno would claim for it; indeed, the most insistent theme of the book's vast ensemble of theme-and-variations is that art and philosophy are phases of a continuous activity; neither is valid without the other: they need each other; they enlarge each other; they complement and complicate each other. Adorno is tireless in urging that the restoration of critical force to art involves the 'labor of the concept'; but he is pretty tight-lipped about the complementary program, of restoring to philosophy (and critique, theory, science: to what he wants to restore as 'truth-discourses') something of the affective or aesthetic power they only illusorily renounce or repress in any case. This reticence raises two embarrassments for my argument. The smaller one is that Adorno's reticence about affect produces, absent argued discriminations from him, some slippage in my account between 'affect' and such terms as 'feeling', 'cathexis', 'suffering', and the like. On this I can only beg forbearance, and hope my speculations earn their keep. The other embarrassment is more substantial: if Adorno means to 'rescue' affect, then why is 'affect', as a *theme*, so repressed in his work? Why *isn't* he more explicit about it? The answer I'd most like to give is that Adorno counts on the high affective voltages of his writing to make the point, as if coming right out and saying it would be a gaffe on the order of explaining why a joke is funny. Modernism generally plays down affect, in ways sometimes to be read as a kind of (mock-) *ataraxia* (Céline), sometimes as a kind of restraint or understatement (e.g., 'impersonality') meant actually to heighten affect; oftenest, of course, modernism's affective restraint enacts a refusal or critique of the excesses of so much nineteenth-century art (Dickens, academic painting, Chopin, Wagner—too many examples). Adorno shares in that critique, but his own work risks an emotionalism that most tight-lipped moderns refuse. I suppose that Adorno shied away from making the case more explicitly lest it be mis-taken to mean that philosophy (sc. critique, etc.) is a 'merely subjective' expression, i.e., aesthetic in precisely the diminished ideological senses that Adorno means to protest *and* redeem in his dialectical reinvention of it in *Aesthetic Theory*. Adorno regularly protests against the 'merely subjective' gambit, as a reductive psychologism; in Adorno's own account of the subject/object relation, there is no such thing as the '*merely* subjective' because the very condition of subjectivity is its dialectical engagement with the objective.

In any case, the implication of the affects in the 'truth-discourses' is ubiquitous in Adorno—for example in his surprisingly frequent assimilations of philosophy to music: in the very title of *Philosophy of New Music*; in the resonances with Hegel in the *Beethoven* fragments (see any of the numerous references in the book's Index); and in quotations like this one, from the early (1932) essay, 'On the Social Situation of Music':

> Music will be better, the more deeply it is able to express—in the antinomies of its own formal language—the exigency of the social condition and to call for change through the coded language of suffering. . . . The task of music as art thus enters into a parallel relationship to the task of social theory. . . . solutions offered by music in this process stand equal to theories (*EM* 393).

But the premise is put more globally in many places—as in the 1961 essay, 'Opinion Delusion Society':

> The moment called cathexis in psychology, thought's affective investment in the object, is not extrinsic to thought, not merely psychological, but rather the condition of its truth. Where cathexis atrophies, intelligence becomes stultified (*CM* 109).

And in what is undoubtedly his most-remembered and oftenest-quoted utterance—'To write poetry after Auschwitz is barbaric' (*P* 34)—Adorno might seem to be putting a limit to the argument, by citing an atrocity that threatens to beggar all affect, indeed, all expression—which would have to mean, all critique as well. For surely Adorno's anxiety in the question of poetry after Auschwitz encompasses anxiety about the continuance of critique and philosophy after Auschwitz as well—a way of putting it that helps uncover the utopian wishfulness in the famous assertion that 'Philosophy lives on because the moment to realize it was missed' (*ND* 3). But those who deplore what they take to be the hair-shirt defeatism or melodramatizing unhappy consciousness of the 'after-Auschwitz' remark would do well to ponder Adorno's own comment a decade and a half later:

> I once said that after Auschwitz one could no longer write poetry, and that gave rise to a discussion I did not anticipate . . . [I]t is in the nature of philosophy—and everything I write is, unavoidably, philosophy, even if it is not concerned with so-called philosophical themes—that nothing is meant quite literally. Philosophy always relates to tendencies and does not consist of statements of fact. . . . it could equally well be said . . . that [after Auschwitz] one *must* write poems, in keeping with Hegel's statement in his *Aesthetics* that as long as there is an awareness of suffering among human beings there must also be art as the objective form of that awareness. . . . [The question whether one can write poetry after Auschwitz should rather be] the question whether one can *live* after Auschwitz. . . . Since it concerns the possibility of any affirmation of life, this question cannot be evaded. . . . any thought which is not measured by this standard, which does not assimilate it theoretically, simply pushes aside at the outset that which thought should address—so that it really cannot be called a thought at all (*MCP* 110–1; cf. *ND* 362).

This passage brings together a number of themes: the evocation of high ambition, or vocation, or doom ('everything I write is, unavoidably, philosophy'); the adviso that in philosophy 'nothing is meant quite literally'; the rootedness of art *and* philosophy both in 'an awareness of suffering'; the ultimate question of 'the possibility of any affirmation of life'. And indissociable from these thematics is the affect that the writing itself communicates—'communicate' meaning not transmission from sender to receiver, but a communion, a making-common, between writer and reader, and in that sense the evocation of 'an objective form' of 'that awareness [of suffering among human beings]'.

Adorno means to advance the work of affect not only programmatically, but also in the tones and textures, the meanings and the motives, the textual effects or affects, of his writing practice. Adorno's writing, indeed, in the largest sense, his *project*, involves an affective investment—that 'labor of affectualization', or 'work of affects'—and to that extent his project is something like aesthetic in the radically enlarged senses Adorno proposes in *Aesthetic Theory*. Adorno's *aesthesis* is quite the reverse of the glamorous 'strong pessimism' and 'tragic' ecstasies in which Nietzsche affects to find art's 'redemption by illusion'. All such exaltations of strength and tragic heroism Adorno disdains as imaginary consolations; his own ideation tends rather to abjection—and not as the willed asceticism diagnosed by Nietzsche, but as the burden imposed on us by history will we or nill we, the social trauma critique shares, and suffers, and which it can only attempt, however impossibly, to work through:

> Unquestionably, one who submits to the dialectical discipline has to pay dearly in the qualitative variety of experience. Still, in the administered world

the impoverishment of experience by dialectics, which outrages healthy opinion, proves appropriate to the monotony of that world. Its agony is the world's agony raised to a concept (*ND* 6).

'Agony raised to a concept' must entail, reciprocally, that the concept be submitted to the ordeal of agon: again the juncture of—or better, kinesis between—affective 'sense-certainty' and the cognitive apprehension of the concept. The concept of agony must be, must be concretized as, must be *made* (in the writing, in the reading) agonizing—and agonistic. If Wittgenstein famously sneered that the concept of sugar is not sweet, Adorno consistently retorts, in effect, that the concept of suffering ought surely to hurt. Indeed, given the implication of sugar in the development of the Atlantic slave trade, the American plantation system, the development of banking, credit, and other fiduciary devices in the inauguration of capitalism, I would expect Adorno to urge that the *concept* of sugar, however sweet the taste of the white cube you put in your coffee, must be very bitter indeed to the critical intelligence mindful to constellate the concept, including the brutal history, with the sensual and quotidian spatio-temporality of your mocha latte. For Adorno, the proposition that 'the concept of sugar is not sweet' is true only in a trivial (and trivializing) sense; 'agony raised to a concept' can only be a lie if in the raising conceptualization functions as analgesic against the agony. The very phrase protests the habit of thinking that conceptualization 'raises' painful material above (away from) suffering: on the contrary, in Adorno the agony is what 'the concept' raises itself *to*.

'Agony Raised to a Concept'

Hence, in 'lending a voice to suffering', critique itself must be painful: must be anguished, and anguishing. Critique must bear the marks of unhappy consciousness, and not as a mere textual effect appropriate to the sufferings of our brutal civilization, but as fundamental among critique's own constitutive properties. We might call this Adorno's 'after-Auschwitz' imperative, except that in Adorno's work this critical affect long pre-dates Auschwitz—not to mention that Adorno wrote his two most poignant books (*Minima Moralia* and *Dialectic of Enlightenment*) literally '*during*-Auschwitz'. *Dialectic of Enlightenment* scorns the official optimisms of modernity's ideological cheerleaders—from the 'revolutionary' scenario of the orthodox Stalinist left, through the meliorist grand narrative of liberalism, to the apocalyptic fantasias of fascism—since it was the pursuit of these diversely ideological happy endings that unleashed so much horror. Whatever their other conflicts, it was policy in all three camps that the needs of morale-management (propaganda) must cast critical questioning as 'defeatism' and 'pessimism'—reminder enough that critical 'unhappy consciousness' like Adorno's was, in Adorno's own lifetime, quite the reverse of 'mandarin' indulgence. In the context of this optimism/pessimism force-field,

Adorno's citation of Hegel as advocate for an awareness of human suffering is telling, because it was Hegel's 'optimism' as much as Marx's that underwrote the official optimism of Soviet Marxist-Leninism; and for many, especially after the War, Hegel's sanguine view of human history seemed, especially in light of Hegel's professional success post-1816, a 'false consciousness' or worse, a Panglossian dishonesty. (Adorno himself often chides Hegel in these same terms: 'guaranteed roads to redemption are sublimated magic practices' [Cumming 24].) The 'Right Hegelians' did, after all, have a case.

I would argue that *every* critique Adorno mounts of Hegel involves the ideological delusions, imaginary consolations, false consciousness, the bourgeois 'coldness' (*MM* 26) of Hegel's '*happy* consciousness'.[2] But neither does Adorno ever forget the 'darker' Hegel—Hegel's repressed-always-returning 'unhappy consciousness'. The vocation of the concept, the dialectic, mediation, contradiction, negation; the imperative to rethink historically the un- or trans-historical Platonic-Aristotelian hypostases of hallowed philosophical tradition; the deconstruction (if you'll allow the anachronism) of the hallowed metaphysical binary of appearance and reality, noumenon and phenomenon; the insistence on the philosophical dignity of the latter (that phenomena have, *contra* Plato, a 'logos' and that there is, in consequence, a phenomeno-logy): these and many other Hegelian motives attest Adorno's large investment in the critical force of Hegel. Not for nothing does Adorno observe, in one of the Beethoven fragments (# 24): 'In a similar sense to that in which there is only Hegelian philosophy, in the history of western music there is only Beethoven' (*B* 10).

For Adorno as for Hegel, philosophy/critique is no ivory-tower exercise for a 'disinterested' elite, but rather a labor in the service of humankind. Both write in the long 'physician to an age' tradition, which diagnoses unhappy consciousness as primary among the afflictions to be cured: this is the programmatic impulse registered in the serenity of Hegel's own textual voice, which has so often seemed to the politically conscious unduly 'optimistic'—as if Hegel took in the 1793–1815 horrors with a smile of unflappable composure on his face. But Adorno's concern lest such textual effect, or affect, be taken as a merely subjective expression of the author has its analogue in Hegel's own cautions about the solicitations of unhappy consciousness. Hegel, indeed, writes in the historical moment when happiness first became charged with political and social meanings and motives. Thomas Jefferson made its pursuit an inalienable human right in an age when Rousseau, Lessing, Schiller, Wordsworth, and many others dared imagine a 'sentimental' or 'aesthetic education' in which the promise of cultivated pleasures would supplant the threat of corporal punishment as incentive to learning, indeed, to self-making. It was after all the age of Schiller's ethic-aesthetic of 'play', of his Ode '*An Freude*' so stirringly orchestrated by Beethoven (and now the anthem of the EU), of the utopian visions of Fourier, Saint Simon, and Owen. For such dreamers of the Revolutionary age, the thrilling prospect was happiness (or the pursuit of it) as a popular and universal 'right'—no longer the elite privilege exclusive to those fortunate enough to be philosophers that it was for Plato, Aristotle, the Stoics, Epicureans, and after (for all of whom *eudaimonia* was a pursuit conditioned on dispassion).

Hegel of course knew as well as anyone that happiness, especially collective human happiness, is easier said than done: how, in an age of revolutionary and counter-revolutionary violence, to keep from despairing over your morning newspaper—precisely this is the problem Hegel grapples with in the 'slaughter-bench of history' passage in his 1830 lectures on *The Philosophy of World History*. Hegel doesn't merely own that history is a nightmare; his further aim is to pre-scribe for the demoralization that historical consciousness entails. Hegel notes first the simplest defense-mechanism, self-congratulation on having escaped the carnage:

> . . . we draw back from the intolerable disgust with which these sorrowful reflections threaten us, into the more agreeable environment of our individ-ual life—the Present formed by our private aims and interests. In short we retreat into the selfishness that stands on the quiet shore, and thence enjoy in safety the distant spectacle of 'wrecks confusedly hurled'.

But the other, more dangerous temptation, Hegel implies, is ostentatious despair of the too-familiar breast-beating and hand-wringing sorts that, Hegel warns, become self-perpetuating—for

> it is not the interest of such sentimentalities, really to rise above those depress-ing emotions; and to solve the enigmas of Providence which the consider-ations that occasioned them, present. It is essential to their character to find a gloomy satisfaction in the empty and fruitless sublimities of that negative result (*Philosophy of History* 21).

Only Terry Eagleton still chides Adorno's despair as a 'defeatism'; but to many others it can still seem just such a sentimentality: at best a self-regarding whin-ing, at worst a kind of moral Pecksniffery, in either case a source of (Hegel) 'gloomy satisfactions' that can become compulsive or addictive in the fashion most recently theorized ('Enjoy your symptom!') in Slavoj Zizek's ingenious rein-ventions of Lacan, or protested in accents of Nietzschean brio (sc. 'cheekiness') in the 'kynicism' of Peter Sloterdijk. Adorno, as it happens, anticipates these very objections in a fragment in *Minima Moralia* (written contemporaneously with *Dialectic of Enlightenment*, in the last year of World War Two):

> Subjective reflection, even if critically alerted to itself, has something senti-mental and anachronistic about it: something of a lament over the course of the world, a lament to be rejected not because of its good faith, but because the lamenting subject threatens to become arrested in its condition and so to

fulfill in its turn the law of the world's course. Fidelity to one's own state of consciousness and experience is forever in temptation of lapsing into infidelity, by denying the insight that transcends the individual and calls his substance by its name (*MM* 16; on the following page the 'name' is spelled out: it is 'society [that] is essentially the substance of the individual').

I take 'good faith' here to be ironic: Adorno is accusing 'such sentimentalities' (Hegel) of something very like a Sartrean '*mauvaise foi*', a (dubiously) 'good faith' that Adorno wants to turn, like a Nietzsche in reverse, into a 'bad conscience'.

Some qualifications are necessary here: Hegel posits unhappy consciousness (*Phenomenology* 111–38) to diagnose precisely the sort of moral addiction or compulsion outlined above. He presents it as coincident historically with the advent of Christianity in the Mediterranean world, and its confluence with Greco-Roman Skepticism and Stoicism. For Hegel, unhappy consciousness expresses a relation to some 'beyond' that is inaccessible in this world; it thus encourages an 'abstract negation' of this-worldly attachments, and of the very possibility of this-worldly happiness as such. For this specific but chronic historical-spiritual disorder, Hegel believes that the fullness of history has, in the modern age, at last enabled a (philosophical) remedy, which the *Phenomenology* prescribes: a critical self-consciousness that will redeem the promise of this-worldly happiness by sublating the abjection instigated by our alienation from a 'beyond' entoiled, by reason of its limitlessness, in all the regressions of 'bad infinity'—a formula anticipating the implacably punitive super-ego diagnosed by Freud. The later Hegel was wont (as his younger self was not) to portray this sublation—this redemptive historical project that philosophy was destined to complete—in providential Christian terms: Christianity originated in the 'abstract' (or 'symbolic') Asiatic consciousness of ancient Judaism, but by virtue of its long and shaping experience in Western history—the Hellenization that assimilated it with art and philosophy, the Romanization that politicized it and accommodated it to the needs of statecraft, and the Germanization that suffused it with the spirit, even the libido, of freedom—Christianity so evolved as to realize, in modern times, the qualitative fulfillment or incarnation of its (originally, merely abstract) promise: the progress, from the Asiatic premise that 'one is free', through the Greco-Roman republicanism in which 'some are free', to the democratic ideal emerging in the revolutionary events of Hegel's own lifetime that 'all are free'.

Hegel's 'performativity' is to diagnose unhappy consciousness as a symptomatics that is now—happily—curable. Adorno's just-quoted passage also diagnoses the malaise in question, but confesses its own unhappy infection as well: 'the lamenting subject' suffers this malaise or unhappy consciousness will he or nill he—'even if [especially if?] critically alerted to [him]self'. Where Hegel proposed a rationale for overcoming 'unhappy consciousness' and attempted to realize it as an effect or affect in his philosophical writing, Adorno more conflictedly stipulates that the despair of the critic cannot and should not be so complacently 'overcome' in the critique: critique's own textual affect must answer to 'the matter in hand'; a textualization affecting to have transcended or 'sublated' 'unhappy consciousness' would seem from Adorno's vantage a false consciousness, 'an imaginary solution to a real contradiction'.

Hegel's 'Happy Consciousness'?

For Adorno, clearly, the premise of Hegel's 'optimism' generally circulates too uncritically; every chapter of the *Phenomenology*, after all, rehearses variations of the same scenario, in which the human race, groping after happiness, relapses into ironically inventive and original new forms of misery. Indeed, the narrative of Hegel's *Phenomenology* is scarcely less insistent than the Bible itself that moral suffering is not only chronic but productive for humankind, from Genesis 3's access of shaming knowledge, or knowledge-as-shame, to Paul's 'I had not known lust, except the law had said, Thou shalt not covet' (Romans 7:7), and John of Patmos's 'Revelation' of the fury of divine vengeance. In the Bible, consciousness regularly figures as both effect and cause of pain, fear, suffering, and anguish of Spirit—'For in much wisdom is much grief; and he that increaseth knowledge increaseth sorrow' (Ecclesiastes 1:18). Greco-Roman culture likewise, from the tears of Achilles and Priam, the family curse driving the *Oresteia*, and the fated suffering of Oedipus, to the *lachrymae rerum* of Vergil. Greek philosophy projected a relief from such suffering, and in the narrative of Hegel's *Phenomenology*, 'Reason' makes its 'first, and therefore imperfect, appearance' with 'the beyond' of the 'supersensible world' (*Phenomenology* 87–8), a passage allegorizing the advent, in Socrates and Plato, of the high philosophic tradition. The elite subculture of Greek 'philosophy' invested heavily in overcoming affective unhappiness, and often philosophy seems virtually identifiable with *eudaimonia*, a happiness whose condition is liberation not merely from unhappy affects, but from affect as such. In the Plato-and-Aristotle tradition, affect itself is unhappy, and the *eudaimonia* of the philosophers is prescribed precisely as antidote or narcotic (Eagleton's 'anaesthetic') against the vagaries of affect rather than as a redemption of happiness in any *affective* sense.

Viewed through the historical lens of Hegel's unhappy consciousness, the Greek 'discovery of transcendance', of what Hegel calls 'the supersensible', appears as too complacently oriented to the *apatheia* of 'the beyond'; on Hegel's showing, not until Christianity anthropomorphized the transcendent as God incarnate, and abjected itself before this God as a slave before its master, could unhappiness provide Reason with its proper (because at last duly cathected) challenge, that of overcoming abjection as such. Greek 'Reason' was de-anthropomorphized; it could not thus appear as 'master' in relation to the philosopher-'slave'. Only as projected in human form, and as 'master' in dyadic relation to abjected humankind, can God, *or* Reason, incite the kind of misery that

becomes consciousness in the first place. To say that in Hegel's phenomenology, it is Reason that incarnates itself in human form, is to indicate Hegel's
most fundamental reinscription of Christianity. 'Reason is the slave of the
passions': Hume's aphorism, read Hegel-wise, may illuminate the point here,
stipulating of course that 'the passions' are the unhappy ones, the implacable
thanatoid superego passions mobilized in the moralizing monotheisms, given
their definitive modern theorization by Freud, and, mediated by Lacan, ingen-
iously put to the uses of *Ideologiekritik* by Slavoj Zizek. Hegel projects 'Reason' as
the slave destined, in abjection to the master, first to conceive, and finally to
attain, an 'independent [and "happy"] self-consciousness' that the master will
never know. Try to project this allegory onto the Greek philosophical tradition,
and you get a notably chillier picture: something like Plato's *Republic*, with the
philosophers as 'guardians' in serene service to *Logos* itself as represented, but
precisely *not* personified or incarnated, in the philosopher-king, spinning the
ideological fictions necessary to keep the benighted populace in the fearsome
dark of the benignly ideological cave. Not for Plato and Aristotle, elite 'masters'
of a 'some are free' society, any consciousness or idealization of the self as
slave. Only in Diotima's allegory of Eros in the *Symposium* does ancient Greek
'philosophy' approach imagining an abjected self-idealization, and an 'unhappy
consciousness' that is dynamic and productive, because affective, in anything
like Hegel's way. How telling that its name should be 'love'.

So much, on Hegel's showing, for 'the first, and therefore imperfect appearance of Reason'. By contrast, at the close of the 'unhappy consciousness' section,
Hegel stages for 'Reason' a more consequential second coming. The closing
paragraph dramatizes the unhappy consciousness's search for 'relief from its
misery' (*Phenomenology* 137); its very last sentence announces the advent to
consciousness of 'the idea of *Reason*'. What immediately follows, the next
unit of the text, is the section (about a fifth of the whole *Phenomenology*) called
'Reason'. In the 'unhappy consciousness' section, alienation from 'the beyond'
drives early Christianity's abjected sense of sin and guilt—Spirit's 'action . . .
remains pitiable, its enjoyment remains pain' (*Phenomenology* 138)—and the
search for a 'relief' from such 'miseries' involves the 'sublation' of such antithetical categories as action and obedience, guilt and forgiveness, particular
self-surrender and universal will by the ministrations of a 'mediator', a word
whose antithetical connotations for a Protestant (Christ/priest) Hegel leaves
in play, as if to register the ambivalence of the Christian legacy. The driving
force in Hegel's narrative is 'the negative', the 'unrest', and 'counterthrust'
associated with the not at all Platonic/Aristotelian theme of 'freedom': markers
of Hegel's determination to portray the very conflictedness of his World-Spirit
history—and the affective no less than the logical extremity of its painful contradictions—as the agonizing but creative ordeal from which 'the idea of
Reason' first emerges in a form sufficiently 'dialectical' to meet (or inaugurate)
the challenges of the human story Hegel wants to tell. Only as incited by affect
('unhappy consciousness') does (Hegelian) 'Reason' enter, and change, history.

Qualifying Hegel's supposed optimism is that the Hegelian grand narrative projects the fulfillments of Spirit as still far off, as 'not yet'. The 'slaughterbench of history' passage amply attests Hegel's own 'mental torture' at the state of the world, the misery against which the 'optimism' of his writing, style as well as substance, attempts something like an exorcism, a performativity in the spirit of 'fake-it-till-you-make-it', a veritable therapy for the *Weltgeist* at large, anticipating 'joyful sciences' from Nietzsche and William James's 'healthy-mindedness' to Wilhelm Reich, Norman O. Brown, and the self-esteem or 'recovery' movement of today—that 'triumph of the therapeutic' (Philip Rieff) whose happy-consciousness good-news makes so many moralists among us uneasy. One of Hegel's own most striking ideograms for this project is reserved for the climactic lines that conclude the *Phenomenology*, where the 'Calvary of absolute Spirit' is juxtaposed to the secularized image of the sacramental chalice of communion from Schiller's 'Ode to Friendship' (*Phenomenology* 493; for shrewd comment on Hegel's misquotations of the Schiller, see Kojève 165–8). Here what Hegel had earlier, in the 1802 'Faith and Knowledge', called 'the speculative Good Friday, which used to be [considered] historical' (qtd. Kaufmann 100), meets, if not quite a speculative Easter, at least a speculative chalice of the wine that, for Hegel, should not merely betoken, but should actually *be* the communion of Spirit with, or *as* Human Consciousness, Reason, even the Absolute as such. The Cross first, then the Resurrection: this Christian ur-narrativization of the evil/good, damned/saved binary makes bold to reverse that of Genesis 3; and it reenacts itself in Hegel's paradigmatic assumption that happy consciousness can only be—eventually *will* be—wrested from the unhappy kind. This is the ordeal Hegel calls 'the labor and the suffering of the negative', an ordeal he pictures, indeed, as Spirit's harrowing descent into hell, to own or become death itself, to risk its 'utter dismemberment' as the necessary condition of 'finding itself':

> . . . this is the tremendous power of the negative; it is the energy of thought, of the pure 'I'. Death, if that is what we want to call this non-actuality, is of all things the most dreadful, and to hold fast what is dead requires the greatest strength. . . . But the life of Spirit is not the life that shrinks from death and keeps itself untouched by devastation, but rather the life that endures it and maintains itself in it. It wins its truth only when, in utter dismemberment, it finds itself. . . . Spirit is this power only by looking the negative in the face, and tarrying with it. This tarrying with the negative is the magical power that converts it into being. This power is identical with what we earlier called the Subject . . . (*Phenomenology* 19).

Spirit's near-death experience here—it makes unhappy consciousness sound like a euphemism—lends itself to our thematics of the 'labor of affects': overcoming *ataraxia* in a liberation or re-animation of affect, as fundamental to, even constitutive of Spirit's project, and its eventual reward—a project proleptic of many nineteenth- and twentieth-century reinventions of heroic quest as psychological ordeal, from Wordsworth and Coleridge, Baudelaire ('Voyage à Cythére'), Browning's 'Dark Tower' to Eliot's *The Waste Land*, from the sensationalisms of Delacroix and Géricault to Nietzsche's 'strong pessimism' and Wagner's grandiose dooms, to Freud (Everyman an Oedipus of anguishing self-inquiry) and Mann and Valéry. And, of course, Adorno. The point: Hegel's supposed 'optimism' has obscured his part in the ethos of 'tarrying with the negative'.

Diagnosticians of Critique

So, then: 'unhappy consciousness' as the fundamental human problem, recurrent, chronic, world-historical, something like, if not a 'human nature', then a constant foible of our 'species-being'. But there is a more (so to speak) parochial manifestation of the problem, the 'unhappy consciousness' very specifically *of critique*—for both Hegel and Adorno turn their diagnoses of modernity's pathologies directly onto philosophy or critique itself, and the more urgently for the physician-heal-thyself imperative enjoined in their hope to make philosophy (a.k.a. critique, theory) physician (and midwife!) to their (modern) age. Adorno presents the indictment that critique has shirked the 'labor of the concept' with a plangency, an unhappy consciousness palpable and audible in the very tone and voice of his prose, in a way to forbid the forgiving thought that critique's fault has been merely a kind of laziness, or stupidity; the further premise that the labor of conceptualization implies also a 'labor of affectualization' evokes deficits more morally cathected, deficits of honesty and of courage as well. *Dialectic of Enlightenment* points the irony that enlightenment prides itself on facing a demythologized world stripped of the comforts of traditional illusions, but turns out to be motivated, no less than 'myth' itself, by a drive to master (deny) fear, to achieve an imaginary comfort or self-assurance in face of a world more threatening than enlightenment dares to acknowledge.

Hegel makes similar observations, though usually more as satiric jabs at common sense than, as with Adorno, lamentation over culture-wide pathologies. Hegel, indeed, diagnoses every possible reason for what we might call a 'resistance to philosophy'—fear of a death-like 'loss' of the self in 'doubt and despair' (*Phenomenology* 18–20, 49–51), 'shame' before the intellectual challenge and the 'alien authority' of the new (*Phenomenology* 35), 'the conceit that will not argue' (*Phenomenology* 41), narcissistic 'enjoyment' in or fixation on one's own unwittingly tautological 'explanations' (*Phenomenology* 94, 101). The one stumbling block that seems never to occur to Hegel is sheer intellectual incapacity: Hegel writes not only as a writer/thinker utterly undaunted by the prodigious complexities his inquiry generates for itself, but as if in entire confidence that any reader not debilitated by the moral deficits just mentioned will be fully capable of following where he leads. (I confess to moments of thinking this the most extravagant of Hegel's many 'optimisms'.) Warning that 'a fear of falling into error sets up a mistrust of Science', Hegel advises that we should 'mistrust this very mistrust':

> Should we not be concerned as to whether this fear of error is not just the error itself? Indeed this fear takes something—a great deal in fact—for granted as truth . . . [e.g.,] certain ideas about cognition as an *instrument* and as a *medium*, and assumes that there is a *difference between ourselves and this cognition*. Above all, it presupposes that the Absolute stands on one side and cognition on the other, independent and separated from it, and yet is something real; or in other words, it presupposes that cognition which, since it is excluded from the Absolute, is surely outside of the truth as well, is nevertheless true, an assumption whereby what calls itself fear of error reveals itself rather as fear of the truth (*Phenomenology* 47).

Hegel goes on to diagnose what here appears as merely intellectual error in psychological terms, as a vanity and insecurity vitiating the intellectual courage of the inquirer. (Hegel becomes thereby something of a psychologist of the foibles specific to intellectuals, an impulse Adorno continues.) Hegel explains this 'fear of the truth' as 'intended to ward off Science itself, and constitute an empty appearance of knowing'. What Hegel calls 'natural consciousness' (empiricism, i.e., 'sense certainty' elevating itself to a scientific claim) resists the 'path' of the Notion (a.k.a. 'the labor of the concept') because 'the realization of the Notion, counts for it [natural consciousness] as the loss of its own self . . .' (*Phenomenology* 49). 'The road can therefore be regarded as the pathway of doubt, or more precisely as the way of despair'; and 'natural consciousness', economizing its experiential investments to maximize pleasure and minimize pain, cowers away from that path. But for Hegel, this despair and doubt are part of the 'necessary progression and interconnection of the forms of the unreal [sc. "natural"] consciousness [that] will by itself bring to pass the completion of the series' (*Phenomenology* 50). Hegel goes on to outline, in effect, a therapy of *Geist* in its struggles with such despair and doubt, with the 'anxiety' that attends them, with the 'sentimentality' that resorts to a wishful optimism or eudaemonism against them, with the 'conceit' that will tempt *Geist* to fortify its 'vanity' in the face of such threats of 'loss of self'. Hegel ends with the promise that the 'unrest' of thought will eventually overcome the 'inertia' these despairs induce, to renew the quest for truth or 'the Absolute' (*Phenomenology* 51–3).

For Adorno, of course, Hegel's concluding promise rings false because Hegel overoptimistically speaks as if it were not a '*broken* promise' in the here-and-now world. Hegel's genial and confident tone, in effect, belittles the resistance to philosophy—as if to laugh us out of our intellectual timidity—and offers its own brio as, so to speak, a down-payment on the world-historical promise of eventual redemption and happy consciousness. By contrast, Adorno, especially in *Dialectic of Enlightenment*, means to frighten us into new awareness: not only of our very real peril, in the age of industrialized total war, but of the numbness and despair with which we have so far confronted it—or rather, contrived *not* to confront it. What Hegel satirizes as failures specific to the philosophic guild, Adorno diagnoses as a culture-wide pathology, with lethal consequences all too evident in the age of Auschwitz and Hiroshima.

Fear and Enlightenment

The relevant response to that lethality is *fear*—a response, however, that enlightenment and all its powers of reason work to 'dominate', i.e., to repress. To lift or undo that repression, to raise our culture's numbed fear to consciousness, is among the ambitions of *Dialectic of Enlightenment*. Which is why, in *Dialectic of Enlightenment*, fear figures as both key theme and overarching effect. In the philosophical and critical tradition in which Adorno participates, fear, as among the principal components of 'unhappy consciousness', has held a special, even a rather glamorous, place. In Hegel's master/slave narrative, the 'struggle for recognition' surmounts nature only if the stakes of the struggle are mortal. For the slave who buys life at the cost of bondage, the trauma of mortal fear in the combat remains the necessary condition of the subsequent achievement of 'independence', 'self-consciousness', and an instigating intimation of 'being-for-self'. Nietzsche similarly finds an authenticating experience of 'pure terror', 'original pain', and the like as the *sine qua non* of (just what wimpy modernity has closed its eyes to) 'tragedy'; absent such experiences of terror, there arises (has already arisen) what Francis Fukuyama calls, following Kojève's famous splenetic 'end of history' footnote (Kojève 158–62n6), the 'last man' problem: the fear that, should utopia ever arrive, humankind, delivered at last from all mortal challenges, will devolve into a thumb-sucking limbo of material complacency and moral insignificance. This anxiety motivates the conflicted attachment of so many to violence, as a guarantee (in ways René Girard diagnoses) of the values lost to and on anti-heroic, now consumerist, mass culture. And, to be sure, anxieties lest the revolution happen too non-violently seem overblown. But the prospect that revolution might banish suffering and unhappiness altogether arouses ambivalence. Even Marx, in the most utopian of the 1844 manuscripts, 'Private Property and Communism', avows that come the revolution, not *all* suffering will end, but only the 'alienated' kind: 'for suffering, apprehended humanly [i.e., not 'alienatedly'], is an enjoyment of self in man' (*Marx-Engels Reader* 87). We need our fear, to make ourselves heroic.

Further ideological uses of a glamorized motif of fear also figure in the more individualized inflections of these themes running from Kierkegaard to Heidegger and (early) Sartre, in which fear is the guarantor of spiritual maturity and courage, a sort of *macho philosophique*, an openness of the self (as in Hegel's 'tarrying with the negative') to moral extremities of fear and anxiety, refusal or innocence of which would be inauthenticity or *mauvaise foi*. In Kierkegaard, although the 'religious' is the valorized other of the merely 'aesthetic' life—Kierkegaard's version of the 'last man' vacuity—the political itself appears as, categorically, aesthetic: an evasion of the more challenging fears and tremblings that Kierkegaard projects as the exclusive (shall we say) 'enjoyments' of a life authentically lived. Similarly Heidegger, whose courageous 'being-towards-death' individuates and valorizes the existential *Dasein* as against the massed, faceless, inauthentic 'they' (*'das Man'*); compare Lacan's grammatologized and historicized version of the devolution of 'modern man' from subject-'*je*' into object-'*moi*'. Adorno warned that such rhetorics resonated all too readily with the political vulgarizations of the cheerleaders for Thanatos ('Viva la muerte!') and the SS *Übermenschen* flouting death's-head insignia, encouraged by Himmler in explicitly Nietzschean language ('self-overcoming', etc.) to withstand the urgings of conscience that would impede them in their heroic task of massacring the innocents.

For Adorno, by contrast, 'The goal of the revolution is the elimination of anxiety. That is why we need not fear the former, and need not ontologize the latter' (*CC* 131). To me, indeed, one of the most attractive things about Adorno is his visceral refusal of any such glamorization of fear, not least because the 'violence' of which intellectuals so grandiosely speak is so often merely figurative—indeed, sheerly 'imaginary'—as if to lay a me-too claim on the heroism of the literal kind. Hegel's 'tarrying with the negative' ('to hold fast what is dead requires the greatest strength') becomes in Adorno the more muted formula, 'the embittering part of dialectics' (*ND* 151). Not for him the accents of Zarathustrian bravado, snook heroically cocked at the void. Adorno is more like Freud (and, with qualifications, Marx) in conceiving fear as a humiliation, a non-elective ordeal imposed on us by brutal historical circumstance, a suffering that may or may not elicit heroism from some of the sufferers, but sure to damage and debase, not to ennoble, the vast majority of its victims. Like Freud, Adorno distrusts all rhetorics that align the experience of fear with moral heroics, including those, like the 'last man' anxiety, that put the case negatively. For Adorno, indeed, the 'last man' debasement as argument against utopia would be ideological delusion: as if the 'last man' demoralizations weren't *already faits accomplis* in our nightmarish 'administered world'.[3] The motive Adorno most readily shares with Lacan, though Adorno's moral plangency is at the farthest possible remove from Lacan's knowing *Schadenfreude*, would be precisely his alarm at the masochistic human addiction to misery and sentimentalizing rhetorics of *amor fati*, the problematic neatly summarized by Slavoj Zizek in the sarcastic injunction, 'Enjoy your symptom!', and instantiated by most of the names above (Kierkegaard, Nietzsche, Heidegger, Kojève).[4] Like Lacan, again, Adorno aligns this 'weakening of the ego' with a 'neutralization of sex', a 'desexualization of sexuality' (*CM* 72–5) that sounds notes oddly joining Freud's 'psychic impotence' and Marcuse's 'repressive desublimation' with de Rougemont's extension of the Nietzschean 'last man' lament to Eros. For the administered world's 'castrated hedonism, desire without desire' (*AT* 11), the diagnosis would be very much the Lacanian shake of the head at having given way on desire.

So Adorno affects no pose, à la Kierkegaard, Nietzsche, and Heidegger, of courageously facing down the abyss from which others cower; nor does he make as if to smile it away, as Hegel does, or affects to do. If Adorno's critical unhappy consciousness avoids the Scylla of Hegelian 'optimism', it equally steers clear of the Charybdis of self-regardingly 'strong pessimism[s]' of the anti-utopian type so often mobilized in critique of modernity. Adorno's anxieties about modernity are not Huxleyan, but Orwellian, conjuring not the narcotized 'last man' whom Nietzsche so haughtily disdains, but rather the brutalized 'administered subject' whose abasement before the domination of a 'rationalized' world is achieved at the price of a 'weakening of the ego' to produce the 'authoritarian personality', disciplined and conditioned in the regimes of the workplace and the routines of commodified pleasure as managed by the culture industry, an expropriation, 'for others', of all 'spirit', of all subjecthood, of all subjectivity itself.

The 1944 'Introduction'

I want now to bring this evocation of affect and fear to bear on *Dialectic of Enlightenment*. Written during the darkest days of World War Two, while Horkheimer and Adorno were refugees in the United States, this text motivates the 'unhappy consciousness of critique' as a deliberate cathexis of *fear* in the writing. *Dialectic of Enlightenment* is meant to be a frightening book: meant to declare the fear of the writers, and to arouse the fear that has gone numb in the reader, in the culture, in society at large. Keeping the date of composition in mind—late 1943 to early 1944: 'during Auschwitz'[5]—the book aims to arouse the fear narcotized in enlightenment *chorismos*, the 'division of labor' which assigns feeling and thinking to different faculties (art and science) to the detriment of both. ('The narrow-minded wisdom that sorts out feeling from knowing and rubs its hands together when it finds the two balanced is—as trivialities sometimes are—the caricature of a situation that over the centuries of the division of labor has inscribed this division in subjectivity' [*AT* 331].) Horkheimer and Adorno diagnose bourgeois *ataraxia* as programmatic, and foundational to the 'dialectic of enlightenment' the book diagnoses. Later in his career Adorno will frequently attempt 'rescue' of this or that ambition, program, or value that modernity represses or forgets; the project of excavating the 'emotional force' of Kant's philosophy (above) is an example, but it is a dim after-echo of the much more urgent effort in *Dialectic of Enlightenment* to reawaken the energy of terror that traumatized modernity has numbed itself against feeling. Fear is not merely the textual effect or affect of *Dialectic of Enlightenment*, but also the motivation of its thematic or indeed thetic burden, announced in the book's opening sentences:

> In the most general sense of progressive thought, the Enlightenment has always aimed at liberating men from fear and establishing their sovereignty. Yet the fully enlightened earth radiates disaster triumphant. The program of the Enlightenment was the disenchantment of the world; the dissolution of myths and the substitution of knowledge for fancy (Cumming 3).

The book will go on to urge that so far from 'liberating men [us] from fear', our very fear of fear, our anxious repression of our cultural and historical anxieties, has left us enslaved to fear every bit as much as the primitive trapped in the cycle of 'myth', with its compulsive repetition of rituals that palliate the terror even as they confirm the 'fact' of our impotence in a terrifying world. Enlightenment prides itself on having escaped that cycle, but this very pride has itself become an illusion and a denial, a 'sympathetic magic' against dreads cognate with those that entrap the primitive; the devolution of philosophy into positivism and technology has made of 'scientific method' a denial of the unknown, an ethos that assimilates the unknown to the known, the new and the different to the 'same old same old'.

And hence our aborted enlightenment, 'disaster triumphant', progress reverting to barbarism, in obedience to an as-if fated 'compulsion to repeat'. Hence 'The curse of irresistible progress is irresistible regression' (Cumming 36). The fear of fear itself has driven enlightenment to an illusory exorcism of fear, made this impulse its analgesic, its will-to-denial, in short, its 'imaginary victory' over fear, a freedom from fear the more delusional, and (therefore) the more compulsive, the more terror threatens to engulf it. The dislocations of modernity produce turmoil because the new is frightening—and in societies engulfed by rapid change, it's a collective reflex to try to master collective fear by refusing the new. Hence enlightenment, though priding itself as the very vanguard of the new, is only the more thoroughly regressive for the very 'rationalization' with which it has elaborated its defense mechanisms *against* the 'new'. Whatever perplexes enlightenment's canons of reason arouses 'fear', which enlightenment preemptively represses: 'the prime cause of the retreat from enlightenment into mythology is not to be sought so much in the nationalist, pagan and other modern mythologies manufactured precisely in order to contrive such a reversal, but in the Enlightenment itself when paralyzed by fear of the truth' (Cumming xiii–xiv).

I foreground all this as 'motivation' for the writing of *Dialectic of Enlighten-ment*, that is, for the difficulty of its prose. I want to show how what the book *argues* about fear, repression, the anxiety of the new, it also *enacts*—a labor as much of the affects as of the concept—in the writing. Against the backdrop of World War Two, the contrast of Horkheimer and Adorno's authorial carriage with Freud's will be a useful handle. Freud's diagnosis of cultural pathologies is no less comprehensive and disturbing (arguably more so) than Horkheimer and Adorno's, but Freud's tone of calmly bleak realism is notably affectless. Some might argue that Freud's writing, too, is 'enacting' one of his fundamen-tal themes, the 'nirvana principle', that all mental activity has as its goal to defuse dangerous affects. In his account of 'The Dream Work' (chapter VI of *The Interpretation of Dreams*), Freud demonstrates how the unconscious and lan-guage interact through devices that seem as much rhetorical as psychological—'displacement' (sc. metonymy), 'condensation' (sc. metaphor), 'the rebus', the slide from either/or to both/and, the circumvention of repression under the sign of the negative, etc. These insights were seized on by many modern artists as ways to crank emotion *up*, but Freud's consistent point was that the express function of these detours was to dial emotion *down*: to 'strip the elements which have a high psychical value of their intensity', to effect '*a transference and displace-ment of psychical intensities*' (*Interpretation of Dreams* 342–3; Freud's emphasis). Freud's 'stoic' composure—the shocking disclosures delivered in tones of meas-ured calm; the outrages to common sense and morals rendered only the more stinging for the *sang froid* of the delivery; the serene (and accurate) anticipation of scandalized 'resistance' to his work, taken as confirmation of it—all this is at the furthest possible remove from *Dialectic of Enlightenment*, whose prose is so notably overwrought and so willfully obscure.

Yes, willfully—as we can read in the book's 1944 'Introduction', a manifesto in justification of the obscurity and difficulty of the book's writing. The argu-ment evokes and coordinates three axes of 'difficulty', each motivating, and motivated by, the others: the psychological difficulty of our traumatic history, past, present, and future; the intellectual difficulty of the philosophic-critical tradition whose materials the argument mobilizes; and the darkly enigmatic carriage of the self-consciously, deliberately difficult prose style of *Dialectic of Enlightenment* itself. I'll mention again here the (symptomatic) rarity of com-mentary on Adorno that does more than merely remark the difficulty of the writing as prelude to discussion that then proceeds as if the text's meaning were, at least to the commentator, crystal clear. Yet: 'Since that notion [of linguistic and conceptual clarity] declares any negative treatment of the facts or of dominant forms of thought to be obscurantist formalism or—preferably—alien, and therefore taboo, it condemns the spirit to increasing darkness' (Cumming xiv). Ironic that so much commentary on *Dialectic of Enlightenment* should manifest the very compulsivities of falsifying and anodyne clarity the book so explicitly indicts as symptom of 'the dialectic of enlightenment'.

In the 1944 'Introduction', the dark themes and dark affect of *Dialectic of Enlightenment*—'dark' meaning at once 'unhappy', 'obscure', and 'repressed'—are explicitly conjured as making imperative the difficulties of the book as reading matter, the darkness or obscurity of the way its writing is written. Dated 'May 1944' (just days before the allied landings in Normandy), and reprinted without change in subsequent editions and translations, the 'Introduction' is insistent that the difficulties of the text are *not* to be set aside, that they are bone and blood of the book's argument and intended effect, indeed, of its project and its problem: that they are 'motivated' in ways the authors 'make thematic' in the 'Introduction' itself. If the text proper enacts or performs—the *mot juste* here is *suffers*—the difficulties of 'the matter in hand', the 'Introduction' more explicitly reflects on them, and thus makes the best possible initiation to the challenges the text before us is going to present. From almost the opening sentence, the difficulties of the project are foregrounded:

> . . . the more intensively we pursued our task, the clearer it became that our own powers were disproportionate to it. . . . we had set ourselves nothing less than the discovery of why mankind, instead of entering into a truly human condition, is sinking into a new kind of barbarism. We underestimated the difficulties of interpretation . . . (Cumming xi).

The echo of Rousseau's famous lament—'man', born free, lives everywhere in chains—announces (as in Rousseau) an attempt at 'the discovery why' this should be so; the following sentence similarly conjures the 11th thesis on Feuerbach to suggest, Marx's exorbitant provocation notwithstanding, that 'interpreting' the world is quite difficulty enough, even in default of changing it, and assumes (what Marx can only rhetorically have seemed to question), that there is continuity, not antithesis, between interpreting the world and changing it. In any case, consciousness is not a problem Horkheimer and Adorno are prepared to dismiss:

> We underestimated the difficulties of interpretation, because we still trusted too much in the modern consciousness. Even though we had known for many years that the great discoveries of applied science are paid for with an increasing diminution in theoretical awareness, we still thought that in regard to scientific activity our contribution could be restricted to the criticism or extension of specialist axioms. Thematically, at any rate, we were to keep to the traditional disciplines: to sociology, psychology, and epistemology.
>
> However, the fragments united in this volume show that we were forced to abandon this conviction. . . . in the present collapse of bourgeois civilization not only the pursuit but the meaning of science has become problematical . . . What the brazen Fascists hypocritically laud and pliable humanist experts

naïvely put into practice—the indefatigable self-destruction of enlightenment—requires philosophy to discard even the last vestiges of innocence in
regard to the habits and tendencies of the spirit of the age (Cumming xi).

What had initially looked to be a set of specialist problems ('sociology, psychology, and epistemology') turn out to challenge 'philosophy' itself—and not only
on its wonted ground of 'theoretical' awareness but also, more radically, on
the higher-stakes ground of politics, culture, science, and the very fate of civilization, grounds on which philosophy has wanted to maintain a detached 'innocence' that, Horkheimer and Adorno charge, even the most willfully innocent
can no longer pretend is tenable. The urgency of the crisis is to be read in the
very texture, the very 'fragmentary' quality, of the text before us: we might have
expected that the move from specialist disciplines to the discipline of disciplines,
philosophy, would promise the integration and comprehensiveness (undoing
chorismos) that the specialisms renounce on principle; instead, Horkheimer
and Adorno's effort to overcome the fragmentariness of intellectual culture can
itself yield only 'fragments'. In the context of 1944, a phrase like 'the tireless
self-destruction of enlightenment' would have recalled images from front pages
and newsreels of bombed-out cities, whole cultures reduced to rubble, to fragments. As we'll see, Horkheimer and Adorno diagnose enlightenment as a
rapaciously 'analytic' (i.e., atomizing, separating, distinction-making) habit or
drive, or driven-ness, of thought that has already, in the name of science, frag-
mented the very infra-structure of thinking, the field of intellectual labor, from
within. Enlightenment's divvying-up of disciplinary turf, modernity's settlement
of the 'contest of faculties' thematized by Kant, this 'innocence', this refusal
of the larger, integrated theoretical self-consciousness that opens itself to the
largest problems of the culture, is itself one of the largest problems, a major
symptom of the 'dialectic of enlightenment' Horkheimer and Adorno aim to
address.

'[T]he discovery of why mankind, instead of entering into a truly human
condition, is sinking into a new kind of barbarism' will oblige philosophy to
overcome its wonted (ideological) 'innocence', and like Oedipus (avatar of the
Freudian analysand) face repressed horrors past and present. To meet the challenge of this self-renewal Horkheimer and Adorno prescribe a resolute attempt
at *Verfremdung* or *ostranenia*, to estrange or defamiliarize habits of thinking and
of language long since turned ideological:

> When public opinion has reached a state in which thought inevitably becomes
> a commodity, and language the means of promoting that commodity, then
> the attempt to trace the course of such depravation has to deny any allegiance
> to current linguistic and conceptual conventions, lest their world-historical
> consequences thwart it entirely (Cumming xi–xii).

This seems a very 'period' modernist/avant-garde disavowal of received conventions, and fair warning that we must expect provocations of expression and of thinking whose departure from what we're used to is much of the point—for to use 'an impoverished and debased language to recommend renewal' only 'strengthens the established order [the critic] is trying to break' (Cumming xiv). The renewal of our debased language will contravene conventional cultural 'demands' that are both 'linguistic and conceptual'; the antinomy long dominant in Western critical discourses between (to put it in the most current terminology) 'textual' and 'thetic' is to be collapsed, abolished, even something like deconstructed, not only in the argued theory but in the self-consciously *difficult* writing practice of *Dialectic of Enlightenment*.

But in dissenting from 'current linguistic and intellectual demands', *Dialectic of Enlightenment* declares a critical difference from avant-gardism as usual, for in the modern arts, the search for new and uncorrupted expressive means typically identifies the 'concept', generically, with (even as) the enemy, and mobilizes against it in the name of the 'concrete' particular, whose redemptive *quidditas* or 'authenticity' the familiarizations of intellect have allegedly habituated and debased. (This axiomatic replicates itself, of course, in many philosophical texts, and hence some of the Frankfurt School's particular 'existentialist' *bêtes noirs*, e.g., Heidegger, Jaspers, Scheler.) The twentieth-century arts, too, declare the ambition to reclaim 'truth', but usually by circumventing the very conceptuality that Horkheimer and Adorno set in place as a *sine qua non* of their project, and conceiving 'truth' aesthetically, as 'immediate [i.e., unmediated] experience'. From the Hegelian viewpoint of Horkheimer and Adorno, 'mediation' is indissociable from 'the labor of the concept'; its repudiation, in the arts as in the empirical sciences, is itself a telling symptom (Adorno's frequent name for it is 'nominalism') of the predicament of modernity, the 'dialectic of enlightenment', that they mean to expose and indict. And redeem or 'rescue', in large measure, again, by the 'labor of the affects', i.e., affectualizing or cathecting 'the labor of the concept' itself.

'Mythic Fear Turned Radical'

I want now to read a lengthy quotation that will display these difficulties together. It is only one of the many projections in *Dialectic of Enlightenment* of the arc from prehistory to the present, from animism to Enlightenment, and it enacts the 'progress/regress' motif in the paradoxical gesture of a narrative whose point is to stage the failure of its own progress, to narrate its own continual relapse or regression to its initial (steady-) state, to display the disintricability of progress and regression even at the risk of seeming to identify terms whose non-identity would seem, on Adorno's showing certainly, to be the very condition of dialectic itself. So we have a thematic burden carried less in the details of what the sentences state or argue, than in the formal character of a passage that conducts itself as a quasi- or (even) pseudo-narrative. And, crucially, the theme— the failure of progress, the regression to primitive unreason—is charged with its cathexis of dread by reason of the very cryptic-ness of the oracular carriage of the text itself, its broad-brush laying about with complex and loaded terminologies whose meanings or connotations are not clarified or delimited, and above all its rhythm or tempo, its air of driven and breathless urgency:

> The gloomy and indistinct religious principle that was honored as *mana* in the earliest known stages of humanity, lives on in the radiant world of Greek [i.e., Olympian] religion. Everything unknown and alien is primary and undifferentiated: that which transcends the confines of experience; whatever in things is more than their previously known reality. What the primitive experiences in this regard is not a spiritual as opposed to a material substance, but the intricacy of the Natural in contrast to the individual. The gasp of surprise which accompanies the experience of the unusual becomes its name. It fixes the transcendance of the unknown in relation to the known, and therefore terror as sacredness. The dualization of nature as appearance and sequence, effort and power, which first makes possible both myth and science, originates in human fear, the expression of which becomes explanation. It is not the soul which is transposed to nature, as psychologism would have it; *mana*, the moving spirit, is no projection, but the echo of the real supremacy of nature in the weak souls of primitive men. The separation of the animate and the inanimate, the occupation of certain places by demons and deities, first arises from this pre-animism, which contains the first lines of the separation of subject and object. When the tree is no longer approached merely as tree, but as evidence of the Other, as the location of *mana*, language expresses the contradiction that something is itself and at one and the same time something other than itself, identical and not identical. Through the deity, language is transformed from tautology to language. The concept, which some would see as the sign-unit for whatever is comprised under it, has from the beginning been the product of dialectical thinking in which everything is always that which it is, only because it becomes that which it is not. That was the original form of objectifying definition, in which concept and thing are separated. The same form which is already far advanced in the Homeric epic and confounds itself in modern positivist science. But this dialectic remains impotent to the extent that it develops from the cry of terror which is the duplication, the tautology, of terror itself. The gods cannot take fear away from man, for they bear its petrified sound with them as they bear their names. Man imagines himself free from fear when there is no longer anything unknown. That determines the course of demythologization, of enlightenment, which compounds the animate with the inanimate just as myth compounds the

inanimate with the animate. Enlightenment is mythic fear turned radical. The pure immanence of positivism, its ultimate product, is no more than a so to speak universal taboo. Nothing at all may remain outside, because the mere idea of outsideness is the very source of fear (Cumming 14–16).

This passage illustrates, as I've suggested, what turns out to be the fundamental, and deliberate formal contradiction of *Dialectic of Enlightenment*, for the momentum of the passage as one reads is narrative—we are reading a story—and yet it is a rum question at the close what, if anything, has been narrated. The passage ends much as it began, enlightenment ends where animism began, in fearful denial of what is new or 'outside'; here as elsewhere, what is narrated is the failure of the narrative to achieve narrativity, that is, to accomplish the development, to unfold the new, which would be the *sine qua non* of narrative, the crucial change or 'event' (outcome), the indispensable thing-to-be-narrated in the first place. The burden of this (specifically *narrative*) 'performative contradiction' is that 'The curse of irresistible progress is irresistible regression' (Cumming 36)—and the non-transitive steady-state syntax of that sentence, subject and predicate joined by the present-tense copula, could stand as emblem of just what the narrative's progress/regress enacts, or rather prevents being enacted. A particularly cryptic crux is the word 'tautology', here anticipating Adorno's later assault on 'identity thinking'. In the passage, 'tautology' is not, to be sure, simply identifiable with 'identity', but it acts as something like the surrogate of identity—of the retro- or primary identity of the origin (*archē*), needless to say; not of the ultimate and final identity (*telos*) of the 'Absolute'. As narrative *actant*, 'tautology' appears here as the fated antagonist of 'language', of 'separation', of apprehension of 'the Other', of non-identity, and of 'dialectical thinking' itself: at the recurrence of 'fear', all achieved differences relapse, as if in obedience to the irresistible downward pull of a gravitational field, back to the ground of 'tautology' again.

But Horkheimer and Adorno want to (seem to) 'preserve' the Hegelian narrative as well as to 'cancel' it; hence, near the middle of the passage, 'language', 'concept', and 'dialectic' come onstage, as potentially effectual terms that seem momentarily capable of breaching the closure, the regime from animism to enlightenment, of 'tautology', and enabling a truly narrative movement of change. 'Tautology' figures as their fated antagonist, and in the agon of progress/ regress, as their nemesis, the ruin of all that they would seem to promise. From the primitive awe of the spirit-name that 'fixes . . . terror as sacredness', the mere utterance of which becomes 'expression' and then 'explanation', there arise 'the first lines of the separation of subject and object', and hence the (very Hegelian) sense that 'language expresses the contradiction that something is itself and at one and the same time something other than itself, identical and not identical. Through the deity, language is transformed from tautology to language'. Note that it is as much or more from the interaction of these terms as from any extant notion we might have of their meaning that we infer what 'tautology', 'language', 'dialectic', and so on, connote here, what role they play in the 'night of the world' drama unfolding on the page.

We note the entry here of 'contradiction', a key term in Frankfurt School discourses; and of the problematic of 'identity/non-identity' that Adorno will later elaborate so richly in *Negative Dialectics*. In this passage, these terms conjure the possibility associated with the next such term to agitate the text, 'dialectic' itself, here staged as the condition of a redemption of the 'concept' from its demotion to 'the sign-unit for whatever is comprised under it', a ('nominalist') formulation that reduces 'the concept' to a mere enabling fiction in a positivist construction of the function of language in a world of (readily, and metaphysically, separable) words and things. Against all such 'nominalist' dismissals of 'the concept', the text goes on to retroject 'the kinetic force of [the] concept' (*PMM* 26) back into antiquity, in the assertion that the concept 'has from the beginning been the product of dialectical thinking in which everything is always that which it is, only because it becomes that which it is not'. The language of 'dialectic' and 'becoming' here summons the highest Hegelian vocation of the concept and of philosophy, which sets what can be thought against, and as the critique or 'negation' of, 'what is': as a volitional element in the temporal stream (or narrative) of 'becoming'. Having introduced the terminology, and the promise, of the dialectic, the passage now reverts to program, to stage the miscarriage of that promise: for 'this dialectic remains impotent to the extent that it develops from the cry of terror which is the duplication, the tautology, of terror itself'. ('Develops from': enlightenment may suppose it has surmounted the primal terror, but it has merely repressed it, and thus, unconsciously, prolonged it.) The passage then moves to enlightenment, which seeks to escape 'the duplication, the tautology, of terror itself' via 'demythologization', by a systematic conquest of the source of fear, the unknown, and its conversion to knowledge—but this impotent dialectic cannot help, despite itself and unwittingly, but repeat, rather than undo, the 'tautology of terror'.

That some such reversal or catastrophe befalls the enlightenment program, the general drift of the passage makes clear—though neither narratively nor, so to speak, syllogistically, is the exact course of this miscarriage spelled out. Rather there follows a sequence of problematic assertions, and oddly it is in the obscurer of these that the extent and irony of the failure emerge most clearly in, for instance, the most challenging sentence here, which is also the shortest—'Enlightenment is mythic fear turned radical' (Cumming 16)—and well worth a look at the German: '*Aufklärung ist die radikal gewordene, mythische Angst*' (*GS3* 32). Jephcott's translation reads: 'Enlightenment is mythical fear radicalized' (Jephcott 11). The English 'radical' in both translations is an obvious choice for '*radikal*' in the German; but that buzzword makes harder rather than easier the question of what the sentence might mean. For the politically left reader Horkheimer and Adorno address, the first suggestion of 'turned radical' would be of progress, of 'radicalization' as a desirable conversion or development: something has advanced from a complacent, ideological superficiality, has been 'made conscious', has been made *political* radicalized. So far, the sentence might be read as endorsing the very ideology ('broken promise' indeed) of enlightenment that the authors mean to question.

Another first-take reading, not incompatible with the first, might read 'radicalized' or 'turned radical' to suggest something like an eruption or explosion of mythic fear, as if announcing a sudden and transforming release of affects hitherto repressed and held in check—and of course the sudden unblocking of long-repressed energies is a familiar figure for revolution. But again, context counsels otherwise—the 'universal taboo' is clearly a universal repression—which would skew 'radicalized' or 'turned radical' away from their accustomed meanings: in a direction, indeed, virtually the opposite, toward something like, 'enlightenment is primordial fear precisely *not* bursting up into expression from below, but on the contrary driven downward, back to the atavistic, to the roots'. 'Radicalized', in short, here means 'repressed'—the reverse of its usual connotation.[6] An apposite model to adduce here is Freud's account of trauma in section IV of *Beyond the Pleasure Principle*, according to which an onset of frightening stimuli 'invade' the sensorium, which responds according to the nirvana-principle, with a defensive 'hypercathexis' whose paradoxical aim is to achieve an 'anticathexis' by means of which the floods of overwhelming stimuli can be 'mastered' and 'bound', and thus rendered 'quiescent'.

Freud is elaborating here the 'compulsion to repeat'—a model whose pertinence to *Dialectic of Enlightenment* seems the more compelling for going unmentioned by the authors. ('Anxiety of influence'?) Adorno much more explicitly owns Freud's relevance in *Philosophy of New Music*, which he wrote roughly contemporaneously with, and describes as a 'detailed excursus' to, *Dialectic of Enlightenment* (*PNM* 5). The book contrasts Schoenberg and Stravinsky as 'extremes' of 'new [or modern] music'; Adorno praises Schoenberg for acknowledging, but even (much) more, for *arousing* fear and terror as 'shocks' to break through the narcotizing conventions by which modernity numbs itself against the horror and guilt of its violent social order:

> The genuinely revolutionary element in [Schoenberg's] music is the transformation of the function of expression. Passions are no longer faked; on the contrary, undisguised, corporeal impulses of the unconscious, shocks, and traumas . . . attack the taboos of the form because these taboos submit the impulses to their censorship, rationalize them, and transpose them into images. Schoenberg's formal innovations were closely related to the change in emotional content. They serve the breakthrough of its reality. . . . The scars of this revolution in expression . . . [are] emissaries of the id, distressing the surface and as little to be wiped away by subsequent correction as are the traces of blood in fairy tale (*PNM* 35).

This passage, written in 1941 (before *Dialectic of Enlightenment*), stakes all on Schoenberg's mimesis of the id's fearful impulses; and as the passage continues, Adorno could be charged with commending Schoenberg for rendering these impulses 'immediately', *without* (and as a 'Critique of') 'Semblance and Play'. Adorno achieves a more sophisticated, more critical concept of mimesis in the Stravinsky section of the book (1948), in which he indicts (in terms reversing his praise of Schoenberg) Stravinsky's 'domination' of his audience's emotions, whether in the imitation of 'primitive' effects in the *Sacré* or his later 'neo-classicism', in which the manipulation is mediated by imitation of past musical styles with all their established sentimental associations.[7] At issue throughout is Schoenberg's genuine readiness to 'tarry with the negative', versus Stravinsky's controlled, merely sensationalizing evocation of it (when we wasn't forthrightly offering anodynes against it) in a sort of program music for highbrows. A similar 'tarrying with the negative', a deliberate effort not merely to discuss modern anxiety, but actually to *arouse* it, animates *Dialectic of Enlightenment.*

But in addition to a diagnosis of the etiology of the 'compulsion to repeat', Freud also proposes a therapy of release from it—a process, a 'working-through', whose key term, 'transference', also poses suggestive analogies with the workings of 'immanent critique' (more on this in the next chapter). So, then, again: 'Enlightenment is mythic fear turned radical': having worked through the twists and turns of the argument, the obscurities of the writing, and the cryptic 'antithetical' meanings, there persists—not cancelled but preserved in all this conflictedness of suggestion and connotation against context and larger thought-rhythms (sc. form)—some residue, some still-utopian potential, of the first reading, that is, of the primary association of the word 'radical': that enlightenment is indeed, or may somehow again be, a radicalization of mythic fear in the sense projected in the 'labor of affectualization', in effect the program (I am arguing) of *Dialectic of Enlightenment* itself: to awaken the fear, terror, angst, dread that 'the dialectic of enlightenment' has (so far) narcotized and repressed, and to draw from the jolting accesses of affect thereby released a newly radicalizing energy that shall make of 'the unhappy consciousness of critique' an engine of advance and of the new, rather than a pitfall, a syndrome— an *ataraxia*—of defeat and repetition.

This quasi-'transferential' power of immanent critique, I want to argue, is the 'dialectical' condition and/or effect of Adorno's so agitated and agitating—so affective and affecting—prose. And it is why readings of Adorno that officiously vouchsafe his 'meaning' over the head (so to speak) of his difficult writing seem to me to miss much of the point of reading him in the first place. And again, the challenge is as much moral and emotional as intellectual, as much about confronting fear—as immediate affect, as mediated concept, as meta-fear: the fear of fear itself—as about meeting the interpretive and cognitive challenges of a difficult text in the daunting tradition of Hegel-and-after. The *difficulty* of

Adorno's writing may initially seem an obstacle to reading; but it reflects difficulties—cognitive, moral, and emotional—that the authors fully share with the reader: preeminently, the difficulty, and the shared but too-often repressed bond of *anxiety* itself—remembering that the anxiety most relevantly belongs not to the authors personally or subjectively, but to the objective 'matter at hand', the horror of the Hitler period. All of these challenges or 'difficulties' motivate and are motivated by the complexity and obscurity of the allusive, learned, and restlessly (even recklessly) urgent prose of a text that, both in the writing and in the reading, enacts, or suffers, what it argues: the imperative labor of facing, in thought and in feeling, the *Angst* that has paralyzed thought and feeling both. The difficulty of the prose is meant to inflict on the reader, too, this *Angst*, this 'labor and suffering of the negative'. But it is meant to agitate as well anxiety's antithetical or dialectical other, hope—however unemphatic in the argument, however merely implicit in the movement, the form, of the text.

Most of my description here has made *Dialectic of Enlightenment* sound like a very despairing book indeed—extravagantly, floridly despairing: operatic, even 'hysterical' in the sense Zizek has elaborated from Lacan. It is indeed a text answering to Harold Bloom's fine formulation, 'an achieved anxiety' (Bloom 96). But of course Horkheimer and Adorno do not mean to incite affects of fear for their own sake; that would be 'mimesis' of the merely ideological kind—mere repetition of symptom, not critical negation. On the contrary, their 'immanent critique' intends a 'working-through' that must begin by making the traumas and anxieties of the World War Two ordeal available to consciousness, even at the cost of accesses of terror, as indispensable prerequisite to any breach of the paralyzing captivity in which modern consciousness has languished for too long. Adorno says as much in an unwontedly straightforward passage from a 1967 essay, originally a radio talk, called 'Education after Auschwitz' (a title resonating with Adorno's most famous, and most despairing watchword):

> . . . anxiety must not be repressed. When anxiety is not repressed, when one permits oneself to have, in fact, all the anxiety that this [after-Auschwitz] reality warrants, then precisely by doing that, much of the destructive effect of unconscious and displaced anxiety will probably disappear (*CM* 198).

Hence the paradoxical textual effect or affect of *Dialectic of Enlightenment*, that what might seem Horkheimer and Adorno's *ne plus ultra* of despair nevertheless achieves—antithetically, or dialectically—a kind of climax, intensification and 'relief' all at once, by way of a return to or repetition of the very affects from which relief is sought. The next chapter will consider the complaints of figures as consequential as Georg Lukács and Jürgen Habermas that Frankfurt School 'immanent critique' lapses into 'myth' in the very way it purports to critique.

But Horkheimer and Adorno aim at a 'working-through' (*Durcharbeitung*, cf. Adorno's 'The Meaning of Working Through the Past' [*CM* 89–103]) on, again, the Freudian model of 'transference': a controlled regression designed to make the repressed experientially, affectively, not merely cognitively, available to consciousness. (Here one recalls Freud's adviso that neurosis is 'already a step', and indeed the *first* step, 'toward cure' [*General Psychological Theory* 41; cf. *Moses and Monotheism* 97].) The aim is not dispassionate 'insight' but a 'transferential' reawakening, or becoming-conscious, of the very affects that are causing the trouble. These affects must be evoked, their repression partly lifted, before they can be 'relieved' in a newly conscious 'repetition' that will be in some measure freeing.

What Adorno foregrounds in this Freudian model is a sense that the affects are not merely there to be worked on, but themselves exert their own peculiarly potent 'agency' among the conflicting forces seething in the labor of 'making the unconscious conscious'. So the transaction or transference between consciousness and affects is mutual, a confluence in which we might look for the 'labor of the affects' to rejoin the 'labor of the concept' in a productive collaboration to freeing effect. Thus is 'agony raised to a concept', the concrete *realia* of suffering 'apprehended as thought', the concept quickened by being opened up to (not narcotized against) the feeling of this agony. Only after an evocation of the pain and fear that have paralyzed us can there be any release of affective energies whose freeing might augur possibilities more hopeful: affects agitated by some intimation that there remain potentials of consciousness (thought and feeling, agony and concept, Eros and knowledge)—potentials, in short, of critique—still to be mobilized. The critical is 'not yet' the utopian, nor is the promise (Stendhal's '*promesse du bonheur*') quite vouchsafed, let alone realized, or its 'broken'-ness repaired. Nevertheless, for all its extremities of *Angst* and terror, *Dialectic of Enlightenment* manages actually to arouse hopes that a Freud or a Weber would dismiss with a sadder-but-wiser shake of the head.

Critique and/as Utopia

I want to close this chapter with one further consideration of how this happens—this 'labor of affectualization', this dialectical transubstantiation of despair into something like hope. The example above derived hope as a negatively stated motif inferable from what looks to be on its face a very dark passage indeed. I want now to locate such effects in, and ascribe them to, the compositional rhythm or movement—the *form*—of Horkheimer and Adorno's text: in the climax of chapter 1 of *Dialectic of Enlightenment*. We have been looking so far at passages from that program chapter of the book, passages—'Enlightenment is mythic fear turned radical', e.g.—that have evoked the evil, the 'triumphant calamity', of the dialectic of enlightenment. For more than three quarters of its length, the chapter has diagnosed the 'repression' of fear under whose pall enlightenment since Homer has sleep-walked into ever-increasing terror, and evoked the fear itself in the spirit of an effort to undo that repression. At a determinate point (as we'll see) the text introduces, then prosecutes, its case for the necessity of critique—'thought' itself—as the only possible relief of our predicament, and as antidote to both the terror that has paralyzed us and the terrifying world our paralysis has allowed to come into being. But from this sanguine argument, I want to elicit something more elusive: what I might call an intimation of the utopian, or (perhaps better) a utopia-effect, that is less argued in the book's propositional content or logic (the *Bilderverbot* against representing utopia remains in force), than enacted in its verbal energy, and even more in the book's larger structural rhythms, what Adorno elsewhere calls the 'agency of form' (*NL2* 114). This 'utopia-effect' results, that is, not from a propositional or syllogistic drawing of deductions from initial premises to terminal QED, but rather from something like a musical movement, a trajectory more performative than constative, as much affective as conceptual, enacted as much in the text's orchestration of the sequence of ideas, figures, and tones as in any content or thesis the prose expounds. We undergo the text's utopia-effect not in any excerptable point it makes along the way, but rather in the 'form' of the text's own progress as a piece of writing.

The peroration, in the very last paragraphs of the chapter, reprises the motif of 'thought' and its agency (here evoked as 'revolutionary imagination' and 'unyielding theory'):

The suspension of the concept, whether in the name of progress or of culture—which had already long before tacitly leagued themselves against the truth—opened the way for falsehood. And this in a world that verified only evidential propositions, and preserved thought—degraded to the achievement of great thinkers—as a kind of stock of superannuated clichés, no longer to be distinguished from truth neutralized as a cultural commodity.

But to recognize domination, even in thought itself, as unreconciled nature, would mean a slackening of the necessity whose perpetuity socialism itself prematurely confirmed as a concession to reactionary common sense. By elevating necessity to the status of the basis for all time to come, and by idealistically degrading the spirit for ever to the very apex, socialism held on all too surely to the legacy of bourgeois philosophy. Hence the relation of necessity to the realm of freedom would remain merely quantitative and mechanical, and nature, posited as wholly alien—just as in the earliest mythology—would become totalitarian and absorb freedom together with socialism. With the abandonment of thought, which in its reified form of mathematics, machine, and organization avenges itself on the men who have forgotten it, enlightenment has relinquished its own realization. By taking everything unique and individual under its tutelage, it left the uncomprehended whole the freedom, as domination, to strike back at human existence and consciousness by way of things. But true revolutionary practice depends on the intransigence of theory in the face of the insensibility with which society allows thought to ossify. It is not the material prerequisites of fulfillment—liberated technology as such—which jeopardize fulfillment. That is asserted by those sociologists who are again searching for an antidote, and—should it be a collective measure—to master the antidote. Guilt is a context of social delusion. The mythic scientific respect of the peoples of the earth for the *status quo* that they themselves unceasingly produce, itself finally becomes positive fact: the oppressor's fortress in regard to which even revolutionary imagination despises itself as utopism and decays to the condition of pliable trust in the objective tendency of history. As the organ of this kind of adaptation, as a mere construction of means, the Enlightenment is as destructive as its romantic enemies accuse it of being. It comes into its own only when it surrenders the last remaining concordance with the latter and dares to transcend the false absolute, the principle of blind domination. The spirit of this kind of unrelenting theory would turn even the mind of relentless progress to its end. Its herald Bacon dreamed of the many things 'which kings with their treasure cannot buy, nor with their force command', of which 'their spials and intelligencers can give no news'. As he wished, they fell to the burgers, the enlightened heirs of those kings. While bourgeois economy multiplied power through the mediation of the market, it also multiplied its objects and powers to such an extent that for their administration not just the kings, not even the middle classes are necessary, but all men. They learn from the power of things to dispense at last with power. Enlightenment is realized and reaches its term when the nearest practical ends reveal themselves as the most distant goal now attained, and the lands of which 'their spials and intelligencers can give no news', that is, those of the nature despised by dominant science, are recognized as the lands of origin. Today, when Bacon's utopian vision that we should 'command nature by action'—that is, in practice—has been realized on a tellurian scale, the nature of the thralldom that he ascribed to unsubjected nature is clear. It was domination itself. And knowledge, in which Bacon was certain the 'sovereignty of man lieth hid', can now become the dissolution of domination. But in the face of such a possibility, and in the service of the present age, enlightenment becomes wholesale deception of the masses (Cumming 40–2).

At the top of this final paragraph there is some wordplay in the German on the hoary Marxian figuration of economic 'base' and cultural 'superstructure' (*'Indem er für alle Zukunft die Notwendigkeit zur Basis erhob und den Geist auf gut idealistisch zur höchsten Spitze depravierte, hielt er das Erbe der bürgerlichen Philosophie allzu krampfhaft fest'* [*GS3* 58]) that Cumming captures deftly: 'By elevating necessity to the status of the basis for all time to come, and by idealistically degrading the spirit for ever to the very apex, socialism held on all too surely to the legacy of bourgeois philosophy' (Cumming 41). The irony here indicts with equal point both the 'realism' of bourgeois prudentialism (self-preservation) and the materialism of 'official' Marxist-Leninism, and does so most dazzlingly by way of its witty reversal of the usual terms of the figure: bourgeois and social-ist thought alike have 'elevated' necessity to the 'basis', and 'degraded' spirit ('*Geist*') to the 'apex'. And for good measure, Horkheimer and Adorno charac-terize this officially 'materialist' gesture of Stalinist orthodoxy as 'idealist'. Con-sciousness as volatile as that seems almost to revoke its own 'unhappiness' by the sheer force of its wit: or at least, putting thus in play (or standing on its head) the cliché pyramid-image for the tired materialism/idealism shibboleth, such wit twists materialism's all-too-righteous (and literal-minded) tail.

Still, utopian consciousness isn't given its head; these critical (crypto-utopian?) gestures are intermitted, even checked, throughout, by recurrences to our ideological condition: 'By taking everything unique and individual under its tutelage, [enlightenment] left the uncomprehended whole the freedom, as domination, to strike back at human existence and consciousness by way of things'. But the recurrence works both ways, in what has by now begun to mani-fest as a regular rhythm or dialectic of ideological condition alternating with revolutionary possibility: 'But true revolutionary practice depends on the intransigence of theory in the face of the insensibility with which society allows thought to ossify'.

The gesturings, orchestrations, rhythms, tones, structurations of this prose enact the unremitting agon of a heroically 'unyielding theory' against the pow-ers of what the passage licenses us to call 'domination uncomprehended': in the passage's own terms, the agon is against 'the suspension of the concept'; in the Hegelian terms Horkheimer and Adorno evoke throughout, their struggle is for a renewal of '*die Arbeit des Begriffs*', the 'labor of the concept'. But 'the insen-sibility with which society allows thought to ossify' is a deficit not merely of intel-lect; it is a deficit of feeling as well: *ataraxia*, apathy, anaesthesis, asceticism, 'coldness', Odysseus roped to the mast, the rowers with ears artfully deafened against art. In saying the passage 'enacts' this agon, I mean, of course, to imply that the motion and energy of the prose actually *performs* the 'labor of affectuali-zation' that, I have been arguing, Horkheimer and Adorno stipulate as the necessary complement or completion of the making-conscious 'labor of the concept'. Almost as if to forestall any binary (i.e., non-dialectical) opposition of the labor of *concepts* to that of *affects*, the passage fuses concept and affect when it includes diagnosis of the affects, and of the disease or debilitated psychology or 'learned helplessness' of the affects, that its own dialectical 'labor' means to 'work through', redeem, overcome.

Like Freud, Horkheimer and Adorno adapt categories of individual psycho-logical analysis to the domain of the social; more audaciously than Freud—here they align rather with Hegel—they also mean to prescribe, for the social

psychology of the 'damaged life', a 'labor of concept *and* affect' that offers an
amelioration of unhappy consciousness that would seem to promise more than
Freud's '*ordinary* unhappiness'. As in Hegel and Marx there is the premise
that unhappy consciousness results when people are alienated from their own
powers and creations, so alienated that they can no longer recognize them as
their own ('The mythic scientific respect of the peoples of the earth for the
status quo that they themselves unceasingly produce'): resentment against what
we take to be an externally given reality becomes at once shame at our impotence to change it and guilt at our debilitated desire (and vestigial 'imaginary'
power) to do so. In Horkheimer and Adorno's social diagnostic, 'guilt' is not
the irredeemable liability wisdom resigns itself to (at best) merely coping with;
rather, 'Guilt is a context of social delusion', in a resignation to complicity
in collective misery that paralyzes the very energies that might undo the self-
perpetuating structure of collective injury. 'That might undo': sounds utopian?
It can sound no other way, in an 'administered world' in which we have guiltily
relinquished our power, in which our deluded guilt converts our Promethean
potentialities into self-contempt and abjected, defeated passivity before 'what is':
what Fredric Jameson calls the 'Promethean shame' in which 'even revolutionary imagination despises itself as utopism and decays to the condition of pliable
trust in the objective tendency of history' (*Postmodernism* 315)—a way of putting
it, please note, as critical of Soviet orthodoxy as of liberal hand-wringing;
Adorno would presumably have seen Lenin's tough-guy put-down of 'infantile
leftism' as an anti-utopian pathology functionally equivalent to that of bourgeois 'supposed, even if delusional, *Realpolitik*' (*CM* 198).

  Needless to say, I want to stipulate as premise for the arguments to follow that
in the energy of Horkheimer and Adorno's prose, there is a 'making conscious'
as much affective as conceptual, a labor as much of feeling as of thinking,
and more, a labor aspiring to overcome the separation or *chorismos*, habitual in
Western culture generally and in the European enlightenment particularly, that
disjoins thought from feeling to the detriment of both. 'Consciousness without
shudder', we have quoted Adorno as saying above, 'is reified consciousness'.
The implication is that unreified consciousness, full subjectivity, involves affect
as well as cognition: 'What later came to be called subjectivity, freeing itself
from the blind anxiety of the shudder, is at the same time the shudder's own
development; life in the subject is nothing but what shudders, the reaction to
the total spell that transcends the spell'. In this 'self-transcending' work Adorno
sees something very different from Aristotelian catharsis, prototype of the
instrumentalization of the affects whose culmination is the culture industry.
Adorno opposes catharsis, if that would mean simply the neutralization of
affect, the de-cathexis of what had been cathected: as he says elsewhere,
'[Aristotelian] catharsis is a purging action directed against the affects and
an ally of repression' (*AT* 238). In Adorno's model, the 'shudder' persists in,
indeed *as*, 'the reaction to the total spell that transcends the spell'—it is both

the spell and the transcendence. Just such casting-and-transcending of the 'spell' under which enlightenment has lain numbed is the textual effect I have wanted to elicit in *Dialectic of Enlightenment* and other writings of Adorno—a 'labor and suffering of the negative' that 'joins eros and knowledge' (*AT* 331), affect and concept, and not merely evokes, but enacts, what such labor, sufficiently impassioned, can actually *make* of 'the unhappy consciousness of critique'. We turn to the *how* (and as always in Adorno, the *why*) of that *making*—the 'poetics'—in the next chapter.

Chapter 2

Rewriting the Dialectic

But the essay ['as form'] is also more closed [than 'systematic' thought], because it works emphatically at the form of its presentation. Consciousness of the non-identity of presentation and subject matter forces presentation to unremitting efforts. In this alone the essay resembles art.

—Adorno, 'The Essay as Form' (NL1 18)

Criticism has power only to the extent to which every successful or unsuccessful sentence has something to do with the fate of humankind.
—Adorno, 'On the Crisis of Literary Criticism' (NL2 307)

The dialectic's protest against language cannot be voiced except in language.
—Adorno, 'Skoteinos' (HTS 121)

The Dialectic of Writing, the Writing of Dialectic

This book, again, is about how Adorno writes, and how self-consciously; in this chapter we confront what Adorno had to say about the theory and practice of 'doing philosophy'—that is to say, *writing* it. This chapter, then, might have come first—but I wanted to begin by addressing the question of affect in (Adorno's) critique, to introduce a major problematic his work engages, and to indicate how it enlarges our sense of what Adorno's work is trying to do, what ambitions he entertains, and what burdens he incurs, as thinker and as writer. Adorno's imperative that critique must own *affect* places large demands on the writing itself, the writer him- or herself. In Adorno's usage such terms as 'constellation', 'dialectic', 'concept', 'negation', and 'immanent critique' bear as much on questions of (to adapt Gertrude Stein) 'how the writing of critique should be written'—how Adorno's own writing is written—as on questions of theory. Their *point d'appui* is how to write as much as how to think. It is usual in this connection to cite Adorno's mid-'50s essay called 'The Essay as Form', because it is so patently a manifesto for so many of Adorno's own values or programs or ambitions as a writer-critic.[1] I want here, however, to treat an essay much more charged and thus more suggestive for Adorno's own writing practice and his view of language, the important late text dating from 1963,

'Skoteinos, or How to Read Hegel'—an essay not only about reading Hegel, but about the problems of philosophical writing and expression in practice, and specifically Adorno's own critical practice.[2]

The premise that Hegel's writing—his 'textuality'—should be an access to discussion of him was just emerging in the period (1962–1963) when Adorno was writing 'Skoteinos'. It doesn't feature, for example, in early Heidegger, Gadamer, or Kojève, nor in Hyppolite's magnum opus of 1946, *Genesis and Structure of Hegel's* Phenomenology of Spirit. The later Heidegger's 'linguistic turn', however, put the problem of 'literature and philosophy' on the agenda, and by 1966, Hyppolite appropriated the theme in 'The Structure of Philosophic Language According to the "Preface" to Hegel's *Phenomenology of the Mind*', his contribution to the 1966 Johns Hopkins conference that brought 'French theory' (then called 'structuralism') to America. Younger participants included Lacan and Derrida (and de Man, in attendance, though not on the program), for whom Hegel on the one hand and problems of 'representation' on the other were equally central preoccupations. Philippe Lacoue-Labarthe and Jean-Luc Nancy developed the relevant questions in a series of texts, most interestingly for our purposes, *The Literary Absolute* (1978), whose titular provocation was to engage the Jena circle's negotiation of the tensions between what the authors inventively termed 'eidetics' (philosophy) and 'aesthetics' (literature) in an 'eidaesthetics' that in effect, though against the intentions of these figures, foregrounded the writing of the philosophical text, and perforce also its writer, as intrinsic to its condition or horizon of thought; thus the dynamic that made 'the Subject' absolute could not but entail 'the literary absolute' as well. While Lacoue-Labarthe and Nancy in *The Literary Absolute* mentioned Hegel only glancingly, others, preeminently Andrzej Warminki, were conducting extensive and close-focus treatments of passages in Hegel as 'allegories of reading' and writing. (I'll also mention here Paul de Man's only two essays specifically on Hegel, 'Sign and Symbol' and 'Hegel on the Sublime'.) None of these treatments, though, adduces 'Skoteinos'.

As we know, this style of commentary proscribes virtually any resort to 'the Subject' as a critical category: 'the Subject' is summoned almost exclusively as an object of ideological unmasking. Programmatic taboos can, however, be constraining. It's one thing to deconstruct Hegel's prose; it's something else to foreclose inquiry into Hegel's avowed motivations and investments in (his own) writing. (For me, Werner Hamacher's Hegel commentary, *Pleroma*, negotiates the conflicting demands most satisfyingly.) Just such an inquiry into Hegel is what 'Skoteinos' undertakes, and the project is all the edgier because Adorno is not aiming at a dispassionate assessment; on the contrary 'Skoteinos' engages with problems of philosophical writing that are clearly close to the quick for Adorno's own project. (We sense how personal it can get when Adorno remarks Hegel's 'appalling academic rancour towards anything clever and witty [*das Geistreich*]—in other words, towards those who know how to write' [*H&F* 46].) Adorno's objections to Hegel's lapses *as writer* tell us much about Adorno's self-consciousness about his own effort to get right what his great precursor got wrong; hence 'Skoteinos' elicits some of the subtler intimations of Adorno's philosophical-critical poetics, a poetics specifically modernist in its take on problems of language, expression, and representation.

Adorno's view of language rejects the *adaequatio* paradigm current since Plato, that the ideal of representation, never achieved in practice, is *adaequatio rei atque cognitionis,* adequacy or 'adequation' of word to thing: the measure of representation is the precedent, extant 'truth' of the thing (so imperfectly) represented. Adorno nowhere works out programmatically his case against that view and its metaphysics, but it's sufficiently pervasive throughout his corpus as to have struck many as an anticipation of Derrida. Adorno's theory and practice of language, of philosophical writing-and/as-thinking, emphatically dissent from any value-scheme rooted in the subservience of language to any *a priori* 'reality'. This refusal extends equally to 'the concept' and its putative Platonic original, which is to say, to the 'adequacy' of thinking to reality: in an interview Adorno insisted that the crucial thing is

> the *historical* adequacy of consciousness, [which isn't] restricted to academic knowledge . . . [but rather] is expressed with equal force in art, which is after all also a form of consciousness and at the same time . . . a configuration of cognition—or even of truth—in the face of which the question of adequacy also can be asked . . . the adequate consciousness of an epoch is that consciousness which is most advanced at any given time ('Adequacy' 97).

Neither, though, is critical 'negation' an affair of *adaequatio* to 'what *should* be', the usual come-back, since at least the Renaissance, to Plato's dismissal of art: that what art copies is a 'golden [or "second"] nature', closer than nature itself to the Platonic ideal. Adorno's presuppositions are Hegelian, and modernist, as if having 'overcome metaphysics' in advance—though Adorno makes this move not, as Hegel and Nietzsche do, with the air of liberating philosophy from a false problem, but rather of forcing upon it a problem far heavier.

As I read him, Adorno's view of language is close to the Nietzsche of 'Truth and Lie in an Extramoral Sense': language as not a re-presentation of some precedent standard-setting reality, but rather a tool, or even a weapon, a survival adaptation, like the claws and fangs of the tiger. Like Hegel, Nietzsche, Lacan, etc., Adorno finds in the 'nonidentity' between reality and language— 'the non-identity of presentation and subject matter' in the epigraph above— the space where desire and will, and critique, and art, make their case against 'what is'. Adorno reconceives 'dialectic', 'concept', and 'negation' and other such Hegelian properties as functions of that performative agon language incites between conflicting human interests and indeed between human interests and material circumstance itself. To say that 'Dialectics means intransigence towards all reification' (*P* 31) is to say that 'dialectics' operates in language and in thought—or rather, in language-and-thought, since Adorno would distrust any separation of these two things: indeed, their correlation is not only everywhere assumed in the Adorno force-field, but virtually named in the category of 'the concept'. When Adorno alludes to 'the kinetic force of [the] concept' (*PMM* 26), he is evoking what Hegel memorably called 'the power of the negative' to unfreeze, unfix, set back into kinesis, the congealed and hardened petrifications of ideology. 'Negation' is the alternative to, indeed, the critique of, *adaequatio*: not the mind's deplorable failure to see things as they really, ontologically, are, but on the contrary, the mind's dialectical dissonance or non-identity with what is, in which is coiled all the critical potential rejoining affect and critique. This 'power of the negative', convertible with the power of dialectic itself, activates in semiosis, in language and in thinking: in *making* meaning, not more or less accurately (or 'adequately') 'representing' it. For Adorno, as for Hegel, much of the point of dialectic is to put 'negation' in the place where 'representation' used to be.

This sketch will flesh out in what follows; but for now, the preceding paragraph will at least have indicated the extent of Adorno's immersion and investment in Hegelian themes and vocabularies—a way of introducing some of the interest attaching to 'Skoteinos, or How to Read Hegel'.

'Skoteinos': Rewriting Hegel

The Greek word '*skoteinos*'—it means 'the obscure one'—was an ancient epithet for Heraclitus; and it announces one of the essay's motives, to valorize Hegel as a Heraclitean alternative to the Plato-and-Aristotle legacy (a.k.a. 'Western metaphysics', 'logocentrism', etc.) so implicated in modernity's 'dialectic of enlightenment'. For Hegel's (and Adorno's) program of undoing the 'fixities' of received thought, Heraclitus is, of course, an apt totem. More programmatically, the titular 'Skoteinos' reprises Adorno's chronic (and Hegelian) animus against (Cartesian) 'clarity' and '*certitudo*' ('the cold and brutal commandment of clarity . . . amounts to the injunction that one speak as others do and refrain from anything that would be different and could only be said differently' [*HTS* 106]) in behalf of the more difficult philosophical imperative, namely adhering to 'the matter in hand' at whatever cost in 'obscurity' (*HTS* 99–107; cf. *NL1* 14–15). 'Skoteinos' mounts a powerful critique of Hegel precisely on the score of how his failures as *writer* compromise his 'claim to truth' (*HTS* 146) as *philosopher*; but Adorno is far from agreeing with those who rebuke Hegel's obscurity. Indeed, 'Skoteinos' begins with an uncompromising assertion (not, for once, an 'exaggeration') of Hegel's difficulty or 'obscurity':

The ways in which Hegel's great systematic works . . . resist understanding are qualitatively different from those of other infamous texts. With Hegel the

task is not simply to ascertain, through intellectual effort and careful exami-
nation of the wording, a meaning of whose existence one has no doubt.
Rather at many points the meaning itself is uncertain, and no hermeneutic
art has yet established it indisputably. . . . For all their pettiness and *ressentiment*, Schopenhauer's tirades about Hegel's alleged bombast evidenced a
relationship to the matter itself, at least negatively, like the child and the
emperor's new clothes, in a situation where respect for culture and fear of
embarrassment merely dodge the issue. In the realm of great philosophy
Hegel is no doubt the only one with whom at times one literally does not and
cannot conclusively determine what is being talked about, and with whom
there is no guarantee that such a judgment is even possible (*HTS* 89).

On the following page Adorno declares a quoted sentence from Hegel
'a match'—i.e., comparably difficult—'for Hölderlin's most advanced prose of
the same years' (*HTS* 90; cf. *NL2* 134). Adorno urges that Hegel's thematic
of the disintricability of part and whole is enacted in Hegel's writing, with the
consequence that Hegel's word-by-word meaning must be inferred by the light
of the reader's (developing) sense of Hegel's overall 'conceptual structure',
not, as per usual, the other way around. Hence a typically knotty passage
'becomes susceptible of interpretation in the light of knowledge of the general
train of Hegel's thought, especially the conceptual structure . . . but it cannot
be interpreted from the wording of the paragraph alone' (*HTS* 91). Despite
Adorno's (presumably pointed) non-mention of the 'hermeneutic circle' here,
his account of interpretation as a process of continual back-and-forth, of inter-
adjustment between the larger 'conceptual structure' and the more immediate
processing of 'the wording' evokes the textual habitus of modernist literature,
in which 'structure', 'form', 'figuration' and the like are not mere epiphenom-
ena of textual meaning, but its very constituents:

> To the person who holds doggedly to the wording and then in disappoint-
> ment refuses to get involved with Hegel because of his unfathomable quality,
> one can offer little but generalities . . . There is a sort of suspended quality
> associated with his philosophy, in accordance with the idea that truth cannot
> be grasped in any individual thesis or any delimited positive statement. Form
> in Hegel follows this intention. Nothing can be understood in isolation,
> everything is to be understood only in the context of the whole, with the awk-
> ward qualification that the whole lives only in the individual moments. . . .
> however, this kind of doubleness of the dialectic eludes literary presentation
> . . . it cannot in principle achieve the unity of the whole and its parts at one
> blow . . . Every single sentence in Hegel's philosophy proves itself unsuitable
> for that philosophy, and the form expresses this in its inability to grasp any
> content with complete adequacy [cf. '*adaequatio*']. If this were not the case,
> the form would be free of the poverty and the fallibility of concepts that
> Hegel tells us about (*HTS* 91–2).

At issue here are not deficits in Hegel's skill as a writer; rather Hegel's fore-grounding the failures elicited here amounts to a paradoxical kind of success: the evocation of an experience that is the very 'truth' of our condition, and indissociable from predicaments that Hegel registers as endemic to language as such, indeed to *Geist* as such:

> . . . if Hegel's verdict that no individual sentence can be philosophically true holds outside his own work, then each sentence should also be confronted with its linguistic inadequacy. . . . the unclarity for which [Hegel] never ceases to be reproached is not simply a weakness; it is also the force that drives him to correct the untruth of the particular, an untruth that acknowledges itself in the unclarity of the individual sentence (*HTS* 105).

Adorno here speaks of the 'doubleness of the dialectic [that] eludes literary presentation' as a predicament (an 'obscurity') incumbent on philosophy generically and as such. But later in the essay, Adorno charges some measure of this deficit in Hegel to Hegel's carelessness as a writer, his 'stylistic indifference' to 'linguistic praxis', his lapse from the 'skeptical relation to language' that he had 'raised . . . to a stylistic principle' (*HTS* 118):

> Constellation is not system. Everything does not become resolved, everything does not come out even; rather, one moment sheds light on the other, and the figures that the individual moments form together are specific signs and a legible script. This is not yet articulated in Hegel, whose mode of presenta-tion is characterized by a sovereignly indifferent attitude toward language; at any rate it has not penetrated into the chemism of his own linguistic form. In its all-too-simpleminded confidence in the totality, the latter lacks the sharpness derived from the critical self-awareness that, in combination with reflection on the necessary disproportion, could bring the dialectic into lan-guage. . . . Vagueness, something that cannot be eliminated in dialectic, becomes a defect in Hegel because he did not include an antidote to it in his language . . . The loyal interpreter of Hegel has to take account of this deficiency. It is up to him to do what Hegel failed to do: to produce as much conciseness of formulation as possible in order to reveal the rigor of the dialectical movement, a rigor that is not content with such conciseness (*HTS* 109–10).

Hegel failed 'to bring the dialectic into language'—yet Adorno usually speaks as if dialectic and language were indissociable, as if error could lie only with those (positivists and empiricists) who deludedly set out to purge dialectic from language. 'The loyal interpreter of Hegel' (Adorno himself) offers not merely as reader of Hegel but also as writer 'to do what Hegel failed to do': to elicit the 'critical self-awareness' in which Hegel fell short, and thus to 'bring the dialec-tic into language'.

Adorno seems to me to overstate ('exaggerate'?) his case here; to me Hegel's ad hoc comments on language (the metaphysics of grammar, syntax, and the copula, the form of the judgment, the proposition, the syllogism, etc., as shapes and shapers of consciousness) seem self-consciously and self-referentially operative in Hegel's own writing, in theory if not always so self-consciously in (writing) practice (but as we'll see, precisely there's the rub for Adorno). Hegel's global premise that the result of thought is indissociable from the process of thinking that produced it, linked so firmly in the *Phenomenology*'s 'Preface' to the necessary difficulty of reading and writing philosophy, participates in the period conceptual shift from, in De Quincey's terms, 'literature of knowledge' to 'literature of power', more broadly, a shift from a conception of literature as repository of valuable truths extracted *from* experience, to a conception of reading and writing as themselves a *kind* of experience. Hence Hegel, near the opening of the *Phenomenology*: 'The power of Spirit is only as great as its expression, its depth only as deep as it dares to spread out and lose itself in its exposition' (*Phenomenology* 6; cf. Adorno: 'the presentation of philosophy is not an external matter indifferent to it but immanent to its idea' [*ND* 18]). What Hegel regularly advocates as the 'dialectical movement' of consciousness is enacted in the forms and formats of language, including written language, to the effect that subject and object interact in a participatory *methexis* that anticipates the poetics of Romantic and modernist literature (from the mirror to the lamp), and the linguistic vision developed from von Humboldt (e.g., Hegel's ambition to 'teach philosophy to speak German' [*Letters* 107]) to Sapir and Whorf, all the way indeed to the contemporary meme of 'performativity', so thoroughly does Hegel sublate language's supposed 'representational' or 'constative' responsibilities into its 'negative' or 'performative' powers (*HTS* 109; *NL2* 134).

Such are the stakes when Derrida calls Hegel 'the last philosopher of the book and the first thinker of writing' (*Grammatology* 26). Hegel's philosophical polemic is always also a polemic about philosophical writing—a way of putting it that recalls Richard Rorty's phrase about 'philosophy as a kind of writing': except that Rorty's phrase can too readily seem reductive (as if it means 'philosophy as *nothing but* a kind of writing') in ways often taken to diminish philosophy and writing both. The practice of Hegel (and Adorno, and many others who might refuse Rorty's characterization of 'private ironists') aspires to an achievement that would rather enlarge both terms. Consider, e.g., that astonishing sequence of paragraphs in the 'Preface' to the *Phenomenology* in which Hegel dramatizes the sublation by which the merely 'ratiocinative' import of the philosophical proposition becomes 'speculative'. Crucial to Hegel's account of this 'becoming-speculative' is the figuration of movement versus fixity: whereas the 'proposition' in 'ratiocinative thinking' aims to stabilize or define a meaning, the point of 'speculative thinking' (Hegel urges) is to set the properties thus fixed back into motion, into a jostling 'unrest' that answers to the very movement of the reading-and-thinking consciousness itself, as it scans a sentence, sequentially, word by word, subject, verb, predicate, the will to understanding reaching always forward for the next semantic/syntactic member, even as it processes each new input retrospectively, against what sense has been collected so far, so that the 'movement which is thinking apprehension . . . runs back and forth' until at last—and this is the very point of 'speculative thinking' for Hegel—'the movement itself becomes the object' and 'goes beyond' the grammatical parts of speech thus mobilized, even as this movement is at times itself 'checked in its progress' and 'suffers, as we might put it, a counterthrust' (*Phenomenology* 36–7). In this vertiginous hurly-burly, much more dizzying in Hegel's full text than in these excerpts, the sentence or 'proposition' appears as a sort of conduit through which the 'meaning' sloshes back and forth as in the ebb-and-flow of liquid pulsing in adjoining lengths of pipe— to the effect that 'the general nature of the judgment or the proposition'—the traditional means by which philosophy attempts, syllogistically, to stabilize chains of deduction from premise to QED—'is destroyed by the speculative proposition' (*Phenomenology* 38). 'Power of the negative' indeed: terms that the ratiocinative proposition identifies, virtually equates, the 'speculative proposition' maintains in their difference, arraying the identity and the non-identity before the mind simultaneously.

The trouble, says Hegel, is that the format, the very grammar, of the proposition, its shape and its conventional acceptation (Adorno would say, the ideology of its 'form') conditions us to read ratiocinatively rather than speculatively:

> The philosophical proposition, since it *is* a proposition, leads one to believe that the usual subject-predicate relation obtains, as well as the usual attitude toward knowing. But the philosophical [sc. 'speculative'] content destroys this attitude and this opinion (*Phenomenology* 39).

This remains a complaint today, two centuries later: from the poets, artists, and composers of modernism to the theorists of postmodernism, 'the prison-house of language' has prompted calls to un-make, to 'destroy' if necessary (or possible), the usual ways of making sense—a program ubiquitous in Adorno's own investments: in the modernist art he valorizes, in the philosophical and political commitments his work undertakes, in the burdens and the self-consciousness he assumes for his own writing practice. But Hegel's response to the predicament—his faith in the 'speculative' power of the 'counterthrust'—is sanguine to a point most moderns scorn as complacency. 'We learn by experience', writes Hegel, 'that we meant something other than we meant to mean; and this correction of our meaning compels our knowing to go back to the proposition, and understand it in some other way' (*Phenomenology* 39). The dramatic reflexivity here—as if the 'proposition' just now being 'speculatively' read stands revealed, at a stroke, as a proposition the reader himself (Hegel) had earlier written—sets the writer in a relation to his 'own' words not to be so frontally problematized again for 175 years (Barthes, Foucault, Derrida).[3]

But the prophetic radicalism of Hegel's gesture is softened by his complacency about the incommensurability of (mediated and mediating, irredeemably 'universal') language and (immediate, sensual) perception, a complacency moderns and postmoderns like Adorno do not share. At the opening of the 'Sense-Certainty' chapter, Hegel casts the inevitable 'universality' of language as a sort of saving grace against the solicitations of 'sense-certainty':

> It is as a universal that we *utter* what the sensuous is. . . . Of course, we do not envisage the universal This or Being in general, but we *utter* the universal; in other words, we do not strictly say what in this sense-certainty we mean to say. But language . . . is the more truthful; in it, we ourselves directly refute what we *mean* to say (*Phenomenology* 60).

Hegel is one of the first, and still one of the most thorough, to theorize the dual problematic, that of 'crisis of representation' (no unmediated access to reality) and 'language-speaks-us' (our thoughts are not '*ours*') that Adorno and other modern figures find so anguishing. It's a theme familiar to students of modern culture: we might mention, to start with figures Adorno himself critiques, Husserl's *epoché* of (in effect) 'mediation' itself in the name of a 'return to the things themselves'; and Heidegger's 'jargon of authenticity', a mystification (in Adorno's view) conjuring with fantasies of recovering a 'primordial' immediacy, or achieving at least an immediate sense of the *Angst* that should attach to the loss of that primordiality. Adorno sees something similar at work in the lush orchestral effects of Wagner and the faux-primitivism of Stravinsky; more visceral lunges toward immediacy animated Dada and Surrealism, and the mystiques variously attaching to Van Gogh, Gauguin, and *les fauves*. In literature, writers have been seeking since Romanticism to make their writing more life-like, which has typically meant more 'immediate', less familiarized by the mediations of literary tradition and convention; this is the claim especially staked out by the 'realist' novel; the effort is only the more acute for the more immemorially sanctified (i.e., compromised) art of poetry. Some poets can sound the theme with something of Hegel's sense of the 'happy' potentials peculiar to language by reason of its inevitable 'universality'—Mallarmé's flower absent from all bouquets, e.g., or, more cagily, Stevens, whose frivolous-profound can seem to smile the whole problem away. Programmatically, Stevens ('Not ideas about the thing but the thing itself') or Williams ('No idea but in things') can sound, *pace* Kant, as if purging the abstract should be realizable; elsewhere it takes on the coloration of 'impossible task' attaching, e.g., to T. S. Eliot's lament for the lost Eden of 'immediate experience', as opposed to the fallen world of 'the intolerable wrestle with words'.

The Kantian residues in Adorno can look like a version of this immediacy-hunger, and its association with, or expression as, a distrust of 'the concept' and all its works. Adorno is wary of the liability of the concept to reification or hypostatization: to becoming, as Nietzsche warned, a stale counter of thought and feeling that threatens to become a narcotic against thinking and feeling both; to prevent such hypostatization, to keep the concept concrete, is precisely 'the labor of the concept'. The more complicated liability attaching to the concept manifests most often and most elaborately in Adorno in connection with Kant. Adorno is usually on Hegel's side of disputes with Kant; but perhaps the most important of Adorno's still-Kantian commitments is an entailment of his critique of idealism, the 'identity thinking' that identifies thinking and being, and which, in Adorno's view, ultimately vitiates Hegel's thinking. Here Adorno's construction of the problem is Kantian and materialist at once: Kantian in that the inaccessible, unknowable *Ding an sich* cannot be mastered (though it can be hypostatized, a sort of *illusion* of 'mastery') by 'the labor of the concept'; materialist or Marxist in that the reaches of experience Adorno calls 'non-conceptual' are not merely (as in Kant's trinity) sheerly cognitive, moral, or aesthetic, but social and historical as well.[4] Adorno follows Benjamin in seeking in 'mimesis' an approach to making the non-conceptual available to art and language without conceptualizing, and thus betraying, its non-conceptual character. The point: contra the (modern) ideology of the aesthetic as usual, Adorno repudiates rhetorics of immediacy that call for an 'absolute negation' of the concept in favor of non-conceptual (sensual, concrete, immediate) experience. For Adorno, only through the 'labor of the concept' can the limits of the concept be probed—indeed, *experienced.* Beyond those limits, 'mimesis' and other strategies of the non-conceptual offer not a triumphant victory over or liberation from 'the concept' but rather a tragic or 'unhappy' brake on its potentials, a check to its 'power of the negative'.

And so Adorno consistently scorns, as an ideology that not only shirks the 'labor of the concept', but makes a righteousness of doing so, all aesthetic fetishizations of immediacy. Adorno accepts the imperative to 'make it new', and all the burdens and impossibilities of that task in a numbed, instrumentalized, 'administered world'; and to that extent he can make common cause with many an artist—Proust, for example—who might naively resort to rhetorics of immediacy; still, Adorno joins that understandable and nostalgic longing or 'ontological need' to his own subtler and more challenging Hegelian account of aesthetic experience, according to which the transit from immediacy to mediation is necessary and, though irreversible, may nevertheless sublate further into what Hegel calls 'mediated immediacy': indeed, it's only the 'mediated' part of the response, Adorno would say, that enables the 'reader' of the new artwork (poem, painting, music) not merely to *experience* the freshness (sc. 'immediacy') of the new, but to *know* that immediacy for the complexly mediated experience it is.

Again, Adorno is typically 'modern' in casting the problematic of immediacy in desperate colors, a symptom—even a 'medium'—for 'unhappy consciousness' of a very specifically modern type. Hegel would figure modernity's anguish over lost immediacy as the latest reinvention of the 'unattainable beyond' underlying our species being's chronic 'unhappy consciousness'; Adorno would then be notable only for the intensity with which he renders or performs this problem. And here, too, Adorno's complaints about Hegel's language evince his unease with Hegel's Panglossian 'happy consciousness', for the modern anguish about the irredeemable mediatedness of language is an anguish Hegel simply does not feel. Hegel finds a providential grace of *Geist*, not a tragic fallen-ness, in the circumstance that '[what] is meant [in "sense-certainty"] *cannot be reached* by language, which belongs to consciousness, i.e., to that which is inherently universal' (*Phenomenology* 66). For Hegel, 'because language is the work of thought, nothing can be said in it that is not universal' (*Encyclopedia* [§20] 49)— and for Hegel that is *good*: for from that condition, Spirit will learn the limitations of sense-certainty, of perception, and eventually even of the merely 'ratiocinative' powers of 'Understanding'. Moreover, Hegel seems confident that language can and will do all this by itself: the inadequacy of the 'ratiocinative proposition' to 'speculative' consciousness is a sort of *felix culpa*, that 'seems . . . to recur perpetually, and to be inherent in the very nature of philosophical exposition' (*Phenomenology* 40); hence Hegel is not moved to call for a new language or a new grammar that can express the 'speculative' meaning that eludes the traditional proposition. The challenge is rather to the reader than to the writer: the 'speculative' (new) insight is to be *read out* of the old proposition by the reader, rather than *written into* it by the writer. Hegel's complacent faith in the dynamic of the 'counterthrust' apparently rationalizes his 'sovereign indifference' to his own compositional practice: the counterthrust will wreak its speculative work on the ratiocinative inertia of what the writer 'meant to mean' regardless. By contrast, for Adorno, as for so many modern writers and thinkers, it is upon the writer that the burden falls when historically new predicaments call for historically new ways of writing or representing them—and if the predicaments are chronic, that only makes the more urgent the need for newly defamiliarizing (re- or de-) constructions of them. If Adorno (et al.) bewail the need for new expressive means to escape from old 'familiarized' fixities of consciousness, Hegel enjoys a more robust confidence not only in the power of the new to unfold itself, but also in the fundamental benignity of the past which can thus be more generously and happily sublated—'preserved' in, even as it is 'cancelled' by, the new. (For Adorno and other moderns, the anxiety is that the cancellation part won't take effect.) Hegel would have savored Nietzsche's quip, in *Twilight of the Idols*, that 'we are not rid of God because we still have faith in grammar' (*Portable Nietzsche* 483); but he would have taken the point rather as endorsing the continuity than protesting it.

I'm trying here to 'motivate' the contrast of Hegel's textual effect or affect with the 'unhappy consciousness' of Adorno and, so frequently, of modernity at large. When Adorno writes that 'all philosophical language is a language in opposition to language, marked with the stigma of its own impossibility' (*HTS* 100), many might think of Beckett or Wittgenstein; but Beckett's 'I can't go on' nevertheless entails the sequel, 'I'll go on', as against Wittgenstein's (to Adorno, ideological) adviso about remaining silent. Adorno finds much more threatening than Hegel the potential in language to 'fix' or 'freeze' or 'hypostatize' thought-moments that ought to remain or be rendered fluid—an anxiety widespread, under various aliases, in modernity (Lukács's 'reification', Wittgenstein's 'category mistake', Whitehead's 'misplaced concreteness'). When Horkheimer and Adorno, in *Dialectic of Enlightenment*, warn of 'the universality necessarily assumed by the bad content of language, both metaphysical and scientific' (Cumming 22), they are sounding a familiar modern theme, in which anxieties about feeling and thinking fuse with issues of writing. No less than the poet must the philosopher struggle to get the 'exact curve of the thing' (T. E. Hulme) down on the page; to quote 'Skoteinos' again:

> The moment of universality in language, without which there would be no language, does irrevocable damage to the complete objective specificity of the particular thing it wants to define. The corrective to this lies in efforts to achieve [an] intelligibility . . . [that is] the opposite pole to pure linguistic objectivity. The truth of expression flourishes in the tension between the two (*HTS* 106).

The complaint here about Hegel's over-estimation of the universal is a legitimately philosophical point—that 'the truth of expression' involves both the (bad) universality of language and its inevitable contravention of the 'concreteness' of the particular—but 'the bad content of language' ('*der schlechte Inhalt in der Sprache*' [*GS3* 39]) also encodes a 'higher-level' version of the 'tension between the two'. In translation, the English suggests a 'content' distinct from the container (à la Plato's 'form' and 'matter'); whereas the German ('*Inhalt*') can imply rather an Aristotelian fusion of form-and-content, substance substantiating form, form in-forming substance as indissociable correlatives in a single spatio-temporal manifold. Cumming's 'bad content' suggests, better than Jephcott's 'faulty content' (Jephcott 17) that the 'bad content' is formal beyond any particular content: the 'bad content', along the lines of 'bad infinity', involves the 'universality'-effect itself. But Adorno's point is not that this 'bad content' should be overcome; the point is that it *can't* be—with the consequence that this 'bad content' itself must be part of what a critique of universality must perform.

The difficulty of that task—what Hegel called 'the labor and the suffering of the negative'—is just the *askesis* Adorno charges Hegel with having shirked. Hence what might seem the near-*ressentiment* of Adorno's complaint that Hegel is 'sovereignly indifferent' to language—to the extent at least that it amounts to the complaint that Hegel doesn't share Adorno's *Angst* in addressing a historical crisis that requires crisis-agitations in critique's own expressive means. Patently, Adorno reflects on his writing (and thinking) practice more explicitly, more often, more self-consciously and above all more anxiously, than Hegel: there are no motifs in Hegel corresponding to such chronically and insistently self-reflexive evocations of thematics-and-technics, theories-and-practices, of Adorno's as 'immanent critique', 'dialectical image', 'constellation', 'mediation', 'expression', 'parataxis', 'mimesis', and the like. The further question for Adorno is, What can a practitioner of 'immanent critique' (an Adorno) *do* in the face of the reification, 'the [false] universality necessarily assumed by the bad content of language'? Adorno considers that the strategies usual to the modern literary arts mistake their medium if they propose to eliminate 'universality' by reverting (Keats) to 'sensations rather than thoughts', mobilizing the mantra of 'concrete-not-abstract' against the supposed pitfalls of thinking as such—as if not noticing (perfect illustration of Hegel's point about language 'speaking the universal') that when they evoke 'the concrete' in this way, they are using the word abstractly.

Adorno, of course, carries no brief for 'abstraction': his imperative is to concretize the abstract—as here, from 'The Essay as Form':

> Higher levels of abstraction invest thought neither with greater sanctity nor metaphysical substance; on the contrary, the latter tends to evaporate with the advance of abstraction, and the essay [i.e., philosophical writing as Adorno would prescribe it] tries to compensate for some of that.

The point is that to concretize the abstract is to grapple with it, not to refuse it, as so many Romantic-to-modern aestheticisms make a glamorous 'impossibility' of attempting to do:

> Thought's depth depends on how deeply it penetrates its object, not on the extent to which it reduces it to something else. . . . The essay quietly puts an end to the illusion that thought could break out of the realm of *thesis*, culture, and move into that of *physis*, nature (*NL1* 11).

To Adorno, all such efforts to *escape* the predicaments incumbent upon language—to escape from the mediations of culture into un-mediated nature—are not only futile, but (variously) ideological: dupes of a false consciousness more insidious than the false universality they would evade. For Adorno, it is the *askesis* specific to the agon of philosophical (critical, theoretical) labor, to confront head-on—not to evade, but fully to *suffer*—the dilemma that 'all philosophical language is a language in opposition to language, marked with the stigma of its own impossibility' (*HTS* 100):

> To the extent to which philosophy makes an ongoing effort to break out of the reification of consciousness and its objects, it cannot comply with the

rules of the game of reified consciousness without negating itself, even though in other respects it is not permitted simply to disregard those rules if it does not want to degenerate into empty words. Wittgenstein's maxim, 'Whereof one cannot speak, thereof one must be silent', in which the extreme of positivism spills over into the gesture of reverent authoritarian authenticity, and which for that reason exerts a kind of intellectual mass suggestion, is utterly antiphilosophical. If philosophy can be defined at all, it is an effort to express things one cannot speak about, to help express the nonidentical despite the fact that expressing it identifies it at the same time. Hegel attempts to do this (*HTS* 101–2).

The expressive demand for 'a philosophical language that would strive for intelligibility without confusing it with clarity' (*HTS* 105) engages contradictions rather to display and dramatize than to reconcile them; the differences between them can not and *should* not be 'resolved': to preserve the 'objective contradictoriness' (*ND* 151) of the dilemma must be one of the conditions— 'the labor and the suffering', indeed—of philosophy as such.

On the other hand, Adorno warns against another downside to Hegel's project of 'freeing determinate thoughts from their fixity so as to give actuality to the universal, and impart to it a spiritual life' (*Phenomenology* 19–20), that it can succeed too well:

> The substance of Hegel's philosophy is process, and it wants to express itself as process, in permanent *status nascendi*, the negation of presentation as congealed, something that would correspond to what was presented only if the latter were itself something congealed. . . . Hegel's publications are more like films of thought than texts. The untutored eye can never capture the details of a film the way it can those of a still image, and so it is with Hegel's writings. This is the locus of the forbidding quality in them, and it is precisely here that Hegel regresses behind his dialectical content (*HTS* 121).

The 'film' metaphor insinuates that Hegel's rush and blur, however admirably it may 'reliquify' what had been congealed, can generate an 'immediacy'-effect that goes too far in the other direction, thus imperiling the 'speculative' consciousness that would maintain the 'content' as 'dialectical', and rather 'regress[ing] behind' it.

Here, as elsewhere, Adorno charges such deficits to Hegel's 'lack of sensitivity to the linguistic medium' (*HTS* 121)—again, that 'sovereignly indifferent attitude toward language' (*HTS* 109)—a lack or lapse with more than merely stylistic consequences: Hegel's failure 'to reflect on his own language', Nicholsen writes, 'is the failure of his philosophy'; she goes on to confirm that it is on this ground that Adorno 'differentiates himself from the Hegel who failed to reflect on language' (*Exact Imagination* 93). It might sharpen a point to draw a contrast: Nicholsen takes Adorno as defending Hegel's mimetic or gestural, non-conceptual language, and deploring his apparently unwitting or inadvertent lapses into anti-mimetic, over-abstract expression. I'd rather put it that Adorno regards the mimetic and musical features of Hegel's prose as the persistence of a sort of linguistic unconscious, that intermittently subverts Hegel's programmatic determination to transcend the 'limits of language':

> Perhaps however, the antilinguistic impulse in his thought, which perceives the limits of any particular existing thing as limits of language, was so deep that as a stylist Hegel sacrificed the primacy of objectification that governed his oeuvre as a whole. This man who reflected on all reflection did not reflect on language; he moved about in language with a carelessness that is incompatible with what he said. In the presentation his writings attempt a direct resemblance to the substance. Their significative character recedes in favor of a mimetic one, a kind of gestural or curvilinear writing strangely at odds with the solemn claims of reason that Hegel inherited from the Enlightenment. . . . The romanticism that the mature Hegel treated with contempt, but which was the ferment of his own speculation, may have taken its revenge on him by taking over his language . . . Abstractly flowing, Hegel's style, like Hölderlin's abstractions, takes on a musical quality (*HTS* 122).

Here Hegel seems to succumb, against his own principles, to an unwitting 'romanticism', and thus lapses into a kind of 'mimesis' that merely replicates, repeats (or 'reflects') the 'substance' his 'dialectic' should be rendering speculative, should be subjecting to a 'determinate negation' whose force and effect would be ineluctably critical, a 'counterthrust' to the substance's received, 'fixed', 'congealed', reified and reifying acceptance. But as the passage continues, Hegel's unwitting contravention of his own anti-mimetic commitments seems to realize some redemptive potentials:

> No doubt Hegel's style goes against customary philosophical understanding, yet in his weaknesses he paves the way for a different kind of understanding; one must read Hegel by describing along with him the curves of his intellectual movement, by playing his ideas with the speculative ear as if they were musical notes. Philosophy as a whole is allied with art in wanting to rescue, in the medium of the concept, the mimesis that the concept represses, and here Hegel behaves like Alexander with the Gordian knot. He disempowers individual concepts, uses them as though they were the imageless images of what they mean. Hence the Goethean 'residue of absurdity' in the philosophy of absolute spirit. What it wants to use to get beyond the concept always drives it back beneath the concept in the details. The only reader who does justice to Hegel is the one who does not denounce him for such indubitable weakness but instead perceives the impulse in that weakness: who understands why this

or that must be incomprehensible and in fact thereby understands it (*HTS* 122–3).

Both Nicholsen (*Exact Imagination* 92) and J. M. Bernstein (Huhn 43–4) take this passage as commending Hegel's 'musical' and 'romantic' (Nicholsen) or (Bernstein) 'more than logical' (i.e., 'non-conceptual') effects as attesting Hegel's deliberate effort 'to rescue, in the medium of the concept, the mimesis that the concept represses'; I read it as staging a more conflicted apprehension of Hegel than that. In writing that 'Philosophy as a whole is allied with art in wanting to rescue, in the medium of the concept, the mimesis that the concept represses', Adorno suggests that Hegel's prose, whether abetted or duped by his 'sovereignly indifferent attitude to language', achieves such an effect *against* its author's intention: it is rather 'philosophy' than Hegel that has willed this 'rescue' of the 'mimetic'. We've already seen Hegel anticipating the post-modern maxim that 'language speaks us'—'We learn by experience that we meant something other than we meant to mean' (*Phenomenology* 39)—and just as, above, 'The romanticism that the mature Hegel treated with contempt' took its 'revenge' by infusing his 'abstract' style behind his back with a Hölderlinian musicality, here Adorno intimates that Hegel's unwittingly mimetic *practice* has gotten the better of his avowedly anti- (or trans-) mimetic *theory*. It's the practice that 'rescues' what the theory 'represses'. Thus Hegel, impresario of 'the con-cept', aspiring to soar 'beyond' the concept, suffers instead a (sometimes) for-tunate fall 'back beneath the concept'. The prophet of art's sublation into philosophy reinvents philosophy, despite himself, as a quasi-Romantic kind of art, of music, mimesis. Ironic *Aufhebung*: Hegel's aspirations to 'the end of art' prove rather to prolong ('preserve') it. Or such seems to me the suggestion, the *alchimie du verbe*, of Hegel's 'disempowered concepts . . . use[d] as imageless images of what they mean' (the English-speaker recalls this Plato-haunted prob-lematic in Shelley), not to mention the 'enlightened' sacrilege of Alexander cutting the Gordian knot.

But however we parse the subtleties here, this passage seems to find, as if in despite of what Hegel 'meant to mean', a model for Adorno's own attempt 'to rescue, in the medium of the concept, the mimesis that the concept represses': to undo the '*chorismos*' of philosophy from art, of 'the [allegedly, ideologically "abstract"] concept' from 'the [mimetic] concrete', of thinking from feeling. Adorno's labor to rehabilitate, by 'concretizing', the concept, shows the work of 'rescue' to be a double project: both a rescue of the mimetic *from* the 'bad content' of the concept (i.e., from its liability to reification, abstraction, false universalization, etc.); but also, reciprocally, a rescue *of* the concept from its liabilities by way of a determined discipline of the concrete, maintained in the writing by a mimetic *methexis* between the writing and 'the matter at hand'. The negative project of keeping 'the concept' and 'the concrete' from *betraying* each

other—for the naive de-mediations of anti-intellectual art practices attest that
this is a double danger—are so re-imagined as to open the prospect of 'the
concept' and 'the concrete' *redeeming* each other.

But just such a double redemption had been Hegel's own programmatic
ambition; so Hegel becomes a cautionary example insofar as he unwittingly
betrays this noble program in practice, that is, in his lapses as *writer*. Adorno
charges Hegel with flinching before his own work's 'forbidding quality', that it
is Hegel's commitment, tonally or stylistically as much as substantively, to 'happy
consciousness' that betrays his radical premises, 'regresses behind his dialectical content'. Thus does Hegel's way of writing, his 'sovereign indifference' to
language, compromise—and this time not, contra Hegel, in a providentially
good way—what Hegel 'meant to mean':

> In the *Phenomenology* Hegel still wanted to believe that [philosophical] experi-
> ence could simply be described. But intellectual experience can be expressed
> only by being reflected in its mediation—that is, actively thought. There is
> no way to make the intellectual experience expressed and the medium of
> thought irrelevant to one another. What is false in Hegel's philosophy mani-
> fests itself precisely in the notion that with enough conceptual effort it could
> realize this kind of irrelevance (*HTS* 138).

To 'realize this kind of irrelevance': a cheeky formula for Hegel's noble hanker-
ing after an 'absolute knowledge' that would transcend 'the medium', language,
altogether—as if, in aspiring to the 'end of art', Hegel contravened the very
condition, the achieved immanence, of his own 'absolute philosophy':

> He who entrusts himself to Hegel will be led to the threshold at which a deci-
> sion must be made about Hegel's claim to truth. He becomes Hegel's critic
> by following him. From the point of view of understanding, the incompre-
> hensible in Hegel is the scar left by identity-thinking. Hegel's dialectical phi-
> losophy gets into a dialectic it cannot account for and whose solution is
> beyond its omnipotence. Within the system, and in terms of the laws of the
> system, the truth of the nonidentical manifests itself as error, as unresolved,
> in the other sense of being unmastered, as the untruth of the system; and
> nothing that is untrue can be understood. Thus the incomprehensible
> explodes the system (*HTS* 146–7).

That last quotation, from the closing peroration of 'Skoteinos' (*HTS* 146–7),
pulses with high energies: the 'scar', the problem 'beyond omnipotence', the
'incomprehensible' that 'explodes'—on the next-to-last-page!—Hegel's mighty
'system': this is a peroration, even by Adorno's standards, of unusual *brio*.

How words on a page can propose a system, and then 'explode' it, would be
impossible to explain within the *adaequatio* paradigm of language and 'representation'. Yet an *adaequatio* acceptation of language proves, as the peroration

builds, to have persisted in Hegel's thinking-and-writing, which is to say that Adorno here diagnoses how Hegel himself falls victim to the 'the bad content of language', the falsifying 'universality'-effect that implies, that can only arise from, a logocentric metaphysics of 'representation', of thing and word conceived on the model of original and copy, of which the telling symptom in Hegel is the motif of 'identity':

> For all his emphasis on negativity, division, and nonidentity, Hegel actually takes cognizance of that dimension only . . . as an instrument of identity. . . . This is where the idealist dialectic commits its fallacy. It says, with pathos, nonidentity. Nonidentity is to be defined . . . as something heterogeneous. But by defining it nonetheless, the dialectic imagines itself to have gone beyond nonidentity and be assured of absolute identity (*HTS* 147).

—as if Hegel complacently supposed that 'the identity of identity and nonidentity' really were so simply an identity, and not always and necessarily an irreducible nonidentity as well. (Why Adorno appears *not* to be hoist by his own pétard insofar as his own 'negative dialectics' seems to undertake a comparably 'absolute [rather than "determinate"] negation' of 'identity', is a rum question, which may one day seem richly symptomatic for our period.)[5] But it is along these lines that the closing sentences of 'Skoteinos' aim to clinch a critique of Hegel in which the *philosophical* lapse can't be disentangled from the *literary* lapse, that is, from Hegel's inattention (or 'sovereign indifference') to language as the fundamental condition of 'the concept':

> One cannot move from the logical movement of concepts to existence. According to Hegel there is a constitutive need for the nonidentical in order for concepts, identity, to come into being; just as conversely there is a need for the concept in order to become aware of the nonconceptual, the nonidentical. But Hegel violates his own concept of the dialectic, which should be defended against him, by not violating it, by closing it off and making it the supreme unity, free of contradiction (*HTS* 147).

For Adorno, as we have seen, 'contradiction' is virtually the condition (necessary, not sufficient) of truth; again, our administered world's 'objective contradictoriness' (*ND* 151) is just the 'truth content' critical writing must try to communicate. The very last words of 'Skoteinos' are these:

> . . . only by a Münchhausen trick, by pulling itself up by its own bootstraps, could [dialectic] eliminate the moment that cannot be fully absorbed, a moment that is posited along with it. What causes the dialectic problems is the truth content that needs to be derived from it. The dialectic could be consistent only in sacrificing consistency by following its own logic to the end. These, and nothing less, are the stakes in understanding Hegel (*HTS* 147–8).

These, and nothing less, are the stakes of Adorno's own project. 'The dialectic that eludes literary representation', the 'inexpressible' that the writing of critique obliges itself to (try to) express, are burdens incumbent on the imperative to express *both* the ideological condition *and* (or rather, by way of) its critical 'negation'. Its *critical* (sc. 'determinate') negation, not (à la Hegel) its *ideological* ('absolute') negation: Adorno's diagnosis of Hegel's failure implies his own critical program. The 'embittering part of dialectics' (*ND* 151), the principled 'unhappy consciousness' of critique, prescribe a 'taboo on utopia' as prophylaxis against 'imaginary solutions' and false consolations, which can look to some like 'defeatism' (one commentator has evoked a 'will-to-powerlessness' [Niethammer 138–42]). Hence the conflictedness Adorno's labored 'immanent critique', the 'chemism of [Adorno's] own linguistic form' (*HTS* 109), his 'literary presentation', aims to express: the 'objectivity of [social] contradiction' (*ND* 151–3), to cite one of his pithier formulations; 'dialectics at a standstill', to cite another borrowed from Walter Benjamin. Adorno's performative critique must perform both the 'standstill' and the 'dialectic', both the 'contradiction' and the 'objectivity', both the promise and its broken-ness, both the utopia and the ideology.

The obligation to express this 'inexpressible' conflictedness summons a word skeptical readers might think Adorno overuses, dragoons to do more work for him than any mere word should be asked to do, more than any one word can: 'dialectic'.

'Dialectic', 'Concept', 'Negation'

. . . the dialectic advances by way of extremes, driving thoughts with the utmost consequentiality to the point where they turn back on themselves, instead of qualifying them. The prudence that restrains us from venturing too far ahead in a sentence, is usually only an agent of social control, and so of stupefaction.

(MM *86)*

'Dialectic' and 'concept', words of patently Hegelian lineage, are ubiquitous in Adorno's oeuvre; 'negation' occurs less frequently, and often with the air of (to invoke Austin's speech-act distinction) 'mention' rather than of 'use': that is, when Adorno invokes 'negation' it is often in connection with a specifically Hegelian argument or practice that he wants to qualify or (in the terms of the epigraph just above) 'turn back on itself'. Still, the three words summon a range of related connotations that Adorno's impetuous invention can seem to overextend; the difficulty for the reader, then, is less to determine what these terms 'mean', than to cultivate a sense of the wide range of possible things Adorno can push them to mean. Adorno's appropriation of Hegelian vocabulary is no mere borrowing, but a wholesale reinvention, encoding ambitions both critical (to disencumber these terms of some of the disabling ideological baggage they bear from the Hegel-and-Marx tradition) and redemptive (to refunction these terms to a modern, even modernist, poetics or practice of critique). I foreground here Adorno-the-writer as against Adorno-the-philosopher: not to enforce the distinction but to spotlight Adorno's own virtual abolition of it. Here as throughout, my premise is that what Adorno thinks and how Adorno writes are functions of each other, produce each other—so I intend no instrumental suspension of *what* Adorno is saying in favor of *how* he is saying it. Rather the aim is to consider 'dialectic', 'concept', and 'negation' as philosophical categories with a long and tangled history, but more concretely as devices of Adorno's highly self-conscious critical program whose proof, Adorno insists, is in the performance, that is, the *writing*, of critique. Our procedure will be to inspect specimen usages of these terms, to infer the special kinds of torque Adorno seeks to transmit to them; then to read some passages of *Dialectic of Enlightenment* in which each of these words operates not merely as vehicle or relay in an unfolding process of meaning-making, but as something more like a narrative *actant* in dramatic (historical) conflict with other such terms, and in critical confrontation with its own inner 'equivocations', to dramatize those moments in which 'dialectic' or 'negation' or indeed 'concept' finds itself, as Adorno puts it, 'in contradiction with its own concept'.

To begin, then, a passage chosen almost at random from Hegel's *Science of Logic*:

> That which enables the Notion ['the concept'] to advance itself is the already mentioned *negative* which it possesses within itself; it is this which constitutes the genuine dialectical element (*Science of Logic* 55).

Here, this section's three titular words are set in suggestive relation, indicating the degree to which their usages, in Hegel as in Adorno, can so coincide as to approach functional convertibility. I want here to unfold the three terms together rather than separately, to promote an experiential sense of what 'reading Adorno' should involve, an emphasis that Adorno himself aligns with his disapproval of the usual 'metaphysical' preoccupations with 'definition' (indeed, with any thinking that 'subsumes' the particular under the general or the universal). Adorno's essay, 'The Experiential Content of Hegel's Philosophy' begins by warning that 'initially, the concept of philosophical experience will be left undefined: only the presentation can concretize it' (*HTS* 53). The ambition to 'concretize' implies a critique of 'definition', and it's clearly one of the aims of Adorno's writing program, one of the purposes he intends 'dialectic', 'concept', and 'negation' to achieve. The reflexivity or reciprocity of all this—that 'the concept' needs, and is susceptible to, being concretized; that the 'concrete' needs and is susceptible to 'the labor of the concept'—instantiates the necessity and the use of 'dialectic': to assimilate and differentiate all at once; but more transitively, to 'differentiate' in the sense of changing, negating, making each term *different* from what it was before.

A detail of the textual history of *Dialectic of Enlightenment* is relevant here: in the book's first appearance, mimeographed for circulation among the Institute exiles in America (1944), its title was *Philosophical Fragments*, and the first chapter was called 'The Dialectic of Enlightenment'; for publication in book form (1947), the latter title was transferred to the volume as a whole—giving us the title we now know, *Dialectic of Enlightenment*—and the first chapter was renamed: no longer 'The *Dialectic*', but rather 'The *Concept* of Enlightenment'. The commutativity of the two terms is not, of course, a simple equivalence; but rather something more like what we today would call a recursivity: as if defying Wittgenstein's caution that the concept of sugar is not sweet with the constant insinuation that the concept of the dialectic must be dialectical, the dialectic of the concept, conceptual, and the like. For those fearful, à la Wittgenstein, of the 'category mistake', Adorno poses, against the generalizing proscription, the specificity, the test, so to speak, of the 'concretization' of each particular instance. The recursiveness Wittgenstein and Russell would forbid, Adorno invokes both cognitively and rhetorically as the condition of that 'labor of the concept' by which merely 'reflective' consciousness becomes 'speculative'—a connection more visible in the German, for where English translations of Hegel and Adorno have 'speculative', the German might be '*spekulativ*'; but it is frequently '*begreifend*', the adjectival present participle of '*begreifen*' ('to conceive'), cognate with '*der Begriff*' ('the concept'); the cognate would be clearer if '*begreifend*' were translated not 'speculative' but something like 'conceptual' or 'conceptualizing'. As noted above, Adorno's aim to 'raise agony to a concept' meant that he wanted to *make* the concept of agony agonizing: a model of such (dialectical, conceptual, recursive) 'concretization' as Adorno projects here.

These prescriptions matter because false universalization (the 'bad content of language') constantly threatens to reify the very agencies of resistance to it, concept and dialectic themselves. The familiar suspicion of the concept as reifying, as reification as such, is not wrong, unless we draw the conclusion that therefore we should refuse, rather than reconceive, the labor of the concept. Similarly with the 'nominalist' impatience of 'dialectic', unhappily accelerated (in Adorno's view) by the sanctification of dialectic in Soviet orthodoxy. Just as 'Hypostatized dialectic becomes undialectical' (*PDGS* 26), so also, 'thinking without a concept is not thinking at all' (*ND* 98)—salutary reminders that 'dialectic' and 'concept' can be subject to cognate reifications: hence, indeed, the irony, the protest, of the locution 'dialectic of enlightenment', a liability imperiling dialectic and concept in all their recursive interimplication (dialectic of the concept, concept of the dialectic). For Adorno, neither 'dialectic' nor 'concept' connotes a sure-fire critical panacea; rather they name the condition of a potential whose dereifying efficacy must be a function of critical vigilance— as, for example, in the following polemical aside against 'official' Stalinist orthodoxy, in which the word 'dialectical' persisted, to be sure, but as a piety of party-line optimism, and as such a repetition (not to say: return of the repressed) of the providential God of history nominally under ban in official Soviet atheism. In Stalinist usage, 'dialectic' functioned as an article of reified 'faith', quite the reverse of the dereifying solvent Hegel had projected as 'determinate negation':

> The dialectical method, and it is precisely the one which is placed squarely on its feet, cannot simply treat the separated phenomena as illustrations or examples of something in the already firmly established social structure and consequently ignore the kinetic force of a concept; in this way the dialectic declined to a state religion (*PMM* 25–6).

No one will miss here the allusion to Marx's remark in the 1873 'Preface' about standing Hegel right side up; more suggestive is the Hegelian insistence on the '*kinetic* force of [the] concept' [my emphasis], the specifically Hegelian revision of the stasis and immutability idealized since Socrates and Plato as the *sine qua non* of *to ontos on*, the really real. This, by the way, is why, throughout this study, for this one passage from *Philosophy of New Music*, I cite the 1973 translation by Anne Mitchell and Wesley Blomster. Robert Hullot-Kettor's 2006 version gives 'the movement of the concept' (*PNM* 23; the German is '*der Bewegung des Begriffs*' [*GS12* 33])—but for this passage the Mitchell/Blomster wording more saliently foregrounds not only that 'the concept' is mobile rather than static, but the further implication (in the tension between '*Bewegung*' and '*Feststehenden*'[6]) that 'the concept' *transmits* its motion, and thus *acts* transitively to loosen, 'unfix', 'negate' the reifications that paralyze thought and action both. Hegel saw that the Platonic quest for the 'really real', and its legacy from Aquinian 'realism' to Heideggerian 'ontology', entailed the dialectical backfire of giving philosophic sanction to the 'really real' as reified: indeed, as reification itself— an irony (or 'dialectic') Adorno saw overtaking Marxism, too, as 'official' Soviet dogma, fetishizing and thus reifying Hegelian categories in the name of dialectic, turned them into ideology ('a state religion'). The oft-quoted opening sentence of *Negative Dialectics*—'Philosophy, which once seemed obsolete, lives on because the moment to realize it was missed'—gains a specifically anti-Soviet spin in light of the next sentence's adversion to the 11th Thesis on Feuerbach: 'The summary judgment that it [philosophy] had merely interpreted the world, that resignation in the face of reality had crippled it in itself, becomes a defeatism of reason after the attempt to change the world miscarried' (*ND* 3).

Adorno refunctions Hegel's terminology as Hegel reworked Kant's. In Kant, 'the concept' (*der Begriff*) rises free above the psycho-physiological connotations attaching to the 'percept' into the ozone of a disembodied Reason; whereas in Hegel, 'the concept' is historicized: recognized as mutable historically, and in that sense contingent, but thereby empowered with the potentials of 'the negative' for what Hegel designates as the philosophical or critical 'task nowadays', that of inciting new thought, rethinking habituated ideas, 'freeing determinate thoughts from their fixity' (*Phenomenology* 20). Hegel meant to 'cancel' the 'hypostatizations' of the Platonic 'really real', even as he hoped to 'preserve' or renew 'the universal'. (Compare Hegel's puzzling maintenance of the Plato-redolent term, 'the Idea'; and see Adorno's explanation [*HTS* 38–40].) If Adorno can seem similarly still-entangled in old problems some might prefer he simply abandon (e.g., 'metaphysics' itself: see Part III of *Negative Dialectics* and the contemporaneous lectures, *Metaphysics: Concept and Problems*), it is less a desire like Hegel's to 'preserve' inherited categories than wariness of an over-hasty confidence that they can so safely be written off as 'cancelled'. The point is that for Adorno as for Hegel 'the concept' has 'kinetic [i.e., dereifying] force'; the difference is that, more vigilantly than Hegel, Adorno wants to exert that force against 'the bad content of language', the abstract universality that epitomizes reification and ideology.

Kant, obedient to the law of non-contradiction, finds his philosophy entoiled in the 'difficulty that its concepts become aporetical, that is to say, they must give rise to assertions that are mutually contradictory'; for Hegel's more 'kinetic' or dialectical usage, 'the very essence of [the] concept requires it to contain contradiction, to be antithetical or full of tensions' (*H&F* 254). In the energy of those 'contained' tensions lies coiled the de-reifying potential of 'the kinetic force of a concept'. For Kant, 'the concept' is still an *a priori* Platonic entity, on the model of the eternal 'Forms' or 'Ideas'; for Hegel and Adorno it is rather an effect of the conceiving mind (compare Lacan's axiom that the signified is the *effect* of the signifier, not its precedent 'meaning'). Hence the urgency of 'the labor of the concept': it isn't merely this or that concept that is threatened with reification; it is thinking itself, the labor of the conceiving mind, that is at stake. If 'concrete' is usually deployed as an adjective, or nominalized as 'the concrete', Adorno refunctions it as a (transitive) *verb*—to 'concretize' (*konkretisieren*)—thus making the word not merely a noun, naming an extant state of affairs, but a project, an action, a conation, to be enacted or performed. The critical task is not merely to favor 'the concrete' in experience, but to *make* concrete, to produce as concrete that which, in thought and experience, may have lapsed from or fallen short of concreteness—i.e., reified. 'The concept', in particular, must be 'concretized' precisely because it is *not* 'always already' so: on the contrary, all the derelictions of distracted consciousness—the false universality, the 'bad content of language', the habituation and familiarization that have reified not only our intellects but our emotions and our sensoria as well—mean that even when reading an Adorno, the concretization he labors to achieve in the writing may be lost, absent an answering vigilance in the reader, in the reading. Especially potent in the formulation of 'the kinetic force of the concept' is the apprehension of 'the concept' as not a thing or an entity or an object but an *action*, a 'force'; similarly 'kinesis' mobilizes an active *alchimie du verbe* against any suggestion latent in 'the concrete' of a stable, thing-like solidity. To enact such gestures is to perform a kind of 'mimesis' of the problem 'the concept' attacks, as well as of the event of the attack as the writing itself works it out. Adorno's formulation that 'Philosophy . . . is allied with art in wanting to rescue, in the medium of the concept, the mimesis that the concept represses' (*HTS* 123), evokes the potential of 'the concept' as a 'medium' for that redemptive 'concretization' enacted in 'the mimesis the concept represses'.

Like 'dialectic', 'concept' can be reified, and on two levels: particular concepts can become stale counters that impede rather than incite fresh perception; hence 'the dialectical taboo on concept fetishes' (*CM* 160; in this case, 'progress'). But more pernicious is that 'the concept' itself is often conceptualized in ways that continue the 'logocentric' reifications of the Platonic heritage—even in protest, as in Nietzsche's 'Truth and Lie':

> Every word immediately becomes a concept, inasmuch as it is not intended to serve as a reminder of the unique and wholly individualized original experience to which it owes its birth, but must at the same time fit innumerable more or less similar cases—which means, strictly speaking, never equal—in other words, a lot of unequal cases.

Adorno is no less vehement than Nietzsche in rejecting 'the concept' as figured here: as a generalizing thought-instrument under whose heading particulars are 'subsumed', a ('logocentric') model into which is programmed from the beginning the very 'bad content of language' Adorno wants to circumvent. And Nietzsche's charge that 'Every concept originates through our equating what is unequal' anticipates not merely the overall gist but the very language of Adorno's critique (in, e.g., 'Progress' [*CM* 143–60]) of economic 'equivalence exchange', or more broadly, his critique of 'identity thinking' in *Negative Dialectics*:

> No leaf ever wholly equals another, and the concept 'leaf' is formed through an arbitrary abstraction from these individual differences, through forgetting the distinctions ; and now it gives rise to the notion that in nature there might be something besides the leaves which would be 'leaf'—some kind of original form after which all leaves have been woven, marked, copied, colored, curled, and painted, but by unskilled hands, so that no copy turned out to be a correct, reliable, and faithful image of the original form (*Portable Nietzsche* 46).

Nietzsche's critique of the generalizing tendency of the concept is a philosophical critique, but his vivid rhetoric gives his point a force as much aesthetic as philosophical, in ways that anticipate anxieties about what in our conditioning causes our experience to go stale and dead on us, what numbs perception and feeling, that, in Adorno's generation, the arts in particular took as their brief.

Like Nietzsche, Adorno takes on this ambition (Kafka's axe striking at the ice of a frozen sea) for philosophy as well.

The Nietzschean evocation of habituated thought's role in the alienation from, the narcosis of, sensory and affective experience helps us focus a blur in Adorno's deployment of 'the concept'. Recall the self-congratulation of Monsieur Jourdain, on learning that all his life he'd been speaking in prose. A certain type of modern anxiety, by contrast, cathects worry as to the force of unwittingly thinking in concepts—and hence, one more reason to anathema-tize 'the concept', as if to outwit conceptualization by an act of will. For Adorno, our problem is rather that we 'think' in *familiarized* concepts, concepts we have forgotten *are* concepts, concepts we have mistaken for immediate perception or self-evident truth. The antidote is to make our unconscious concepts conscious, to recall that our thinking is shaped by concepts whose role in our mental pro-cesses we have forgotten (if we ever grasped it in the first place). To 'think thinking' means to make our thinking self-conscious, i.e., 'dialectical', ever alert to 'conceptualize' the particular, and to particularize—or 'concretize'—the concept. Only thus can thought resist the 'deception' and the 'inhumanity' of 'hypostatizing concepts':

> Knowledge can only widen horizons by abiding so insistently with the particu-lar that its isolation is dispelled. This admittedly presupposes a relation to the general, though not one of subsumption, but rather almost the reverse. Dialectical mediation is not a recourse to the more abstract, but a process of resolution of the concrete in itself. . . . The double-edged [i.e., 'dialectical'] method which has earned Hegel's *Phenomenology* the reputation among rea-sonable people of unfathomable difficulty, that is, its simultaneous demands that phenomena be allowed to speak as such—in a pure 'looking on'—and yet that their relation to consciousness as the subject, reflection, be at every moment maintained, expresses this morality [of thought] most directly and in all its depths of contradiction. But how much more difficult has it become to conform to such morality now that it is no longer possible to convince one-self of the identity of subject and object, the ultimate assumption of which enabled Hegel to conceal the antagonistic demands of observation and inter-pretation. Nothing less is asked of the thinker today than that he should be at every moment both within things and outside them . . . (*MM* 74).

As we have seen, Adorno especially despises 'official' Comintern rhetoric for its reification or 'hypostatization' of the term 'dialectic' itself. It can therefore seem questionable that Adorno so frequently nominalizes 'dialectic' and other such abstract nouns (e.g., 'philosophy', 'science', 'concept', 'enlightenment', 'reification', etc.), in ways that can seem to evince the very same 'bad universality'. Anglophone readers often suspect this is a particular foible of the German language. Certainly one can recall, from Adorno's era, plenty of ideological

pronouncements in which 'the dialectic' indeed appears as something like
an ontologized agent or subject of History, the providential *deus ex machina*
wheeled onstage to lend assurance of a happy ending, however lengthily to be
postponed, of whatever ideological scenario is at hand. Hence Adorno's
admonition:

> . . . the dialectic, the epitome of Hegel's philosophy, cannot be likened to a
> methodological or ontological principle . . . The dialectic is neither a mere
> method by which spirit might elude the cogency of its object—in Hegel the
> dialectic literally accomplishes the opposite, the permanent confrontation of
> the object with its concept—nor is it a weltanschauung into whose schema
> one has to squeeze reality. Just as the dialectic does not favor individual defi-
> nitions, so there is no definition that fits it. Dialectic is the unswerving effort
> to conjoin reason's critical consciousness of itself and the critical experience
> of objects (*HTS* 9–10).

But these sentences, in which the (grammatical) subject is 'dialectic', seem to
risk (performative contradiction?) violating the very rule they announce; we
are evidently to read 'dialectic' here as meaning, roughly, 'we, when we are
thinking dialectically'. Adorno's use of such abstract nouns *as if* in the same
reifying way as so many other ideologues of the period is meant to induce vigilance against such ruses of ideology, and to remind us that evading them takes
not a mere policy decree, but concretization: confronting the concept with
'the cogency of its object', a 'relation to the general . . . not . . . of subsumption,
but rather almost the reverse'. It takes not, as in Nietzsche and so many others,
a liquidation of 'the concept' or the 'conceptual' in favor of 'the concrete', but
rather their mutual redemption in experience:

> The task of dialectical cognition is not, as its adversaries like to charge [and,
> Adorno might have added, as its party-line guardians stipulate by decree], to
> construe contradictions from above and to progress by resolving them—
> although Hegel's logic, now and then, proceeds in this fashion. Instead, it is
> up to dialectical cognition to pursue the inadequacy of thought and thing, to
> experience it in the thing (*ND* 153).

Adorno is broadly Nietzschean (and Marxian) in wishing ('transvaluation of all
values') to elevate the low relative to the high: hence Adorno's insistence,
whether against ethereal Hegelian idealists or gritty zealots of materialism, that
'dialectics is a challenge from below' (*ND* 303).

A challenge, not least, to the very idea of 'resolving' contradictions—and
here our discussion can gain from Adorno's contrast with Lukács, whom Adorno
mocked as 'the officially licensed dialectician' (Taylor 152). Adorno's 'dialectic' is conceived as a pointed critique of Lukács's. In, for example, Lukács's

'Realism in the Balance' (1938), the premise of 'totality' produces for 'dialectic' the task of resolving the contradictions of the social fabric, mediating between them in a way to expose the *real* unity concealed under the ideological appearance:

> Under capitalism . . . the different strands of the economy achieve a quite unprecedented autonomy . . . an autonomy so extensive that financial crises can arise directly from the circulation of money. . . . [hence] the surface of capitalism appears to 'disintegrate' into a series of elements all driven toward independence. . . . the movement of its individual components towards autonomy is an objective fact of the capitalist economic system. Nevertheless this autonomy constitutes only one part of the overall process. The underlying unity, the totality, all of whose parts are objectively interrelated, manifests itself most strikingly in the fact of crisis. . . . [Lukács goes on to quote Marx:] 'The crisis thus makes manifest the unity of processes which had become individually independent'. . . . [Lukács resumes:] this means that in periods when capitalism functions in a so-called normal manner, and its various processes appear autonomous, people living within capitalist society think and experience it as unitary, whereas in periods of crisis, when the autonomous elements are drawn together into unity, they experience it as disintegration (Taylor 32).

The subtlety here—precisely when the truth of the system is most salient, its appearance is most false—is Lukács at his best. Lukács is arguing for the realist novel as opposed to the fragmentary, disintegrated, 'subjective' art of modernism; he diagnoses 'the ideology of modernism' as a symptom of the crisis-state of capitalism in his era; and he goes on to prescribe: to argue that art, and of course critique as well, should present the 'underlying unity', the persisting fact of 'totality' that the experience of crisis should reveal, but experientially obscures. For Lukács, to demonstrate the 'underlying unity' in the 'surface' appearance of disintegration is the ordained task of the 'dialectical method'. For both art and critique, Lukács stipulates that history is and should be projected as a 'living dialectical unity' (Taylor 55).

    For Adorno, as we've seen, 'the dialectic . . . cannot be likened to a methodological or ontological principle' (*HTS* 9–10); in Lukács it is both, with the methodological implicated in the ontological and vice versa (see the opening chapter of *History and Class Consciousness*). Lukács insists on an 'objective dialectics of Being and Consciousness' (Taylor 43); and in his chronic Stalinist *mea culpa* excoriates his own masterwork, *History and Class Consciousness*, for 'its denial of a dialectics in nature' (Taylor 50). For Adorno, by contrast, 'concept' and 'dialectic' belong not to nature, but to the human, to 'the labor and the suffering of the negative', to the agency and powers of thinking itself: hence Adorno's sweeping refusal of the metaphysical pathos of Lukács's avowedly materialist 'underlying unity'. If Lukács regularly reproaches his modernist *bêtes noirs* for being 'undialectical', Adorno replies that such figures as Nietzsche and Freud are far more dialectical in spirit than Lukács himself, whatever their scorn (Nietzsche) or indifference (Freud) to the philosophical letter, the mere *word*, 'dialectical' (Taylor 152; *NL1* 217). We recall here the motif of 'Dialectic in Spite of Itself' (*AE* 49–50): just as 'dialectic' can be made into a fetish, so the refusal of dialectic can comport with a critique of fetishized dialectic every bit as 'dialectical' as Adorno's own.

Negation, Determinate and Absolute

As we've seen, Adorno's critique of Hegel turns on Adorno's imperative to maintain what Hegel promises to 'sublate', a (negative) 'dialectic' in which 'the kinetic force of the concept' (*PMM* 26) sustains a tension between 'subject and substance', between itself ('the negative', thinking as such) and 'what is':

> The concept, which some would see as the sign-unit for whatever is comprised under it, has from the beginning been instead the product of dialectical thinking in which everything is always that which it is, only because it becomes that which it is not (Cumming 15).

Here again we find all three of this section's key terms ('concept', 'dialectic', and 'negation', this last appearing here in the guise of 'nonidentity'). As with the linguistic 'sign' or word, so with the 'concept' (and recall that in German, in some contexts, '*der Begriff* ['concept'] can mean 'word'): 'the concept' does not 're-present' something—does not, in speech-act terms, 'constate'; rather, it enacts the performativity called 'negation'; indeed, so intrinsic are these terms to each other that, as we've seen, Adorno can cite Hegel to the effect that 'the concept' actually arises from negation, here again called 'nonidentity':

> According to Hegel there is a constitutive need for the nonidentical in order for concepts, identity, to come into being; just as conversely there is a need for the concept in order to become aware of the nonconceptual, the nonidentical (*HTS* 147).

'The concept', in short, is not only the product or result of 'negation', but the agent or subject of it as well.

If we grasp 'negation' as act, and transitive, a *gestus* rather than a (reified) thing, state, or condition, then 'the concept' and 'dialectic'—and, let's add, 'critique', 'theory', 'thinking' as such—appear as ineluctably 'performative', to the degree that they function (again) not to *represent* 'what is', but to *negate* it. But crucially, Adorno prescribes that negation should always be 'determinate' (specific, concrete, conceptual), rather than 'absolute' (sc. 'abstract'). 'Determinate negation' critiques something particular and concrete; 'absolute negation' negates or refuses whole generalized domains or categories of experience or thought, and thus traffics in the 'bad content of language' critique should labor to overcome. In the theater of temporality and historicity, 'determinate negation' performs the function of *Aufhebung*: what it 'cancels' or 'negates' it also (thereby) 'preserves'. What is *aufgehoben*, 'sublated' persists, negatively, insofar as 'negation' as Adorno prescribes it—'*determinate* negation'—is, in Husserl's sense, 'intentional', that is, negation *of* some very specific ('determinate') thing or concept. Like 'concept' and 'dialectic', 'negation' can be gotten wrong—but not in the same way, the way of 'familiarization' and reification. Rather the bad kind of 'negation' is '*absolute* negation', which makes a taboo, a 'political unconscious', of what is negated, thus forbidding critique any access to what will persist as crucial aspects of its problem. Hence the recurrence of 'metaphysics' and 'religion' throughout Adorno's oeuvre. (They are certainly not 'personal' preoccupations of his.) Adorno consistently credits Hegel with theorizing-and-practicing philosophy as 'determinate negation', and specifically as antidote to the intellectual pathology of 'absolute negation'; hence the critique of Hegel mounted in *Dialectic of Enlightenment*, that his determinate negations too often lapse into the 'absolute' kind:

> By ultimately making the conscious result of the whole process of negation—totality in system and in history—into an absolute, he of course . . . lapsed into mythology (Cumming 24).

'Determinate negation' is an infinite process (an avatar of 'infinite interpretation'); A prompts its negation in B, B further provokes C, and so on. 'Absolute negation', by contrast, oscillates between locked-in, polar oppositions, as in math: the negative of variable x is minus x; the negative of minus x merely reverts to positive x again. We'll see below, in some cryptic passages from the first chapter of *Dialectic of Enlightenment*, that Horkheimer and Adorno figure 'absolute negation'— of 'the labor of the concept', of the 'mimetic', of 'quality' itself in favor of 'quantitative' judgment—as something like the original sin, the *culpa* in no way *felix*, of the 'dialectic of enlightenment'. Indeed, the distinction between 'determinate' and 'absolute' negation is foregrounded in the opening chapter of *Dialectic of Enlightenment* as diagnosis of how the Enlightenment converted good 'dialectic' (and 'concept') into bad: how, in short, Enlightenment thinking reversed its own radical potential. Hence, as we've noted, the rich 'equivocation' in the chapter's alternative titles: 'The *Dialectic* of Enlightenment' can mean the dialectic of the Enlightenment's self-cancellation, or it can mean the Enlightenment's mistaken and trivializing version (or refusal: 'absolute negation') of dialectic; likewise 'The *Concept* of Enlightenment' suggests enlightenment's too-facile self-idealization (or -conception), Enlightenment's arrogant repudiation of 'the labor of the concept', as well as the rethinking, the critique, the 'negation' of that concept that Horkheimer and Adorno mean to incite.

'Determinate negation', counter-intuitively enough, can regularly appear as, so to speak, *weak* negation. Hegel, as 'diagnostician of critique', might have explained the appeal of 'absolute negation' as simply that absolute postures or psychologies can *feel*, seductively, like power (Nietzsche's 'imaginary revenge', etc.). It's my own experience learning to read Adorno and Hegel that, at least in English, 'negation' itself functions as a 'strong' term: as if 'absolute negation' were the default setting of 'negation' as such—an effect abetted in *Dialectic of Enlightenment* by the book's angry rhetorical force. 'Absolute negation' means a sweeping, categorical, all-or-nothing negation, akin to a taboo or a repression— e.g., 'Plato banned poetry with the same gesture that positivism used against the [Platonic] theory of ideas' (Cumming 18): the irony (sc. dialectic) of enlight-enment's self-liquidation, from Socrates to Bertrand Russell, in one sentence. By contrast, 'determinate negation' means negation of some 'determinate' (particular, concrete) thing, concept, argument, rather than the totalizing all-or-nothing proscription; moreover, it can also be obliquely, rather than frontally, 'negative' to that 'determinate' thing: as in Spinoza's maxim, *omnis determinatio est negatio*, which casts determinateness as such as 'negation' in the sense of mere individuating difference, a condition of particularity as such. This 'weak', but determining negation has the advantage of affording ways to think 'relationality' in other than rigidly binary terms; it also underwrites Adorno's deployment of such terms as 'mimesis', 'expression', 'affinity', 'allegory', and of course 'negation' itself—even, more distantly or obliquely, 'constella-tion' and 'form'—as alternatives or implicit critique, *avant la lettre Derridéenne*, of the logocentric metaphysics of representation-as-*adaequatio*.

So far, 'negation' designates the very purpose or program of 'dialectic' and 'concept'. But I want to elaborate one more variation on the theme of 'nega-tion'. If 'negation' is what critique or theory *does*, it feeds on a corresponding phenomenon in critique's object, namely 'contradiction', which Adorno con-ceives as the object's own (determinate) self-negation. When Adorno says that some bourgeois fetish—'progress', 'enlightenment', 'philosophy'—is 'in con-tradiction with its own concept', he is adverting to 'the power of the negative' and 'the labor of the concept', of dialectic itself as 'unrelenting theory', to hold administered reality to its own word. Lukács, as we've seen, spoke of dialectic as a way to 'mediate', i.e., make sense of, and in that sense reconcile, the contra-dictions of the social fabric. The reconciliation in thought was to anticipate the rectifications in social relations that revolution would eventually deliver. Adorno regarded such 'reconciliation under duress' as an ideological false conscious-ness ('imaginary solution to a real contradiction'). In Adorno, on the contrary, 'dialectic' acts not to harmonize or mediate, but to highlight, dramatize, indeed, 'exaggerate' contradictions:

> To proceed dialectically means to think in contradictions, for the sake of the contradiction once experienced in the thing, and against that contradiction. A contradiction in reality, it is a contradiction against reality (*ND* 144–5).

'Contradiction' in Adorno can mean, as usual in Marxist discourse, social contradictions which ideological (false) consciousness conceals or falsely reconciles, and which critique should expose; but for Adorno, 'immanent critique' should so insinuate itself into the problematics it targets that the 'contradictions' it exposes would, so to speak, declare themselves in the critique: hence the 'voice [of philosophy, sc. critique] belongs to the object . . . It is the voice of contradiction, which would otherwise not be heard, but triumph mutely' (Cumming 244). Critique evokes (or performs) a 'contradiction *in* reality' as a 'contradiction *against* reality': converts it into a contestation *of* 'what is'. In enacting 'contradiction', 'dialectic' finds its very *raison d'être*—and thus contradiction becomes method: becomes central to Adorno's poetics of critique.

An Historiography of Contradiction: *Dialectic of Enlightenment*

I want now to bring all this to bear on a detailed reading of some difficult passages from the opening chapter of *Dialectic of Enlightenment*, in which the themes we've been developing—language, the tasks and problems of philosophy and philosophical writing, 'dialectic', 'concept', and 'negation', as well as 'mimesis' and enlightened anti-mimesis—perform and interact. Contradiction as method—as poetics—of critique becomes a drama of performative contradiction in the narrativity of *Dialectic of Enlightenment*. The point of the foregoing has been less to provide backgrounds for an interpretation or explication of the text's *meaning* than to prepare for a reading in which 'dialectic', 'concept', and 'negation' (etc.) function not merely as complex pieces of terminology, but as narrative *actants*, conflicted, contradictory, highly unstable agents, *dramatis personae* indeed, of a fateful world-historical drama. As we'll see, Horkheimer and Adorno do not organize their text around key binaries that the reader must learn to decode as good/bad; rather, the text's key terms appear as variously 'good' or bad from one moment to another, inducing cognitive dissonances meant to set all such static good/bad binaries into kinesis and collision—so that we must read with unusual vigilance to track the drama of the argument enacted on the page as antithetical meanings generate such friction as to abrade their internal contradictions into mutual exposure. 'Dialectic', 'concept', 'philosophy', 'theory', and the rest prove 'non-identical', self-different, and as such behave in radically contradictory, highly conflicted ways, now promising genuinely critical force and power, now devolving into craven hypostatizations of their better potentials, at once dupes and abettors of ideologies their properly critical powers should defeat. Among the most consequential of the book's conceptual protagonists will prove to be 'writing' itself.

From the first pages of *Dialectic of Enlightenment*, the impulse of enlightenment since the pre-Socratics appears as 'demythologization', the refusal of earlier belief systems as illusions, and their rejection wholesale:

> The disenchantment of the world is the extirpation of animism. Xenophanes derides the multitude of deities because they are but replicas of the men who produced them . . . and the most recent school of logic denounces—for the impressions they bear—the words of language, holding them to be false coins better replaced by neutral counters. . . . There is said to be no difference between the totemic animal, the dreams of the ghost-seer, and the absolute idea. . . . in the authority of universal concepts, there was still discernible fear of the demonic spirits which men sought to portray in magic rituals, hoping thus to influence nature. From now on matter would at last be mastered without any illusion of ruling or inherent powers (Cumming 5–6).

This totalizing rationality discredits its own 'enlightened' values as readily as any other values it attacks: the dismissive refusal of 'difference' (between, here, primitive animism, Swedenborg, and Hegel) is a typical instance of 'absolute negation', a negation that doesn't 'cancel yet preserve', but merely, indiscriminately, 'absolutely' cancels. The irony or dialectic of such enlightenment is that the 'power of the negative' thus absolutized constitutes an unwitting regression to 'myth'; and thereby brave, new enlightenment incurs the numbed terrors and self-punitive paralyses attending, as we saw in the previous chapter, 'the return of the repressed'. Enlightenment's 'absolute negation' reduces quality to quantity, multiplicity to unity, the infinitude of concrete particularity to the 'bad infinity' of abstract number:

> Enlightenment recognizes as being and occurrence only what can be apprehended in unity: its ideal is the system from which all and everything follows. . . . Bacon's postulate of *una scientia universalis*, whatever the number of fields of research, is as inimical to the unassignable as Leibniz's *mathesis universalis* is to discontinuity. The multiplicity of forms is reduced to position and arrangement, history to fact, things to matter. . . . Formal logic was the major school of unified science. It provided the Enlightenment thinkers with the schema of the calculability of the world. . . . number became the canon of the Enlightenment. The same equations dominate bourgeois justice and

commodity exchange. . . . Bourgeois society is ruled by equivalence. It makes the [qualitatively] dissimilar comparable by reducing it to abstract quantities. To the Enlightenment, that which does not reduce to numbers, and ultimately to the one, becomes illusion; modern positivism writes it off as literature. Unity is the slogan from Parmenides to Russell. The destruction of gods and qualities alike is insisted upon (Cumming 7–8).

A later passage will develop the theme of the 'Galilean mathematization of the world' (Cumming 25) as precisely Enlightenment's 'anti-mimetic' strategy to eradicate wholesale, at least from 'truth-discourse', not merely the 'mythic' but the qualitative as such. The taboo on the mimetic entails a taboo on the conceptual as well:

Thinking objectifies itself to become an automatic, self-activating process; an impersonation of the machine that it produces itself so that ultimately the machine can replace it. Enlightenment has put aside the classic requirement of thinking about thought . . . Mathematical procedure became, so to speak, the ritual of thinking . . . [and] turns thought into a thing, an instrument . . . (Cumming 25).

Note that 'objectifies itself' here means the opposite of what it would mean in Hegel, something closer to what it means today in discourses on gender and race: not an uttering or outering of self such as the slave achieves in labor, but rather a new kind of slavish subjection, a loss rather than an augment of self-consciousness and independence, enforced in a systemic devolution from *für Sich* to *an Sich*, and indeed, *für Anderes*: an ironic reversal of Hegel's utopian vision of an 'all are free' society into an 'administered world' (ours) in which all are equally oppressed—as in the 'repressive equality' of the Hitler Youth (Cumming 13).

But the 'absolute negation' of difference and quality, their 'reduction' to a homogenized 'unity', is in contradiction with Enlightenment's atomizing, dissecting, analytic impulse, the *chorismos* or separation of related problems into specialized discrete disciplinary domains. Adorno's constant ambition to contest the instrumental separation of 'the aesthetic' from the 'truth'-discourses of science manifests in the following passage, which protests the instrumentalization of the Spirit, the degradation of the concept, and the separation of concrete from abstract, of particular from universal, of art from science, of the aesthetic from 'truth':

With the clean separation of science and poetry, the division of labor . . . was extended to language. For science the word is a sign: as sound, image, and word proper it is distributed among the different arts, and is not permitted to reconstitute itself by their addition, by synesthesia, or in the composition of the *Gesamtkunstwerk* (Cumming 17).

That last word evokes Wagner's 'total work of art' that unifies (Adorno argued, homogenizes) the separate arts, with orchestral music, vocal song, lyric poetry, dramatic narrative, the visual arts of stage-setting and costumery, all joining to a single 'total' effect; by this light, the other, minimalist kind of modernism (Mallarmé, Whistler, Debussy, Corbusier, Adolf Loos, the Bauhaus) aligns with 'Enlightenment' imperatives to 'separation' of the distinct arts (division of their labor) so that each of them may be 'pure', as theorized most rigorously in Clement Greenberg's briefs for the emancipation of painting from pictorial representation and thus free, in abstract expressionism, to be simply 'about paint and canvas', etc. To overturn such an acceptation of Schoenberg is part of Adorno's apologia for twelve-tone music; compare his dismissal of Stravinsky's 'Music About Music' (*PNM* 134–6).

But the point of these 'aesthetic' observations is to register a more-than-aesthetic protest against the instrumentalization of the aesthetic itself, and of language:

> As a system of signs [i.e., in scientific usage], language is required to resign itself to calculation in order to know nature, and must discard the claim to be like her. As image [i.e., as 'mimetic' or 'aesthetic'] it [language] is required to resign itself to mirror-imagery in order to be nature entire, and must discard the claim to know her. . . . Nature must no longer be influenced by approximation, but mastered by labor (Cumming 17–19).

The passage engages a problematic extending from Hegel's opposition of 'picture-thinking' and 'speculative' philosophy to Lacan's *gradus* between Imaginary and Symbolic. Enlightenment positivism forces language into a rigid either/or: *either* (as science) 'to *know* nature', *or* (as art) 'to *be* nature entire': art's portion, 'to *be* nature', sounds like a fall into a subhuman condition, as well ('required to resign itself to mirror-imagery') as a (low) kind of 'mimesis'. The evocation of nature 'influenced by approximation' seems, by contrast with 'enlightened' and modern mastery (i.e., 'domination'), to imply something like nostalgia for 'sympathetic magic'—or at least acknowledgment that Horkheimer and Adorno's own wish to 'influence' the 'administered universe', their own crypto-'mimetic' practice of 'immanent critique', must suffer the very 'regressions' they are protesting.

Obviously these admonitions about language import much for the language, that is, the writing practice, of *Dialectic of Enlightenment* itself. The passage goes on to assimilate the 'separation of sign [science] and image [poetry]' to philosophy's own complicity in the sundering of the concept from the sensual and the concrete:

> In the relationship of intuition (i.e., direct perception) and concept, philosophy already discerned the gulf which opened with that separation, and again tries in vain to close it: philosophy, indeed, is defined by this very attempt.

Here, 'philosophy' means philosophy as Horkheimer and Adorno think it should
be, and as they mean to practice it: the attempt to close the 'gulf' (*chorismos*)
between 'intuition' and 'concept' is, as we've seen, only the more imperative for
the attempt's being 'in vain'. But as the passage continues, 'philosophy' means
philosophy not as it should be, but as it too often has been, at once victim and
accomplice of Enlightenment instrumentalizations: 'For the most part it [phi-
losophy] has stood on the side from which it derives its name'—i.e., on the side
of science, not of poetry; the betrayal being not that it chose the 'wrong' side,
but that it acquiesced in the division in the first place: that it agreed to take *one*
'side' of the gulf, rather than upholding what the previous sentence had advocated as the program definitive of philosophy as such, the attempt to *close* that
gulf, to undo every such '*chorismos*':

> Plato banned poetry with the same gesture that positivism used against the
> theory of ideas (*Ideenlehre*). With his much renowned art, Homer [in indict-
> ments of poetry from Plato to Bentham and beyond] carried out no public or
> private reforms, and neither won a war nor made a discovery. . . . Art must
> first prove its utility (Cumming 18).

If, in an animistic foretime, art's utility—indeed, its magical power—had been
in influencing nature by 'being like her', its utility under 'Enlightenment' is to
renounce influence over nature, and accept the 'purposelessness' assigned it by
aesthetes from Kant to Wilde to Warhol, its non-utility thus becoming, in a habitus of utilitarian calculation, sheer ideology: 'to be nature entire', and thus, an
object, not a subject—an in-itself, not a for-itself, without purpose of its own,
and thus passively amenable to the ideological purposes, or 'domination', of
the instrumentalizing culture at large, a vehicle, and for the more intellectual
and self-conscious, an emblem and an idealization, of the economization of the
affects so convenient to the disciplines of the 'administered world'.

All of which philosophy, in Horkheimer and Adorno's view, should protest,
by way of an 'immanent critique' that both performs the predicament and tries
to undo it. The passage goes on to grant the unenlightened category of 'magic'
a qualified validation as a 'return of the [mimetic] repressed':

> Reason and religion deprecate and condemn the principle of magic enchant-
> ment. . . . The work of art still has something in common with enchantment:
> it posits its own, self-enclosed area which is withdrawn from the context of
> profane existence . . . This very renunciation of influence, which distinguishes
> art from magical sympathy, retains the magic heritage all the more surely. . . .
> It is in the nature of the work of art, or aesthetic semblance, to be what the
> new, terrifying occurrence became in the primitive's magic: the appearance
> of the whole in the particular. In the work of art that duplication still occurs
> by which the thing appeared as spiritual, as the expression of *mana*. This
> constitutes its aura. As an expression of totality art lays claim to the dignity

of the absolute. This sometimes causes philosophy to allow it precedence to conceptual knowledge. According to Schelling, art comes into play where knowledge forsakes mankind. For him it is 'the prototype of science, and only where there is art may science enter in'. In his theory, the separation of image and sign is 'wholly cancelled by every single artistic representation' (Cumming 18–9)

Recall, again, 'the rescue, in the medium of the concept, the mimesis that the concept represses' (*HTS* 123): if earlier the theme had been philosophy's assimilation to art, here that assimilation is enacted in the other direction. In Schelling's anticipation here of *Aesthetic Theory*, 'art' is art redeemed, as it were, from the domestications of 'the aesthetic' as usual: that is, the passage valorizes a power of 'enchantment' that persists in art, in covert defiance of its 'official' non-utilitarian 'purposelessness' (Kant) and the 'renunciation of influence' that is the contractual condition of such sufferance as the 'administered world' has deigned to grant it. The passage credits this 'enchantment' with some charge of subversive or critical power, whereas Enlightenment casts 'enchantment' as epitome of what critique should subvert. Likewise, the passage implies some cognate vestige of power, influence, 'enchantment', for philosophy itself: if such formulae as 'the appearance of the whole in the particular' or 'lay[ing] claim to the dignity of the absolute' ascribe to art ambitions or motivations that are more-than-aesthetic, it's because the thrust of that 'more-than' must be philosophical and critical in ways intimating the ambitions of *Dialectic of Enlightenment* itself.

So our passage (Cumming 17–20) evokes a narrativization among whose principal *actants* are magic, art, and philosophy itself. And also religion: religion, indeed, frames the passage, which begins with the ancient priestcraft of hieroglyphs and symbols, and ends with Reformation textualism (the attempt to reinvest 'the [desacralized] word itself' with 'symbolic power') as unwitting regression to priestly fetishization and prototype of twentieth-century totalitarianisms. The passage closes, indeed, with an '*écrasez l'infame*' that cathects the book's Hegelian, historicizing, diagnostic thematizations with the vehemence of Voltaire, as religion instantiates yet another failure of 'progress' to enact itself as anything other than 'regress'; for in context, the possibilities opened by art and philosophy are foreclosed insofar as bourgeois civilization opts rather for a diminished faith as mere sentimental relief from the 'enlightened' canons of positivist or scientific 'truth'. (It was in behalf of faith that Kant offered to restrict reason; those still holding that faith *was* 'reason' were excluding themselves from the cachet of 'Enlightenment'.)

But our more immediate point is that in this seeming-narrativization of magic, art, philosophy, and religion, Horkheimer and Adorno would seem, again, to be rehearsing, or reversing, a Hegelian master-theme—namely, the historicization, periodization, the phases and eventual fates of religion, art, and philosophy in modernity—with the difference that in their telling, *contra* Hegel,

Aufhebung unwittingly—and disastrously—preserves what had only illusorily been cancelled between one phase and another: the inauguration of one is not 'the end of' the preceding, but rather its unwitting continuation. Again: progress turns out to be regress; enlightenment relapses to myth. Not merely that the Hegelian theodicy is refigured in *Dialectic of Enlightenment* as nightmare: more pointed is that the Horkheimer/Adorno narrative calls into question the separation of magic, art, religion, and science as these (and the separation itself) are reified or essentialized in positivism. *Dialectic of Enlightenment* prosecutes its case against 'Enlightenment' reification by way of a quasi-'mimesis' of it, a seeming assent to the premise that magic, art, philosophy, and science are something like 'essentially' *the same*: as they necessarily (but ideologically) appear in Enlightenment's reified optic of anti-mimetic, anti-conceptual, anti-qualitative 'absolute negation'. Again, Horkheimer and Adorno's (immanent) critique of reification mobilizes the predicament it targets in ways that risk appearing as something very like an essentialism of its own. (How and why 'immanent critique' risks incurring the ideological liabilities of its object will be a major theme of the next chapter.)

Our next passage (Cumming 20–4) continues on from the one above (17–20), offering yet another telling of the story recounted there, beginning, again, in prehistory and concluding in modernity, this time with Hegel. It is, again, a story about the effects on *language* of the 'dialectic of Enlightenment', a theme the preceding passage had pursued in the precipitation of differentiated cognitive and representational possibilities into 'separated' discourses (art, science, philosophy, religion), increasingly specialized, increasingly estranged from each other, increasingly unable to 'speak the same language', following their agon in a 'contest of faculties' each of them had entered as a 'truth'-discourse in its own right, but in which the victory went to the natural sciences, a contestant not officially on the fight-card at all. Thus positivism emerged with its title to 'truth' so unimpeachable as to amount in the practices of the culture at large to a monopoly. The present passage tells the story again, this time featuring the adventures or misadventures of 'the concept', dramatizing the history that makes 'the concept' such crucial fighting ground for them. The book's opening pages, evoking Bacon, had sketched the early-modern background:

> Substance and quality, activity and suffering, being and existence: to define these concepts in a way appropriate to the times was a concern of philosophy after Bacon—but science managed without such categories. They were abandoned as *idola theatri* of the old metaphysics . . . (Cumming 5).

In the present passage, it's not merely the particular concepts of 'substance', 'quality', and the like that recede under the ban of Enlightenment 'absolute negation', but 'the concept'—'thinking about thought', the 'labor of the concept'—as such.

'When language enters history its masters are priests and sorcerers' (Cumming 20), the passage begins, boldly sketching the primordial division of labor evinced in the emergence of specialists in the sacred, such that 'intercourse with spirits [on the one hand] and submission [on the other] were assigned to different classes: the power is on the one side, and obedience on the other' (Cumming 21; sidelights here on Kant's 'Argue, but obey!'). In such a habitus,

> symbols undertake a fetishistic function . . . the recurrence of nature which they signify is always the permanence of the social pressure which they represent. The dread objectified as a fixed image becomes the sign of the established domination of the privileged. Such is the fate of universal concepts, even when they have discarded everything pictorial (Cumming 21).

We note here the recurrence of the 'image/sign' distinction, and its passage to the problematic of 'universal concepts'; that last clause would appear to rebuke Hegel, who supposed that the *Aufhebung* of 'picture-thinking' in philosophical self-consciousness would work the final, 'absolute' liberation of universals from their false (reifying) antithesis with, and mimesis of, the phenomenal. Hegel meant to historicize 'the concept', to 'unfix' the eternalizing, universalizing force of the Platonic 'Form' or 'Idea'—the *bad* kind of universalizing—in behalf of a *good* kind; Horkheimer and Adorno are more severe in qualifying what might count as a good kind, or perhaps more cagey in finessing the issue, committing themselves neither to grounding 'truth' in universality, nor to a solution along the lines their thinking seems to indicate, of Habermas's 'communicative reason'. What's certain is that they are less sanguine than Hegel about the extent to which 'the labor of the concept'—self-consciousness about the historical and linguistic contingencies of one's own thought-instruments—can counteract the liabilities of 'the bad content of language'.

Nowhere, however, do Horkheimer and Adorno spell any of this out; nor do they anywhere define 'the concept' (or 'dialectic', 'philosophy', etc.); rather we get the hang of these words by watching how they behave in the drama of the text. Their 'equivocations', cathected with all the critical and polemical voltages of a long cultural agon, are historicized, their contestation enacted in their own conflicting meanings and connotations, now in the ideological (false) senses the authors deplore, now in the corrected sense(s) they advocate; and the reader must discern from context what valences each word bears in a given instance. The long passage to follow is typical in using the word 'concept' to designate Platonic and Aristotelian universals, as well as Hegel's antidote to them, *and* as well as Horkheimer and Adorno's antidote to Hegel—in a fashion to enact in the argument the ways that Platonic 'Form' or 'Idea' and their evolution or historicization into the Hegelian and post-Hegelian modern 'concept' so implicate themselves in the 'dialectic of enlightenment' as to compromise the labor of negation and differentiation that should be their proper mission. Note how in the passage, 'the concept' becomes a protagonist: now the accomplice, now the victim, now again the scourge of 'the bad content of language':

> . . . the whole logical order, dependency, connection, progression, and union of concepts is grounded in the corresponding conditions of social reality—that is, of the division of labor. . . . Through the division of labor imposed on them, the power of all the members of society . . . amounts over and over again to the realization of the whole, whose rationality is reproduced in this way. What is done to all by the few, always occurs as the subjection of individuals by the many: social repression always exhibits the masks of repression by a collective. It is this unity of the collectivity and domination, and not [*contra* Durkheim] direct social universality, solidarity, which is expressed in thought forms. By virtue of the claim to universal validity, the philosophic concepts with which Plato and Aristotle represented the world, elevated the conditions they were used to substantiate to the level of true reality. These concepts originated, as Vico puts it, in the marketplace of Athens; they reflected with equal clarity the laws of physics, the equality of full citizens, and the inferiority of women, children and slaves. Language itself gave what was asserted, the conditions of domination, the universality that they had assumed as the means of intercourse of a bourgeois society. The metaphysical emphasis, and sanction by means of ideas and norms, were no more than a hypostatization of the rigidity and exclusiveness which concepts were generally compelled to assume wherever language united the community of rulers with the giving of orders. As a mere means of reinforcing the social power of language, ideas became all the more superfluous as this power grew, and the language of science prepared the way for their ultimate desuetude. The suggestion of something still akin to the terror of the fetish did not inhere in conscious justification; instead the unity of collectivity and domination is revealed in the universality necessarily assumed by the bad content of language, both metaphysical and scientific. Metaphysical apology betrayed the injustice of the *status quo* least of all in the incongruence of concept and actuality. In the impartiality of scientific language, that which is powerless has wholly lost any means of expression, and only the given finds its neutral sign. This kind of neutrality is more metaphysical than metaphysics. Ultimately, the Enlightenment consumed not just the symbols but their successors, universal concepts, and spared no remnant of metaphysics apart from the fear of the collective from which it arose. The situation of concepts in the face of the Enlightenment is like that of men of private means in regard to industrial trusts: none can feel safe (Cumming 21–3).

The satirical force of that last image—the concept as *haut*-bourgeois, facing expropriation by *parvenu* capital—is startling in a discourse nominally Marxist, and one recalls Adorno's rebuke to the taunts of *marxisant* critics in the 'Preface' to *Negative Dialectics* that 'now he was confessing' (xv) his supposedly bourgeois class loyalties. The other pole of the comparison, the assimilation of positivist anti-philosophy to capitalist expropriation of the expropriators, restores the stress to the larger picture in which 'the concept' plays a role comparably ambiguous to that of the bourgeoisie itself in the Marxist grand narrative. For while the passage obviously deplores positivism's effective liquidation of the concept, it equally stresses the concept's own guilt in the ever-increasing reach of 'domination': 'Language itself gave what was asserted, the conditions of domination, the universality that they had assumed as the means of intercourse of a bourgeois society'. Note that this complicity appears at some moments as reluctant (e.g., 'the rigidity and exclusiveness which concepts were generally compelled to assume wherever language united the community of rulers with the giving of orders'), at others as a fatality binding on language as such ('the universality necessarily assumed by the bad content of language').

For Horkheimer and Adorno, though, such moralism is beside the point. Plato and Aristotle claimed 'universal validity' for their 'philosophic concepts', with ideological results ('elevat[ing] the conditions they were used to substantiate to the level of true reality'); but, alas, the record since Hegel and Marx shows that escaping false universalisms is not so simple as calling them false. 'The bad content of language' keeps us universalizing despite ourselves, especially if we are positivists and have exempted ourselves on principle from 'the labor of the concept'—thinking thereby to disarm misleading presuppositions and achieve scientific impartiality, the 'neutrality' that proves to be 'more metaphysical than metaphysics', much as enlightenment becomes more 'mythical' than 'myth'. 'The bad content of language' figures here as something like Hegel's 'bad [merely quantitative] infinity' of number, usurping what should be the qualitative domain of word and concept. (Compare Lacan's diagnosis of the ruses by which the signified, though a mere 'effect of the signifier', nevertheless persuades consciousness of its substantiality as 'sublime object'.) Vigilance against this 'bad content of language' is 'the labor of the concept': not merely critical and self-critical scruple in the formation of concepts, but wariness of conceptualization as such, of its own 'bad content', its penchant for transforming itself operatively from a provisional 'thought form', self-conscious about its limitations, into a reification or 'hypostatization' whose false universality is only the more potent for being unconscious.

If I once more assimilate 'the labor of the concept' to Freud's 'making the unconscious conscious', it's to recall the affective resistances, as remote as can be from the serene *apatheia* idealized by philosophy, besetting the task. The inertial forces that tend to universalize or hypostatize even the most scrupulously concrete historicization, cannot be overcome simply by fiat. Hence another 'motivation' of the difficulty of the Horkheimer/Adorno text, and, again, of what might seem to be its lapses into the very kind of falsely universalizing argument ('mythical thinking') it ostensibly deplores—for as we have seen, the terms 'myth' and 'Enlightenment' themselves, as antagonists in the story the book tells, undergo both a dehistoricization and a substantivization that deliberately take the risk—or we had rather say, perform the danger, mimic the ideological fall—of appearing as hypostatizations, that is, of compromise or defeat by 'the bad content of language'. Again, this edgy practice of 'immanent critique' risks appearing to default to the very condition it critiques. Against Lukács's or Habermas's charge that *Dialectic of Enlightenment* dehistoricizes and universalizes the very terms whose historical specificities and differences it should rather articulate and foreground, one might defend the book by splitting hairs over definitions of the terms at issue; but in my view, Horkheimer and Adorno defy this risk, incur it knowingly and deliberately, as a way of attesting the inescapability of the ideological condition they protest. To have contrived an intellectually satisfying 'solution' to it would have vitiated their evocation of the binding-ness of the predicament they are trying to register.

Meanwhile our passage continues, with further variations on the theme of 'the concept', concluding, by way of some cryptic adversions to Judaism's *Bilderverbot*, with Hegel, and with one of the book's most enigmatic evocations of 'dialectic' itself:

> As a nominalist movement, the Enlightenment calls a halt before the *nomen*, the exclusive, precise concept, the proper name. . . . The substantial ego refuted by Hume and Mach is not synonymous with the name. In Jewish religion, in which the idea of the patriarchate culminates in the destruction of myth, the bond between name and being is still recognized in the ban on pronouncing the name of God. The disenchanted world of Judaism conciliates magic by negating it in the idea of God. Jewish religion allows no word that would alleviate the despair of all that is mortal. It associates hope only with the prohibition of calling on what is false as God, against invoking the finite as the infinite, lies as truth. . . . Admittedly, the negation is not abstract. The contesting of every positive without distinction, the stereotype formula of vanity, as used by Buddhism, sets itself above the prohibition against naming the Absolute with names: just as far above as its contrary, pantheism; or its caricature, bourgeois skepticism. Explanations of the world as all or nothing are mythologies, and guaranteed roads to redemption are sublimated magic practices. The self-satisfaction of knowing in advance and the transfiguration of negativity into redemption are untrue forms of resistance against deception. The justness of the image is preserved in the faithful pursuit of its prohibition. This pursuit, 'determinate negativity', does not receive from the sovereignty of the abstract concept any immunity against corrupting intuition, as does skepticism, to which both true and false are equally vain. Determinate negation rejects the defective ideas of the absolute, the idols, differently than does rigorism, which confronts them with the Idea that they cannot match up to.

Dialectic, on the contrary, interprets every image as writing. It shows how the admission of its falsity is to be read in the lines of its features—a confession that deprives it of its power and appropriates it for truth. Language thereby becomes more than a mere system of signs.* With the notion of determinate negativity, Hegel revealed an element that distinguishes the Enlightenment from the positivist degeneracy to which he attributes it. By ultimately making the conscious result of the whole process of negation—totality in system and in history—into an absolute, he of course contravened the prohibition and lapsed into mythology (Cumming 24).

Judaism here sounds rather like *Dialectic of Enlightenment* itself: most simply, in maintaining the intellectual, moral, and affective *askesis* of 'unhappy conscious-ness' ('Jewish religion allows no word that would alleviate the despair of all that is mortal'); more complicatedly in having pioneered a 'negation' that is 'not abstract' (sc. 'absolute') but, like Hegel's three millennia later, 'determinate'. Buddhism and its 'caricature, bourgeois skepticism' (sc. 'enlightenment' itself) negate abstractly or absolutely—as it were, merely quantitatively: such negation annihilates, reduces its object *ad nihil*, i.e., to zero. 'Determinate negation' negates qualitatively, yielding not a zed but a new 'moment'. Hence, 'The disen-chanted world of Judaism conciliates magic by negating it in the idea of God'. Negation as 'conciliation' implies a relation to 'magic' very different from that 'demythologization' Horkheimer and Adorno invoke as the root-and-branch extirpation ('absolute [or "abstract"] negation') of anything qualitative and non-fungible from the mathematicized ethos of 'equivalence' and 'exchange' sustaining bourgeois (capitalist) enlightenment, and from which the 'sublimated magic practices' enforced along the 'guaranteed roads to redemption', whether Hegelian, Hitlerian, or Stalinist, are too unconscious, too un-conceptual, too abstract to function as a critical alternative, let alone the utopian 'solution(s)' they deludedly, ideologically mistake themselves for. Hegel's own premature appropriation of 'the absolute' is his hubris, his lapse into that very 'dialectic of enlightenment' that he otherwise so acutely diagnosed: 'By ultimately making the conscious result of the whole process of negation—totality in system and in history—into an absolute, he of course contravened the prohibition and lapsed into mythology'.

Implicit here is that the Enlightenment should have sought to 'conciliate' (in determinate negation) at least some of the terms its ferocity wanted to anni-hilate (in absolute negation): 'magic' itself, 'mimesis', and of course the 'anti-thetical words' ('philosophy', 'theory', 'science', 'dialectic', 'Enlightenment') over whose 'equivocations', as we've seen, the text regularly incites something like a Bakhtinian 'dialogical' (sc. dialectical) contention. Call this another

---

* This sentence is missing from the Cumming translation; I quote it here from Jephcott 18.

instance of '*weak* negation': in the agon of *Aufhebung*, transitive, transformative, performative as it may aim to be, the impulse to 'cancel' and the impulse to 'preserve' engage each other with outcomes that might range from fighting each other to a 'standstill' to negotiating an at least nominal 'conciliation'. We might mention in this connection, too, the book's, or its ostensible genre's, troubled relations with 'the aesthetic'—libidinal investments nominally under ban in genres avowing themselves to be 'truth-discourses'. But the more enigmatically 'oracular' moment in the passage comes when 'dialectic' itself appears onstage:

> Determinate negation rejects the defective ideas of the absolute, the idols, differently than does rigorism, which confronts them with the Idea that they cannot match up to. Dialectic, on the contrary, interprets every image as writing. It shows how the admission of its falsity is to be read in the lines of its features—a confession that deprives it of its power and appropriates it for truth. Language thereby becomes more than a mere system of signs (Cumming 24).

The first sentence here recapitulates the case against 'abstract [absolute] negation' as instanced in the 'rigorism' of Buddhism and bourgeois skepticism (Hobbes, Hume, Wittgenstein)—but it's the second sentence that presents the enigma. At issue here is not the 'dialectic of Enlightenment', much less the debased 'official dialectic' of the Stalinist USSR, both of which Horkheimer and Adorno aim to indict, but rather 'dialectic' as they *want* it to be practiced, dialectic as 'determinate negation', as guardian of that 'broken promise' that *Dialectic of Enlightenment* here and there allows itself to hint at, but only obliquely, as if the imperative against any 'word that would alleviate the despair of all that is mortal' places redemption itself under the ban of something like an ideational *Bilderverbot*. It is this 'dialectic' that 'interprets every image as writing'—a puzzling linkage of two terms, 'image' and 'writing', upon whose implications I am wary of laying more weight than they can perhaps bear. But I take it that 'writing' and 'image' conjure the word-and-text ethos of ancient Israel against the image- or idol-worship of Greco-Roman culture—with, of course, a bearing on the Nazi persecution of the Jews current when the book was being written. We've already seen this opposition—'pictorial' versus 'speculative' thinking— operative in Hegel's progressive narrative of the adventures of Spirit and its 'event' in 'absolute' philosophy; as well as Adorno's diagnosis of it as symptom of Hegel's Enlightenment anti-mimetic prejudices; and we recall Adorno's effort to redeem Hegel's lapse by appeal to his unwitting mobilization 'in the medium of the concept, [of] the mimetic that the concept represses' (*HTS* 123).

The point for the present passage is that we must refuse any (Hegelian) temptation to valorize 'writing' absolutely (or abstractly) as *against* 'image': just as mimesis and the concept need each other, so do writing and image—and so: 'Dialectic . . . interprets every image as writing'. In German, the verb is '*offenbart*'

(*GS3* 41); where Cumming has 'interprets', Jephcott has 'discloses'. For '*offen-baren*' the usual dictionary meaning is 'reveal'; the connection with 'open' ('*offen*' [adjective] and '*öffnen*' [verb]) is plain. Jephcott is obviously closer to the dictionary sense, but to my ear, the '-close', even prefixed by 'dis-', generates etymological static with 'open'. Clearly 'interprets' is the more daring—the more interpretive?—translation. But however the verb should be *translated*, let's register that it *is* a verb, that it is *doing* something, that (in the quoted sentence) 'dialectic' is acting transitively on 'image' and 'writing' in a way that brings together two things that forces in the culture from antiquity till now have wanted to keep separate, even to oppose. Compare the transitivity above: 'The disenchanted world of Judaism *conciliates* magic by negating it in the idea of God'; in Jephcott's translation (p. 17) the verb ('*versöhnt*') is 'propitiates'. The action of these verbs might seem a version—a mild, or (again) 'weak' version, perhaps, but a version—of *Aufhebung*, a passage or transaction between two things that changes each by so investing it with the problematics and the cathexes of the other as to 'preserve' (interpret, conciliate) something of what it ostensibly 'cancels' or negates. What it can *mean* to 'interpret' (or 'disclose' or 'reveal') images '*as writing*' (Jephcott has 'script') we can infer only from the follow-through: 'Dialectic [sc. 'determinate negation'] . . . interprets every image as writing. It shows how the admission of its falsity is to be read in the lines of its features—a confession that deprives it of its power and appropriates it for truth'. Here, clearly, a bias like Hegel's in favor of 'writing' to the disadvantage of 'image' is patent, yet 'image' is not 'absolutely' negated, not erased, not dispensed with; rather, 'image' persists: not 'cancelled' but 'preserved'—almost as if 'image' and its 'falsehood' provide 'dialectic' with a kind of raw material for conversion to and appropriation for 'truth'—or as if 'truth' can only emerge as 'negation' of some precedent condition.

Our problem of 'interpretation' is, of course, a problem of translation. Rolf Tiedemann, who reads his Adorno in German, considers our sentence ('*Dialektik offenbart vielmehr jedes Bild als schrift*' [*GS3* 41]) by the light of Adorno's proposal, in his inaugural lecture, 'The Actuality of Philosophy' (1931), that the philosophical project be redescribed as 'interpretation' rather than the quest for an 'adequate' or accurate 'representation' of reality (Huhn and Zuidervaart 132–5). For Tiedemann, to 'interpret' means something very like to 'concretize': as if, by way of 'the image', to preserve perception and thinking from the reifications and hypostatizations that are the bane of 'the concept', the 'bad content of language' itself—'to rescue, in the medium of the concept, the mimesis that the concept represses' (*HTS* 123). 'Language thereby becomes more than a mere system of signs'.

This 'rescue'—this 'more than'—is interpretive also in the performative sense that it 'appropriates [falsehood] for truth'. Building on Tiedemann's persuasive linkage of this passage ('Dialectic . . . interprets every image as writing') with Benjamin's 'dialectical image', we may conceive 'writing' as a figure for, or indeed the very agency of, the 'making-dialectical' of the 'image': the unfixing, or putting back in motion, of that ideological 'standstill' we might call 'the bad content of the image'. Moreover, to reprise the concerns of the preceding chapter, the 'dialectical image' also reawakens numbed perception to the 'shock' of primal *fear*:

> The life process itself ossifies in the expression of the ever-same: hence the shock of photographs from the nineteenth century . . . The absurdity explodes: that something happens where the phenomenon says that nothing more could happen; its attitude becomes terrifying. In this experience of terror, the terror of the system forcibly coalesces into appearance . . . What Benjamin called 'dialectics at a standstill' is surely less a Platonizing residue than the attempt to raise such paradoxes to philosophical consciousness (*CM* 160).

In the appropriation of falsehood for truth, then, there is much reason to associate 'dialectic'—a.k.a. 'negation'—*with* or even *as* writing itself: in the quoted sentence (in German, or in either translation), to render (interpret, reveal, *offenbaren*) the 'image *as* writing' amounts to rendering it *in* writing—amounts, simply, to *writing it*.

'Writing', indeed, has been this chapter's theme. We began by eliciting from Adorno's 'Skoteinos, Or How to Read Hegel' what hints we could on How Adorno Wants to Write, which is to say, How To Read Adorno. The problems of philosophical writing diagnosed in 'Skoteinos' receive a very different kind of 'enactment' (or 'mimesis') in *Dialectic of Enlightenment*. But throughout, 'writing' evokes subtly and diversely nuanced feats of 'determinate negation' or 'weak *Aufhebung*'. In the maxim-like assertion that 'Dialectic interprets every image as writing', 'writing' seems to connote a very deliberate bringing-to-bear of dialectical attention, an ethos of 'critical negation' binding on Critical Theory in much the way of Freud's imperative of 'making the unconscious conscious'. Indeed, this maxim posits 'writing' and 'dialectic' as virtually commutable terms: 'writing' projected as the activity or 'labor' of 'making the undialectical dialectical'.[7]

Which is why, as we continue, the question of 'writing' will remain salient. We have seen how Adorno labors to reinvent such stale, reified Hegelian commitments as 'dialectic', 'concept', and 'negation'; in the next chapter we will examine some of Adorno's own signature 'thematizations' of critical procedure, most centrally, 'constellation' and 'immanent critique'. Such terms will prove to name not merely cognitive proposals for how critique should be thought or theorized, but also programs or devices of critical writing, of how critique should be written. They are terms, that is to say, every bit as much of writing *practice* as of critical *theory*—terms, that is, in which theory-and-practice become indissociable. In them, the problematics we've only just breached, the conciliation/tension between 'image' and 'writing' will play out in rich and inventive ways. If 'image' connotes the static, non-temporal, non-narrative arts of the visual, 'writing' and the arts of language (as well as, if more ambiguously, of music), remain ineluctably temporal, and kinetic, as in 'the [transitively, performatively] kinetic force of the concept'. We've seen Hegel mobilize the temporality of the propositional sentence, the moment necessary for the mind to traverse the array of subject, verb, and predicate, as itself a theater and a model of 'dialectic'; in the next chapters we'll see the degree to which Adorno's practice of the 'paradoxically' anti-narrative or anti-dialectical binary (e.g., enlightenment/myth) draws inspiration from Benjamin's 'dialectical image', and comports with the device Adorno theorizes-and-practices under the name of the 'constellation', a way of yoking heterogeneous ideas together that licenses a release, of a very 'modernist' type, from the imperatives, conventional in historicizing critique from Hegel through Lukács, of *narrative* mediation of the constellated terms. The attenuation of 'realist' narrative into a modernist 'dialectics at a standstill', as much in critique as in fiction is, we will see, only one of the symptoms—or negations—enacted in Adorno's poetics of critique.

Chapter 3

Writing It New

. . . the essay does not stand in simple opposition to discursive procedure. . . . But the essay does not develop its ideas in accordance with discursive logic. . . . It coordinates elements instead of subordinating them . . . In comparison with forms in which a pre-formed content is communicated indifferently, the essay is more dynamic than tradi-tional thought by virtue of the tension between the presentation and the matter presented. But at the same time, as a constructed juxtaposition of elements it is more static. Its affinity with the image lies solely in this, except that the staticness of the essay is one in which relationships of tension have been brought, as it were, to a standstill. The slight elasticity of the essayist's train of thought forces him to greater intensity than discursive thought, because the essay does not proceed blindly and automatically, as the latter does, but must reflect on itself at every moment.

—Adorno, 'The Essay as Form' (NL1 22)

The previous chapter considered Adorno's defamiliarizing reinventions of such shopworn Hegelian-Marxian properties as 'dialectic', 'concept', and 'negation'. The aim was to show how Adorno renewed the meanings and usages of these terms, staled by a century and more of familiarization, then worse, since Lenin and Stalin, corrupted by the power-exigencies of a revolution betrayed. Adorno's effort cast these terms as properties not merely of a cognitive project or theory, but also as practice, as a critical poetics—as ways of writing, doing, making, per-forming critique. As we saw, Adorno often projects 'writing' itself as a figure for 'dialectic' and vice versa: either way, the devices in question were topoi of long-standing (and, Adorno thought, long-debased) in the critical traditions stemming from Hegel-and-Marx. In the pages to follow, we'll see Adorno further refunctioning these and other such terms, e.g., 'mediation'. But besides renew-ing stale critical vocabularies, Adorno (and his colleagues, especially Benjamin) invented some new ones, e.g., 'constellation', 'dialectical image', 'immanent critique', that have become virtually signatures of the Frankfurt School. These, too, are proposed as practice as well as theory. They are techniques as much for the writing of critique as for the more strictly cognitive phases of critical labor; and Adorno mobilizes these devices so insistently and self-consciously as to sug-gest the critical and defamiliarizing Shklovskian effect of 'baring the device'.

As in the modernist arts, Adorno's critical stance is the reverse of *celare artem*: on the contrary, the aim is to foreground the devices, the techniques, the 'signifiers' of critique as a writing practice, to defamiliarize, to provoke, to mobilize enthralled faculties, to turn critique's very means, its *how* as much as its *what*, its 'presentation' as much as its 'matter' (in the terms of the epigraph above), to critical effect.

'Constellation' and Critique

Fredric Jameson years ago characterized Adorno's chief critical device or method as the 'historical trope' (*Marxism and Form* 3–59), so it shouldn't strike anyone as a novel claim that Adorno's 'constellation' displays affinities with such familiar devices of modernist art and literature as Eisensteinian montage, cubist collage, the Joycean 'epiphany', the Poundian 'ideogram', etc. It has its analogues as well in 'high theory'—Lacan's riffs on Freud-and-Jakobson ('condensation' and 'displacement' meet 'metaphor' and 'metonymy'), Lévi-Strauss's 'mytho-poetic bricolage' (*Elementary Structures* 17–18), or Derrida's extensive thesaurus of devices ('hinge', 'joint', 'seam', 'tympanum', 'articulation', '*dérive*'. . .) varying the tactic of 'juxtaposition without copula' (occasionally Derrida even deploys the metaphor of 'constellation' itself). The young Adorno presumably first encountered 'constellation' when he read Benjamin's *Trauerspiel* in the late '20s; and it recurs in his work throughout his career, from 'The Actuality of Philosophy' (1931) to the late pieces collected in *Critical Models*. Its connotations are diverse and often conflicting, and one could make an interesting study of such tellingly divergent usages, as well as an interesting speculation of the rarity of Adorno's own second-level reflections on the word. (In perhaps the most suggestive of these, Adorno links it with Max Weber's 'ideal type', a characterization stressing its heuristic potential [*ND* 164–6].) Here I can attempt nothing so comprehensive.[1] Rather we'll pursue some implications of 'constellation' as a critical practice, and elicit their tension or contradiction with the overall program that Adorno and Benjamin called 'immanent critique', by considering 'constellation' in relation to Walter Benjamin's 'dialectical image', with which it has obvious but also qualified affinities; to the *Gestalt* psychology of Wolfgang Köhler, from which Adorno was evidently keen to distinguish it; and to Adorno's account of Hölderlin's epic device of 'parataxis'.

Again, Adorno first encountered 'constellation' in Walter Benjamin's *Origin of German Tragic Drama* (1928), whose first sentence—'It is characteristic of philosophical writing that it must continually confront the question of representation' (*Origin* 27)—declares the ambition, common to Adorno and Benjamin, to realize philosophical (sc. critical) theory in and as writing practice. Benjamin's first chapter develops the case that in a philosophy so conceived, the literary method must enact the philosophical project in and as 'self-representation, and

[must] therefore [be] immanent in it as form' (*Origin* 30). When Benjamin offers an illustrative analogy—'Ideas are to objects as constellations are to stars' (*Origin* 34)—the primary point would seem to be the 'discontinuity', the de-linking or autonomization of the constituent elements (the stars) from the larger semantic array (the 'constellation'). It's a point obviously bearing, to 'nominalist' effect, on traditional philosophical problems (the relation of 'Ideas' [sc. *noumena*] to 'objects' [*phenomena*], universals to particulars, etc.); it also bears on how those arguments should conduct themselves in writing. Like a good modern, Benjamin argues that the 'Idea' is precisely *not* a question of particulars subsumed under a general or universal heading; on the contrary, Benjamin stresses throughout the arbitrariness of this 'configuration' of 'Idea' and 'phenomena'; but for questions of philosophical writing, the more conse-quential result of this 'discontinuity' is that each becomes thereby the necessary 'representation', the 'objective interpretation', of the other (*Origin* 34). To say that neither is prior to the other is tantamount to saying that, at least as repre-sented in the achieved 'constellation', each will be 'immanent' to the other. 'Immanent', but (to use Adorno-speak) non-identical:

> It is the function of concepts to group phenomena together [sc. to 'constel-late' them], and the division which is brought about within them thanks to the distinguishing power of the intellect is all the more significant in that it brings about two things at a single stroke: the salvation of phenomena and the representation of ideas (*Origin* 35).

Here the Platonic motif of 'saving the appearances' intimates that Kabbalistic redemption always latent in Benjamin in ways that can make his project seem ideological, a work of 'extorted reconciliation'. Adorno would put the critical effect of 'the distinguishing power of the intellect' more strongly: that to the extent that the 'constellation' does *not* 'synthesize', 'totalize', or falsely unify its 'constellated' terms, but, precisely, underlines their 'discontinuity', each of these mutually 'immanent' terms functions not only as the other's representa-tion, but as the other's ('immanent') critique. Adorno's headlong, impetuous prose gives his 'constellations' the air of assembling contradictory and disjunct materials; Benjamin's more typically convey an unemphatic 'analytic' labor of patient decomposition and dissociation—of, to speak anachronistically, 'decon-struction', at a pace much more sedate, and in tones much more affectively subdued, than Adorno's (or Derrida's, for that matter). When Benjamin evokes 'digression' as 'method' ('Representation as digression—that is the method-ological nature of the treatise' [*Origin* 28]), he deploys two terms each of which marks a measure of Adorno's difference from him: for Adorno, 'method' usually connotes a positivist or empiricist ideology (as in 'scientific method') that falsely guarantees value-neutral results; as for 'digression', it aptly suggests the dilatory, diffident, inconclusive, passive-aggressive under-statement of Benjamin's prose (the consensus-word is 'saturnine'), but it could hardly be more different from the energetic, even hectic impetuosity or 'exaggeration' of Adorno's.

Adorno nowhere reflects as lengthily as Benjamin on 'constellation'; his usage suggests that it seemed fairly unproblematic to him. He's more reserved about Benjamin's 'dialectical image', about the theory, the practice, and the effect of which he speaks most suggestively and, for his own practice, most revealingly, in his 'Portrait of Walter Benjamin':

> The [Benjaminian] essay as form consists in the ability to regard historical moments, manifestations of the objective spirit, 'culture', as though they were natural. Benjamin could do this as no one else. The totality of this thought is characterized by what may be called 'natural history'. He was drawn to the petrified, frozen or obsolete elements of civilization, to everything in it devoid of domestic vitality . . . The French word for still-life, *nature morte*, could be written above the portals of his philosophical dungeons. The Hegelian concept of 'second nature', as the reification of estranged human relations, and also the Marxian category of 'commodity fetishism' occupy key positions in Benjamin's work. He is driven not merely to awaken congealed life in petrified objects—as in allegory—but also to scrutinize living things so that they present themselves as ancient, 'ur-historical' and abruptly release their significance. Philosophy appropriates the fetishism of commodities for itself: everything must metamorphose into a thing in order to break the catastrophic spell of things. Benjamin's thought is so saturated with culture as its natural object that it swears loyalty to reification instead of flatly rejecting it. . . . the glance of his philosophy is Medusan (*P* 233).

For us, there is peril in this assimilation of culture to nature, which we regard as the classic ruse of ideology. Our antidote, from Lévi-Strauss and Barthes (indeed, from Marx), is to dissolve the category of nature entirely into culture—to 'flatly reject' the category of nature. But for Adorno, the ruse itself is the first thing critique must grapple with—and it must do so 'immanently', that is, from the inside: critique must *suffer* the ruse of ideology, and even in a sense reproduce it from within, in the very course of the attempt to unmask it and neutralize its power. Hence the use, for Adorno and for Benjamin, of a critical device that permits, or demands, even *risks* just what our usual practice forbids, namely a patience of, or tolerance for, transaction between categories (e.g., nature/culture) that other styles of 'external' critique would disjoin. An 'external' critical practice insistently seeks to separate culture and nature, to fortify or sharpen or harden the antithesis between them, to (as it were) *dis*-ambiguate the mystifying conflation by which ideology sanctifies cultural/historical contingencies as natural necessities. By contrast, Benjamin and Adorno risk a 'motivated' re-ambiguation that again allows culture and nature access to each other in ways that can be critical of the binary from 'inside', ways impossible for

Adorno's Poetics of Critique

any 'external' construction of them as mutually exclusive. As Adorno elsewhere puts it:

> For [Benjamin] what is historically concrete becomes image—the archetypal image of nature as of what is beyond nature—and conversely nature becomes the figure of something historical (*NL2* 226).

Hence it is an opening to critical insight rather than an ideological lapse that 'in Benjamin the historical itself looks as though it were nature' (*NL2* 226), or, even more provocatively, that Benjamin's work 'swears loyalty to reification instead of flatly rejecting it' (*P* 233).

It is this subversive evocation of the ideology of 'nature' from within, 'immanently', that makes Benjamin's '*Denkbild*' or 'thought image' a '*dialectical* image':

> [Benjamin] was right to call the images of his philosophy dialectical . . . the plan of his book on the Paris Arcades envisaged a panorama of dialectical images as well as their theory. The concept of dialectical image was intended objectively, not psychologically: the representation of the modern as the new, the past, and the eternally invariant in one would have become both the central philosophical theme and the central dialectical image (*NL2* 226–7).

The language here leaves room for some unclarity. The 'representation of the modern as the new, the past, and the eternally invariant in one' would, presumably, be ideological—the bourgeois world's own 'universalizing' self-representation—and hence a fit 'object' or 'philosophical theme' for ideological exposé by way of the 'dialectical image'. But the unclarity allows also the suggestion that the 'representation' is itself the theme and the ('dialectical') image. We will recur to this ambiguity—cognate with our culture/nature problem—throughout; for now, the passage implicates in the 'dialectic' that the 'dialectical image' achieves or allows not only nature and culture, but also 'theory' and 'image'—another categorical binary often operative, and often less consciously, than culture/nature, in critical practice. In Hegel, 'picture-thinking' belongs to earlier phases of the unfolding story of the World-Spirit, in which the advent of theory or philosophy is itself an important milestone. And this evocation of the World-story reminds us, too, that for Hegel, 'the dialectic' was ineluctably a temporal process, which is to say conceptualizable only in or as *narrative*. 'Image' by contrast, is spatial, and atemporal—and to that extent a 'dialectical image' would seem to be a kind of paradox. Yet what makes the 'representation of the modern as the new, the past, and the eternally invariant in one' ideological is that it has *already* collapsed the narrative implicit in the given terms (modern, new, the past) into the narrativeless stasis of an 'eternally invariant' condition.

Hence the interest, when Adorno insists that 'There are good reasons why [Benjamin's] is a dialectic of images rather than a dialectic of progress and continuity, a "dialectics at a standstill"' (*NL2* 228)—for Adorno's critical practice generally presents what might seem the paradox or contradiction of an insistently historicizing program, realized in a critical practice that is virtually never motivated by historical argument in the form of historical narrative. Hence the relevance of the formula, 'dialectics at a standstill', which has become almost a slogan for Western Marxists and others for whom the forward momentum of nineteenth-century progressive (liberal) and/or revolutionary (Marxist) narratives of eventual happy endings have stalled in the steady-state nightmare of the twentieth century, where, as Horkheimer and Adorno starkly put it, 'mankind, instead of entering into a truly human condition, is sinking into a new kind of barbarism' (Cumming xi). Benjamin's striking phrase, 'dialectics at a standstill', figures this impasse of bourgeois modernity.

'Dialectics at a standstill' is, then, not only the ideological condition to be contested, but also the contestation's method—as witness Benjamin himself: 'Dialectics at a standstill—this is the quintessence of the method' (*Arcades* 865); elsewhere, quite simply, 'image is dialectics at a standstill'; and: 'Only dialectical images are genuinely historical' (*Arcades* 463). In tension with this ethos of 'standstill' attaching to the 'dialectical image' (and to 'image' *tout court*) is a related contradiction: since Hegel, the project of broaching the 'new' in the domain of Spirit has regularly generated figurations of loosening or liquifying formations inherited from the past that have 'hardened' or 'frozen', and thus become rigid and imprisoning. Hegel himself spoke of philosophy's task in such terms, of 'freeing determinate thoughts from their fixity' (*Phenomenology* 20); and compare Hegel's frequent formula that thought 'sets in motion' thought-objects, former 'certainties', that had been stalled. Adorno likewise figures 'reification' as a process of freezing, hardening, congealing, and the critical process, by contrast, as one of softening, loosening, reliquifying (as in the quotation above praising Benjamin's attempt to 'awaken congealed life in petrified objects' [*P* 233]). The task of 'immanent critique', Adorno elsewhere explains, is that 'congealed' ideological thought 'must be reliquified, its validity traced, in repetition' (*ND* 97). Above we saw what I called a motivated ambiguation (sc. 'reliquification') of culture and nature; here we have a cognate move, in that to 'reliquify' so as to release or engender the new, must begin with 'repetition' of that which had been 'congealed'.

Thus conceived, 'immanent critique' might seem, itself, an ambiguously narrative process putting the forward motion of renewal in tension with the cyclical or static entrapments of repetition. But as we'll see, the dialectic whereby narrative devolves into stand-still, into impasse, into image, has its analogous playing-out in the reversal whereby figurations of critical reliquification are displaced by their very opposite: by imageries of petrification, of hardening, freezing, rigidifying, even killing. Here, for example, Adorno's discussion of 'dialectical image' reprises the baleful image of Medusa (also already seen in the passage above from *Prisms*):

Benjamin's medusa-like gaze . . . turns its object to stone. . . . [It] froze [its object] to a kind of ontology [sc. hypostatization, reification, fetish] from the start. . . . This . . . was the spirit in which [Benjamin] restructured every element of culture that he encountered, as if the form of his intellectual organization and the melancholy with which his nature conceived the idea of something beyond nature, of reconciliation, necessarily endowed everything he took up with a deathly shimmer (*NL2* 228).

Here the 'gaze' of the critic does to its object just what 'immanent critique' and other projects of 'dereification' aim to *un*-do: hardens it, turns it to stone, turns it into a *thing*. Indeed, the critic's gaze does something very suggestive of killing the object ('endowing' it 'with a deathly shimmer'). Hence the pointed connection between, or 'constellation' of, the themes of non-narrative stasis and death, and critical efficacy:

[In Benjamin's] micrological method . . . the historical movement halts and becomes sedimented in the image. One understands Benjamin correctly if one senses behind each of his sentences the conversion of extreme animation into something static, in fact the static conception of movement itself (*NL2* 228).

Here, again, the critic 'immanently' repeats, even suffers, the stasis of our ideological condition in a way to perform ('repeat') that very condition—the 'moment' of the process captured in the Medusa-image being that in which the critic enacts the 'repetition' of that congealed, petrified condition, not (yet) its reliquification.

In his 1959 lectures on Kant, Adorno calls for a hermeneutic that, by entering the (objective) 'force field' of a writer's or a text's problematic, allows the interpreter to 'go beyond the immediate meaning on the page'. The Medusa image, fraught as it is with what Freud would call 'antithetical' motifs, emboldens me to give this a try. In the myth, the Medusa's power to petrify anyone who looks at her is defeated by Perseus, who contrives to approach her without looking, and at the crucial face-to-face moment, holds up to her a highly polished mirror. Medusa, seeing her own image, is herself turned to stone, and Perseus then decapitates her. He keeps her severed head, however, and in further adventures, uses it as a weapon—a fright-object with which to petrify new enemies. Adorno ascribes to Benjamin's 'medusa-gaze' the power to do to ideology something like what Perseus's mirror does to Medusa, *as well as* to do what Perseus uses Medusa's severed head to do to future adversaries. This image—the Medusa's petrifying power turned against Medusa herself, and then appropriated for further use against other threats—suggests something of the reflexiveness, the 'antithetical' character, the capacity for 'dialectical' reversals, as well as something of the ordeal, 'the labour and the suffering of the negative', incumbent on the (hero-) critic.

Adorno versus Benjamin

I have so far expounded Adorno's sense of 'constellation' and critique by way of his remarks on Benjamin's 'dialectical image'—a procedure that risks obscuring some of their more telling differences. Benjamin's critical practice is strongly marked, as is Adorno's, by the work of Freud—though a Freud mediated rather by the Surrealists than, as for Adorno, by Nietzsche. The Surrealist program was to inhabit the madness of the culture, to re-enact it from within, less (directly) to critique it, than to exhibit it—to insert themselves into the Freudian drama, but in the role not of ego, but of id. For the Surrealists, we might say, where ego was, there shall id be—on the evident premise that the ego, whatever its for-or-against posture toward the world, cannot be as 'naturally' or as 'immediately' transgressive as the id. The Surrealists typically embraced what Adorno would have regarded as an irrationalist faith that the real madness was reason, and unreason the only antidote or purge, if not salvation or utopian alternative. Benjamin seems to regard such a resort to madness with some ambivalence—almost as something like a desire unhappily forbidden him by reason of that obdurately quotidian sanity from which neither his brilliance nor his spleen could deliver him.[2] Some such longing, or nostalgia, seems to me symptomatized in Benjamin's sense of the world as a pallid, petrified, undead, fundamentally irrational waking dream, and the resistless momentum by which this 'phantasmagoria' passes into 'allegory' in all the diffuse senses Benjamin lent that word. Benjamin plays with a morbid-seeming identification with the dead and with death itself, as if, in his work, critique were playing possum; one of his most famous quotations, indeed, avows that critique itself long since left the land of the living.

Adorno was moved by the pathos of all this in the life and death of his friend, and doubtless he had Benjamin in mind in section V of the Anti-Semitism chapter of *Dialectic of Enlightenment*, in which the modern subject's protective 'mimesis' of the reified surrounding world is imaged as a feigned death entailing all too literally the spiritual consequences of the real thing. (Adorno might have been remembering Benjamin on Baudelaire's 'capacity to become rigid which—if a biological term may be used—manifests itself a hundredfold in Baudelaire's writings as a kind of mimesis of death' [*Baudelaire* 83].) Adorno's hyperactive prose style could never be confused with Benjamin's passive-aggressive 'melancholy'. As for Freud, Adorno never rose to the bait of assimilating the 'repeat/reliquify' course of 'immanent critique' to Freud's therapy of eliciting the 'compulsion to repeat', i.e., the patient's own transferential resistances, in order to enlist them in the healing labor, the 'making conscious', of the analysis (on this last, see Freud's 1914 paper on technique, 'Recollection, Repetition, and Working Through'). Adorno seems wary of any assimilation of his own project to psychoanalysis; the closest he comes is his late lecture, 'The Meaning of Working Through the Past' (*CM* 89–103);[3] and he holds himself much more aloof from Freud than such colleagues as Max Horkheimer, Erich Fromm, or Herbert Marcuse, let alone Benjamin, whose *methexis* in Freud brings him closer to the Joyce of the 'Circe' episode than to the practice of any member of the Frankfurt School. As we've seen, Adorno has his own distinctively critical 'unhappy consciousness', an 'after-Auschwitz' moral *askesis* that, in his work, long pre-dated the news of Auschwitz itself—but in Adorno this is a vibrant, highly cathected affect, quite different from that of the 'saturnine' or 'melancholy' Benjamin, which rather looks like the resigned, 'stoic' *ataraxia* that Adorno so frequently diagnoses as among the more desperate symptoms engendered by our post-Enlightenment, 'administered world'.

Gestalt

These tensions between Adorno and Benjamin's practice of the 'dialectical image' may be illuminated by a consideration of Adorno's wariness of the *Gestalt* psychology of Wolfgang Köhler. Adorno treats *Gestalt* theory as ideology—'constellation', we might say, in reverse. Adorno sounds caveats about *Gestalt* theory in his 1931 inaugural lecture, 'The Actuality of Philosophy' (*AR* 31–2); and a quarter century later, he makes almost a kind of satire of Husserlian 'intentionality' fidgeting in the unwelcome embrace of *Gestalt* psychology (*AE* 158–62). Pertinent here is Adorno's discussion of Kant's 'unity of apperception', the ground on which, Adorno argues, Kant's 'subjective' and 'objective' sustain each other (*KCPR* 100–1). Adorno is writing here in the late 1950s, when artists and poets often seized on *Gestalt* theory as a validation of avant-garde practices of the quick cut, the elision of transitions, etc.; other kinds of inquirers, too— e.g., Marshall McLuhan—made a sort of ideology, or short-hand all-purpose explanation, of 'pattern recognition' (as *Gestalt* was frequently anglicized) as a key to all manner of novel, putatively 'modern', styles of consciousness. Adorno's discussion projects *Gestalt* as the ideological problem rather than its critical solution: like Kant's 'unity of apperception', the functioning of *Gestalt* is 'unconsciously synthetic', thus effecting (false, familiarizing) integrations of experiential fragmentariness. (The motif of the 'fragment' here touches on Adorno's chronic theme of the false coherence of 'system' and the necessity, in critique, of allowing the unintegratable loose ends of 'the damaged life' to stand as reproach or 'bad conscience' to all mystifying 'extorted reconciliations'.) By these lights, *Gestalt* is an instance or model, indeed an epitome, of ideology as such: reflex and reinforcer of the habitual familiarizations, ideological conditionings, false reconciliations, 'imaginary solutions to real contradictions', of the historically and culturally given.

All of which only matters insofar as we can infer from Adorno's critique of *Gestalt* his ambitions for the 'constellation'. I should caution here that Adorno sometimes uses the word 'constellation' to designate historically given, i.e., already familiarized, ideological arrays or *Gestalten* (e.g., *CM* 138, 260); my usage henceforth will connote 'constellation' in the sense Adorno valorizes, as a device with the potential to be turned, in somewhat the manner of the Brechtian V-effect, *against* such familiarizations—though just this dissident potential, of course, is what mid-century avant-gardists were seizing on in *Gestalt*. And as we'll see, the word's 'antithetical' reversals of meaning are themselves indices of the 'dialectical'-ness of Adorno's 'immanent critique'. We might say that these 'antithetical' meanings—'constellation' as unconscious ideological synthesis, or as consciousness-raising estrangement: 'constellation' as object of critique, *or* as subject of it—themselves form a 'constellation' implying or encoding, concealing or de-familiarizing a narrative, that of the classic Enlightenment project summarized by Freud in the formula, 'making the unconscious conscious'. Adorno may 'repeat' an over-familiar 'constellation' and then 'reliquify' (or, Medusa-like, 'petrify') its 'congelations'; or he may present an unfamiliar and even shocking juxtaposition, whose estrangement is to provoke a new and heightened consciousness of the ideological condition in which we are entrapped. The historical 'image' that results, ideological and critical all at once, appropriates the critical force we saw Adorno ascribing to Benjamin's '*dialectical* image', turning it, 'immanently', to estranging or defamiliarizing, *critical* or 'negative' purposes.

Mediation

Most consequential, for our purposes, in Adorno's critique of *Gestalt* is the issue of *mediation*. According to Kant's 'unity of apperception', Husserl's 'intentionality', and *Gestalt* theory alike, the mind synthesizes or integrates bits of sense-data into a coherent whole or pattern; Adorno, as we've seen, regards this operation, under whatever name or construct, as a virtual model of the operations of ideology. Adorno claims Kant's sanction to urge that the 'fragmentariness' that *Gestalt* synthesizes, or, indeed, the fragments themselves 'stand in need of mediation' (*KCPR* 100)—a complexly ideological indictment, but suffice it for now to say that in Adorno, 'mediation' connotes dialectical self-consciousness, awareness of the negative, of contradiction, of non-identity, of the 'labor of the concept' itself. *Gestalt* theory attracted enthusiasts because it seemed to propose or promote a view of experience as 'immediate' (un-mediated), a specifically positivist or 'nominalist' naiveté or ideological mystification—one might even say, '*Gestalt*'—that Adorno consistently meant to combat. As we've seen, versions of this (to Adorno, naive and ideological) quest for 'immediate experience' are pervasive throughout the early-twentieth-century 'modernist' arts, from the scruffy anarchists of Dada and Surrealism to that most stiffly proper of reactionaries, T. S. Eliot. It would seem to be implicit in Adorno's own frequent motif of 'shock' as a way to awaken numbed perception; and it is clearly the program enacted in such modernist devices as 'montage', 'collage', 'ideogram', devices mobilized by their authors expressly to subvert received habits of synthesizing, modulating, contriving transitions—in short, *mediating*—between the typically incongruous or dissonant elements they contrived to bring together. Precisely to smash, subvert, defamiliarize, 'shock' the habituated 'mediations' of thought-and-feeling 'as usual' is of course the program of 'modernist' radical innovations in technique: and if Adorno here can seem to dissent from the repudiation of 'mediation' as such, his dissent is more in theory and concept than in practice. That is, his practice of 'constellation' differs from 'ideogram' and the like less in the way it actually functions than in the way Adorno conceives it: if others assayed gestures of 'de-mediation' or 'im-mediation'—escapes from mediation—Adorno projected rather a reinvention of it for purposes of critique and theory:

> . . . for Hegel, mediation is never a middle element between extremes, as, since Kierkegaard, a deadly misunderstanding has depicted it as being; instead, mediation takes place in and through the extremes, in the extremes themselves. This is the radical aspect of Hegel, which is incompatible with any advocacy of moderation. Hegel shows that the fundamental ontological contents that traditional philosophy hoped to distill are not ideas discretely set off from one another; rather each of them requires its opposite, and the relationship of all of them to one another is one of process (*HTS* 8–9).

This passage is rewriting Hegel in terms that justify Adorno's 'constellation' (and the modernist devices with which it makes common cause)—devices a Lukács would take as an ideological abrogation from the Hegelian-Marxian imperative of 'mediation'. Like 'ideogram', 'collage', and the rest, Adorno's 'constellation' at the very least *appears*—'juxtaposition without copula'—to dispense with mediation, which to Stalinist orthodoxy of the period was tantamount to dispensing with 'dialectic' itself. Here we might say Adorno is narrowcasting modernist 'shock' very directly to that hidebound paleo-Marxist demographic for whom 'dialectic' and 'mediation' were no less articles of faith than the withering away of the state and the dictatorship of the proletariat. Adorno's own practice was meant, in emulation of the great modernists he consistently advocated against the 'socialist realist' criticisms of Lukács, to repudiate 'official' dialectical materialism as reified and reifying dogmatism. In the Lukácsean optic, Adorno's 'constellation', assembling disjunct elements in (seemingly) unmediated array, would seem as decadent as cubist collage, Eisensteinian montage, Poundian ideogram, Joycean stream-of-consciousness: 'idealist', 'subjective', 'decadent', 'immediate' in the proscribed sense of unmediated. Most pertinently, and in terms deriving from the authority of Marx and Lenin both, it would have seemed 'un-dialectical'. Lukács's prose retains the composure of the platform debater; Adorno more characteristically vents exasperation, rejoining that Lukács, 'the certified dialectician', himself argues 'most undialectically' in, e.g., dismissing Freud and Nietzsche as irrationalists and therefore 'fascists pure and simple' (*NL1* 217).[4]

In Lukács, the adjective 'dialectical' often modifies the word 'unity': 'dialectic' thus names a procedure for unifying or integrating disjunct or incommensurable things; its very point is to achieve unity in matters evincing a deficit of unity. (This impulse to unity, sheer ideology in Adorno's view, is what Lukács's Comintern orthodoxy has in common with both Kant's 'synthetic apperception' and *Gestalt*-theory.) In Adorno's theory-and-practice, contrarily, the aim of dialectic is to emphasize the contradictions that ideological appearance has falsely reconciled: to expose or, indeed, *produce* disunity, contradiction, non-identity where false consciousness has minimized them. 'Constellation' serves this end by so juxtaposing diverse phenomena as to amplify their dissonances. As in Benjamin, the clash of the constellated items is the point. To Lukács, such gaps and disjunctions would be evidence of a failure to have done the dialectical work of unifying that is the *sine qua non* of critical activity—a failure, in short, of 'mediation'. To Adorno, mediation that fills in the gaps between the disjuncta would be ideological, homogenizing, causing the disjuncta to (in Roland Barthes's phrase) 'lose their difference'. For Adorno, the point of mediation is to highlight, even 'exaggerate', the very contradictions that Lukács would unify or reconcile; hence Adorno's anti-Lukács formula: 'Extorted Reconciliation' (*NL1* 216–40). To Lukács, 'constellation' would exemplify the same spurious and 'sick' immediacy on display in Beckett, Kafka, Freud, and the other 'decadent' modernists Lukács so deplored.

For Adorno, by contrast, 'immanent critique' cannot hold itself above (or 'outside') the predicaments on which it aspires to comment; since critique cannot help but participate in the culture's 'symptomatics', it had best own this liability, and make of it, to the extent possible, a quickening instantiation of the challenge to be met, the problem to be addressed. Adorno agrees with Lukács in reprehending false or naive 'immediacy', but his 'constellational' view of mediation gives him a very different take on the evidence from Lukács's. I don't pretend always to understand why Adorno approves one work or artist as dialectical and mediated, and damns another as deficient in these qualities; and to the objection that Adorno is 'merely' contriving philosophical sanctions for his personal tastes, I at least would not always be able to muster a very cogent reply. But worth mention here is the move that we might call, borrowing a rubric from *Against Epistemology*, 'Dialectic In Spite of Itself' (*AE* 49–50), by which Adorno often recuperates (or 'rescues') his critical targets from his own critiques of them (e.g., Kierkegaard [*KCA passim*], Kant [*KCPR* 125], Freud, Weber [*IS* 113, 123], even Wagner [*ISW* 153–6/142–5; *EM* 584–602]). But whereas Lukács casts these matters in figures of decadence and disease—see. e.g., his 'Healthy or Sick Art?'—Adorno stages them rather in terms of ideological appearance, 'magic', and 'myth'.

An especially pertinent instance for our purposes is Adorno's exchange with Benjamin over an excerpt (on Baudelaire) of the *Arcades Project* that Benjamin submitted for publication in the Institute journal in 1938.[5] Adorno reacted unfavorably, for reasons, it's not often noted, quite like those Lukács raised against modernism: 'Motifs are assembled but they are not elaborated'; they sit nakedly on the page, un-'mediated' by 'theory'; the (ideological) result is that Benjamin's 'ascetic refusal of interpretation only serves to transport [the subject matter] into a realm quite opposed to asceticism: a realm where history and magic oscillate':

> Unless I am very much mistaken [writes Adorno to Benjamin], your dialectic is lacking in one thing: mediation. You show a prevailing tendency to relate the pragmatic contents of Baudelaire's work directly and immediately to adjacent features in the social history and . . . economic features of the time. . . . you substitute metaphorical expressions for categorical ones. . . . [so that] one of the most powerful ideas in your study seems to be presented as a mere as-if. . . . I regard it as methodologically inappropriate to give conspicuous individual features from the realm of the superstructure a 'materialist' turn by relating them immediately, and perhaps even causally, to certain corresponding features of the substructure. The materialist determination of cultural traits is only possible if it is mediated through the *total social process*. . . . [such] immediate—and I would almost say again 'anthropological'—materialism harbours a profoundly romantic element . . . The mediation which I miss, and find obscured by materialistic-historical evocation, is simply the theory which your study has omitted . . . one could say that your study is located at the crossroads of magic and positivism. The spot is bewitched. Only theory could break this spell—your own resolute and salutarily speculative theory. It is simply the claim of this theory that I bring against you here (*CC* 281–3).

I don't know whether Adorno at this point knew the passage in 'Convolute N' of the *Arcades Project* in which Benjamin confides that his 'method' is 'literary montage' precisely so that 'I needn't *say* anything. Merely show' (*Arcades* 460). In any case, the 'method' clearly didn't win Adorno's approval. The incident suggests telling contrasts between Benjamin's 'dialectical image', especially as practiced in the *Passagen-Werk*, and Adorno's 'constellation': Benjamin cites or quotes particular *faits divers*, one at a time, each standing distinct in its surround of white space on the page—even typographically, a 'dialectical image', one might say, of that 'separation' or '*chorismos*', the ideological entailment of 'analytic' (bourgeois) philosophical method from Plato to Kant and beyond, that Adorno protested throughout his career.

'Constellation' is of course the vehicle of Adorno's protest, but it could serve as a figure for it as well; his famously boundless paragraphs constellate diverse materials so diffusely as to ground or 'theorize' or mediate them together—albeit, again, that the 'ground' is contradiction rather than unity. Adorno tends, also, to 'constellate' higher-brow materials than Benjamin—Hegel and Beethoven rather than, say, century-old department store brochures: in his 1931 inaugural lecture, 'The Actuality of Philosophy', Adorno sounds the 'materialist' motif of the philosophical worthiness of 'the refuse of the physical world' (he is citing Freud's *'Abhub der Erscheinungswelt'* [*AR* 32]); but Adorno is generally loath to incorporate such materials in his writing as Benjamin did.[6] This difference resonates with Adorno's 'mandarin' fastidiousness, as well as with his greater circumspection—almost, as he says himself, a *Bilderverbot*—regarding the utopian (see Buck-Morss, 90–5); it's arguable that the dissent from Benjamin above helped confirm Adorno in these penchants.

Parataxis

We have been navigating between the stasis of image and the kinesis of narrative, and I want to adduce here another motif in which these preoccupations find yet another way of overlapping: the 'epic' device of parataxis, which lends its name to the title of Adorno's late essay on Hölderlin. Parataxis is a rhetorical device in which narrative units follow one another linked only by the conjunction 'and', thus evading or subverting more complex structures or grammars of narrative co- or sub-ordination (cause and effect, antecedent and consequence, main event and subsidiary, and the like). 'Parataxis: On Hölderlin's Late Poetry' (*NL2* 109–49) praises Hölderlin's subversion of the usual reified, familiarized, domesticated ways of making sense. Hölderlin's parataxes, Adorno writes, are 'artificial disturbances that evade the logical hierarchy of a subordinating syntax', and in particular, 'the judgment' and 'the propositional form' (*NL2* 131–2). In Adorno's modernist account, 'parataxis' does with narratemes something like what 'constellation' is meant to do with the diverse fragments it constellates: presents them in an ensemble undomesticated by the familiar thought-syntax, the habituated grammars, and thus the ideological presuppositions, that familiarize the new, converting it at the very moment it's presented, into the same, the old, the already known—the, as it were, pre-reified. Hölderlin's poetry 'searches for a linguistic form that would escape the dictates of spirit's own synthesizing principle' (*NL2* 131)—thus circumventing the mind's own drive to familiarize the new.

Parataxis thus might seem a solvent, a way of de-composing what 'spirit's own synthesizing principle' too unthinkingly composes or synthesizes. (Compare the formula of 'the logic of disintegration' by which Adorno at about this same time characterized what he acknowledged as a career-long concern [*ND* 144–6; and see Buck-Morss, *Origins* 233n3].) The motive would seem to be to mobilize the dissonant fragmentary contents *against* the larger synthesizing form(s). But Adorno insists that Hölderlin's parataxis achieves not merely an abolition of form, an escape *from* it, but something like a kind of emancipation *of* form itself. And of course, to the extent that parataxis is itself a form, this is an emancipation not conferred on form from above or outside, but form's own self-emancipation, in line with what Adorno evokes as 'the agency of form' (*NL2* 114). Hölderlin's parataxis 'puts explication without deduction in the place of a so-called train of thought. This gives form its primacy over content, even the intellectual content' (*NL2* 131–2). Set free from the 'deductive' regime of thinking as usual, the 'explication' of the matter can enact itself 'immanently', according to its own imperatives rather than those of an external, syllogistic logic given in advance. So far from vanishing, form here rather achieves itself in allowing, being the vehicle for, new potentialities by which the particular 'contents' find their expression. Thus does form become itself a content, content a kind of form, and all *concretely*, thus sublating the classic antinomies (form/content, idea/matter, abstract/concrete, universal/particular, 'the bad content of language' [Cumming 22]) bedeviling philosophy and the aesthetic under the regime of 'spirit's own synthesizing principle'. Hence (and readers familiar with Adorno's Beethoven-olatry will recognize the argument here):

> It is not only the micrological forms of serial transition in a narrow sense . . . that we must think of as parataxis. As in music, the tendency takes over larger structures. In Hölderlin there are forms that could as a whole be called paratactical in the broader sense. . . . In a manner reminiscent of Hegel, mediation of the vulgar kind, a middle element standing outside the moments it is to connect, is eliminated as being external and inessential, something that occurs frequently in Beethoven's late style; this not least of all gives Hölderlin's late poetry its anticlassicistic quality, its rebellion against harmony. What is lined up in sequence, unconnected, is as harsh as it is flowing. The mediation is set within what is mediated instead of bridging it (*NL2* 132–3).

Hölderlin, Beethoven, and Hegel are here arrayed—mediated—in 'constellation' as practitioners of this 'immanent' kind of composition (a 'technique of seriation' Adorno calls it [*NL2* 135]) in which the particular 'takes over larger structures', to produce forms that are 'paratactical in the broader sense'.

This issue of 'larger structures', of parataxis on the large-scale level of form, returns us to the issue of temporality—Hölderlin, Beethoven, and Hegel (and, of course, Adorno) are all practitioners of forms a hearer or reader must experience in time—and thus of possibilities of kinesis within or by way of the structures that form achieves. 'The transformation of language [in Hölderlin's parataxis] into a serial order whose elements are linked differently than in the judgment is musiclike' (*NL2* 131), such that parataxis as a form—as an '*agency of form*'—pushes referential language in the direction of non-referential meaning; moreover, terms like 'serial' and 'musiclike' restore 'temporality' to the stasis of 'constellation'. In the 'Parataxis' essay, although Adorno's focus is on the lyric, narrative in Hölderlin appears (under the sign of the 'epic'; see the discussion of Hölderlin's relation to Pindar [*NL2* 132–4]) as another impulse working against 'the logical hierarchy of a subordinating syntax':

> The narrative tendency in the poem strives downward into the prelogical medium and wants to drift along with the flow of time. The Logos had worked against the slippery quality of narrative . . . the self-reflection of Hölderlin's late poetry, in contrast, evokes it. Here too it converges in a most amazing way with the texture of Hegel's prose, which, in paradoxical contradiction to his systematic intent, in its form increasingly evades the constraints of construction the more it surrenders without reservation to the program of 'simply looking on' outlined in the introduction to the *Phenomenology* and the more logic becomes history for it (*NL2* 134).

Here the animus since Plato between poetry and philosophy is 'sublated'; moreover, Adorno presents the sublation itself as event, that is to say, as narrative. The redemptive or utopian promise is made more explicit in a passage reprising all these themes:

> The logic of tightly bounded periods [i.e., the opposite of 'parataxis'], each moving rigorously on to the next, is characterized by precisely that compulsive and violent quality for which poetry is to provide healing and which Hölderlin's poetry unambiguously negates. Linguistic synthesis contradicts what Hölderlin wants to express in language. . . . [Hölderlin] began by attacking syntax syntactically, in the spirit of the dialectic . . . In the same way, Hegel used the power of logic to protest against logic (*NL2* 135–6).

'Immanent Critique' as 'Repetition'

Given the ubiquity of the phrase 'immanent critique' in Adorno's oeuvre, it's surprising that what Adorno might have meant by it has received such perfunctory attention from commentators, most of whom treat it as an easily explained premise to dispose of on the way to weightier matters.[7] Yet in this phrase, Adorno comes as close as he does anywhere to naming something like a programmatic ambition for his work. It's a term meant not only to distinguish Adorno's work from the conventional critical practices of his era, but to model a riskier, more daring range of critical effort, and thus to challenge criticism-as-usual to enlarge its scope, to take on greater burdens, to attempt, defying the risk of failure, ever more daunting tasks. Adorno means to bring critique itself into the critical crosshairs, to enlarge or arouse the very self-consciousness of critique, and he means the consequences to bear not merely on the kinds of object critique might target, or the kinds or method or scope of the arguments it might mount, but on the very writing practice in which critique realizes itself. So rather than take 'immanent critique' as a given, I want here to trace fault lines and contradictions in Adorno's theory-and-practice of 'immanent critique' that seem to me suggestive and illuminating for the dialectical uses to which Adorno turns it—or (better) allows or suffers it to turn his writing. I aim to set the 'performative contradiction' (Habermas) of Adorno's 'immanent critique' in relation to other constructions (Benjamin's) and/or critiques (Lukács's, Habermas's) of it, in ways that will illuminate all these figures and the issues at stake in their disagreements over what critique can be and how it should conduct itself. Again, I characterize Adorno's immanent critique as not only a *critical* program, but also a 'performative' one, that is, a reflexive self-consciousness about Adorno's own writing practice, and thus a weighty motivation of the flair and drama that are so distinctive to Adorno's writing.

'Immanent critique', then: by this usage Adorno clearly intends more than just to take sides in the long contention over what critique is, or should, or can, be. Rather, Adorno means to enact a critique of the debate itself, and to model larger possibilities and challenges beyond it. A traditional program of critique has been to get 'outside' the critical object, to achieve 'critical distance' from it, or 'objectivity' about it. Both in its Kantian and its Marxist senses, 'critique' has turned on issues of inside/outside; and the pursuit of the 'inside' track has largely belonged to 'hermeneutic', as opposed to 'critique'. 'Hermeneutic' sanctions the interpreter's sympathy, or even identification with the object— precisely the stance 'critique' rejects as imperiling objectivity. As usual, when confronted with a dichotomy in our culture's way of conceptualizing its problems, Adorno takes the dichotomy or *chorismos* itself as the ideological problem or wound that his own critical labor will attempt to overcome or heal. Hence Adorno's 'immanent critique' encodes the ambition to get the critical 'subject' *inside* what we might then no longer so simply be able to call critique's 'object'. Adorno frequently contrasts it with critique 'from outside', what he calls 'external' or 'transcendent critique' (*Prisms* 31–4; *KCPR* 20):

> The immanent approach need not fear the objection that it is without a perspective, mollusklike and relativistic. Ideas that have confidence in their own objectivity have to surrender . . . to the object in which they immerse themselves . . . Transcendent critique avoids from the outset the experience of what is other than its own consciousness. . . . Transcendent critique sympathizes with authority in its very form, even before expressing any content; [for] there is a moment of content to the form itself (*HTS* 146).

Adorno's most sustained contrast of 'immanent' with 'transcendent' criticism comes at the close of the 1949 essay, 'Cultural Criticism and Society' (it is this peroration that rises to the climax of 'To write poetry after Auschwitz is barbaric' [*P* 34]):

> The alternatives—either calling culture as a whole into question from outside under the general notion of ideology, or confronting it with the norms which it itself has crystallized—cannot be accepted by critical theory. To insist on the choice between immanence and transcendence is to revert to the traditional logic criticized in Hegel's polemic against Kant. . . . The position transcending culture is in a certain sense presupposed by dialectics as the consciousness which does succumb in advance to the fetishization of the intellectual sphere. Dialectics means intransigence toward all reification. The transcendent method, which aims at totality, seems more radical than the immanent method, which presupposes the questionable whole. The transcendent critic assumes an as it were Archimedean position above culture and the blindness of society . . . [But] The choice of standpoint outside the sway of existing society is as fictitious as only the construction of abstract utopias can be. Hence, the transcendent criticism of culture, much like bourgeois cultural criticism, sees itself obliged to fall back on the idea of 'naturalness', which itself forms a central element of bourgeois ideology. . . . This explains the inadequacy of most socialist contributions to cultural criticism: they lack the experience of that with which they deal. In wishing to wipe away the whole as with a sponge, they develop an affinity to barbarism (*P* 31–2).

The 'transcendent critic' here is clearly Lukács; in affecting to play Hegel to Lukács's Kant, Adorno here trumps Lukács's own indictment, in *History and Class Consciousness*, of Kant as the 'bourgeois philosopher' par excellence.

Adorno goes on to clinch the contrast of this 'transcendent criticism' with the 'immanent criticism' he prefers: as the passage develops, 'immanent criticism' and 'dialectics' begin to operate as functionally convertible terms:

> [Immanent criticism] pursues the logic of its aporias, the insolubility of the task itself. In such antinomies criticism perceives those of society. A successful work, according to immanent criticism, is not one which resolves objective contradictions in a spurious harmony, but one which expresses the harmony negatively by embodying the contradictions, pure and uncompromised, in its innermost structure. Confronted with this kind of work, the verdict 'mere ideology' loses its meaning. At the same time, however, immanent criticism holds in evidence that the mind has always been under a spell. On its own it is unable to resolve the contradictions under which it labours. Even the most radical reflection of the mind on its own failure is limited by the fact that it remains only reflection, without altering the existence to which its failure bears witness. Hence immanent criticism cannot take comfort in its own idea.

It can neither be vain enough to believe that it can liberate the mind directly
. . . nor naive enough to believe that unflinching immersion in the object
will inevitably lead to truth by virtue of the logic of things . . . The less the
dialectical method can today presuppose the Hegelian identity of subject
and object, the more it is obliged to be mindful of the duality. . . . the very
opposition between knowledge which penetrates from without and that
which bores from within becomes suspect to the dialectical method, which
sees in it a symptom of precisely that reification which the dialectic is obliged
to accuse. . . . No theory, not even that which is true, is safe from perversion
into delusion once it has renounced a spontaneous [sc. 'immanent'] relation
to the object. Dialectics must guard against this no less than against enthrall-
ment in the cultural object. It can subscribe neither to the cult of the mind
nor to hatred of it. The dialectical critic of culture must both participate in
culture and not participate. Only then does he do justice to his object and to
himself (*P* 32–3).

If 'the very opposition between knowledge which penetrates from without and
that which bores from within' is itself a symptom of the problem, then the logic
of that aporia requires a method that aspires to do both: and 'the insolubility of
the task' is not its disqualification, but an attestation of its necessity. Adorno's
practice thus assumes for 'immanent critique' burdens both critical *and* hermeneutic, making each immanent to the other, and *at the same time* making each
the other's critique: critique's 'distance' from the object now appears not as an
objectivity to be striven for, but an alienation, even an *ataraxia* or repression, to
be overcome; while hermeneutic's 'inwardness' with the object, attesting the
interpreter's sympathy with the text, now appears as an ideological entrapment
critique must struggle, however vainly, to breach. 'Immanent critique', then, is
critique of critique, and not merely in the sense of auto-critique. At stake is not
the critic's mere decision in advance between two kinds of critique, internal
and external. Adorno's premise is that all 'critique' is from 'inside'—inside of
history, of economy, of culture, politics, ideology—and that 'external critique'
is ideologically deluded, or self-blinded, or self-trivializing, if it supposes that it
has gotten, or can or should get, 'outside' the determinations of 'the social'.
'Immanent critique', then, is not a lofty ambition critique should aspire to, but
a social predicament critique must try not to flinch from.

   An 'immanent critique' thus conceived incurs complex burdens—as we can
observe in a section of *Negative Dialectics* that proposes an 'immanent critique'
of Heideggerian 'ontology'. Adorno concedes that the Spirit in our age has a
legitimate 'ontological need', to which Heidegger offers false consolation.
Adorno's 'immanent critique' means to interpret the genuine (symptomatic)
need or problem as well as to expose the ideological mystification of the proposed 'imaginary solution'. 'We have no power over the philosophy of Being if
we reject it generally, from outside instead of taking it on in its own structure—

turning its own force against it ... The thought movement that congealed in [Heidegger's ontology]', Adorno explains, 'must be reliquified, its validity traced, in repetition' (*ND* 97). Observe first that this is a critique—a 'determinate negation'—concerned as much to validate what is valid in its object, as to discredit what is not. But the real trouble is 'repetition', a word in all critical usages (including Adorno's) virtually always connoting ideology itself, i.e., everything that forecloses the (utopian) promise of future deliverance from the fated 'repetition' of the past. As part—or as 'moment'—of its effort to 'reliquify' the ideological rigidities it suffers, 'immanent critique' must 'repeat' these rigidities, which is to say, must suffer, indeed, must inflict 'repetition' upon itself *deliberately*. Adorno is Hegel's disciple in holding that the past cannot be merely disowned, or gotten 'outside' of: escaping its cycle of 'repetition' requires a 'working-through' that confronts, 'immanently', all the horror of what we would escape. So solving a problem requires first of all the evocation of the problem, in all its problematicalness. We cannot overcome ideology without a full acknowledgment—more: a full experience, in the writing, in the reading—of the power of ideology.

As writing, therefore—and Adorno never lets a reader (or a critic) forget that critique is, ineluctably, 'a kind of writing'—as writing, critique must labor as mightily to evoke its object, as to sublate or move beyond it. And hence the 'unhappy consciousness' imperative that is palpable in every word Adorno ever wrote. Recall here the theme of an earlier chapter, that the Hegelian 'labor and suffering of the negative' becomes, in Adorno, an insistence on 'the labor of the concept' as part and parcel of a 'labor of affectualization'—the labor of apprehending our ideological condition not only as thought, but also as feeling—with the caveat (again) that Adorno refuses the conventional antithesis, the ideological *chorismos*, of 'concept' and 'affect'. He aims (and this, too, is part of the problem his 'immanent critique' means both to 'repeat' and to 'reliquify', part of the breach he wants to close, the wound he wants to heal, even if doing so must begin by reopening it) to make affects conceptual, and to make the concept affective, to overcome the *chorismos* by which enlightenment has, in separating thought from feeling, impoverished both. Only thus can the wound, and the healing (if any: at any rate, the need for it), be made 'concrete'.

This figuration of wound and healing recalls the motif of Amfortas's spear: to 'repeat and reliquify' the reifications of our 'damaged life' must risk a renewal of the ordeal, a reopening of the wound, which can only be healed by the spear that inflicted the wound in the first place. Again, the dynamic resonates with the Freudian transference—a model that would seem irresistible, though Fredric Jameson is the only commentator I recall evoking it (*Late Marxism* 64); the closest Adorno comes to allowing such a parallel is in the late (1959) essay, 'The Meaning of Working Through the Past' (*CM* 89–104). Like psychoanalysis, immanent critique prescribes a labor at once cognitive and affective; and the 'repeat/reliquify' effect arises from immanent critique's 'transferential' relation to its ideological object, first eliciting from it experientially the very contradictions and impasses it will then try to relieve. Recall also here Freud's adviso that neurosis itself, as a coping mechanism, however dysfunctional, should be regarded as already a first motion toward cure (*General Psychological Theory* 41; *Moses and Monotheism* 97). Freud's sense of the covert affinities between 'antithetical' themes and affects, affinities that can lead to their sudden reversal into each other, might seem 'undialectical' and 'unmediated'— Adorno occasionally implies as much himself, especially when what's at issue is the antinomic force of such quasi-'mythical' Freudian binaries as Eros/ Thanatos—but Adorno more typically honors Freud's evocation of the seemingly unmediated 'antithetical' as if under the rubric of 'dialectic in spite of itself'. Foundational to Freud's project as to Adorno's is the Hegelian imperative or ethos of 'becoming (self-) conscious' (in Freud, 'making the unconscious conscious' [*Introductory Lectures* 435, 455]).

Clearly such experiential, transferential, or 'affective' (even *aesthetic*) burdens puts large demands on the *writing* of critique—the critic must be a writer of peculiar brilliance to meet them—and likewise on the reader, who must be open to a peculiarly challenging, peculiarly difficult text, whose self-conscious expressive 'difficulty' is motivated by the historical, cultural, social, and political difficulties of its subject matter, difficulties it must 'repeat': must *evoke*, experientially, as preliminary to any other hoped for relief, any transformative ('reliquifying') effect upon them. And that imperative, familiar in our period from the great radical innovations of modernism, incurs the dangers that Georg Lukács reprehended as 'the ideology of modernism': that to '*repeat*'the problem will be merely to *replicate* it, so that the radical new work will present merely a 'symptom' of the problem rather than a critical 'negation' of it. Lukács's indictment of 'sick' modernism recalls Karl Kraus's quip against psychoanalysis: that it is the disease for which it purports to be the cure. (Compare, more recently, Terry Eagleton: 'Adorno . . . offers as a solution what is clearly part of the problem, the political homeopath who will feed us sickness as cure' [Eagleton 360].) Hence the decades-long debate between Lukács and Adorno (et al.) over the merits of realism versus modernism. For Lukács, a Joyce, or a Proust was merely an *instance* or *symptom* of bourgeois decadence, not, in any useful way, an anatomist or critic of it. For Adorno, a Kafka, a Beckett, has a critical value far outstripping any more conventionally conceived critique, because they make the contemporary predicament and its anguish real, 'concrete'— they convey its 'objectivity'. Beckett's plays, e.g., 'arouse the anxiety that existentialism only talks about' (*NL2* 90)—and they do so without offering any narrative resolution, such as would be, for Lukács, the *sine qua non* of any 'critical' prospect of release from the predicaments they portray: the failure of any such enactment is what makes them, for Lukács, merely symptomatic of the bourgeois ideology, and thus ideological themselves. For Adorno, such narrative release could only be 'imaginary': not merely ideological, but an epitome of ideology as such. It's not merely that Lukács and Adorno disagree on what's critical and what's ideological: it's that precisely what determines the question for one determines it the other way for the other.

To Lukács, *Dialectic of Enlightenment*, whether as argued theory or as a piece of rhetoric, can only have exemplified 'the ideology of modernism': it transgresses the nineteenth-century conventions of critique Lukács's own practice upheld as radically as Joyce or Proust violated those of the realist fiction Lukács continued to champion. It avows a historicizing and dialectical program, but builds itself around binary pairs—Odysseus as bourgeois, myth as enlightenment—that would seem to be anything but: asserted, rather, as trans-historically or un-historically homogeneous, 'equivalent' or fungible in a way to obscure the need, even foreclose the possibility, of their 'dialectical' mediation, let alone negation or sublation. They so 'constellate' historically disjunct pairs as to preempt any narrative leading from one to the other, much in the manner of Eisenstein's 'montage', Pound's 'ideogram', Joyce's 'epiphany', and other modernist devices in which Lukács saw only symptoms of bourgeois decadence. If this critique of *Dialectic of Enlightenment* remains implicit in Lukács, Jürgen Habermas, epigone of the Frankfurt School generally and protégé of Adorno in particular, spells it out. In Lecture V of *The Philosophical Discourse of Modernity* (106–30), Habermas warns that *Dialectic of Enlightenment* risks incurring the sin it avowedly condemns, namely enforcing the myth/enlightenment binary so insistently as to lapse into a 'mythic thinking' of the very kind the book charges against enlightenment itself. (Habermas is concerned lest the gains of modernity be lost in the cross-fire between anti-modern reactionaries on the right and postmodern radicals on the left; he more charitably concedes Adorno and Horkheimer's commit-ment to 'reason' in the interviews, roughly contemporaneous with *Philosophical Discourse of Modernity*, collected as *Autonomy and Solidarity* [e.g., 98, 154–5].) But Habermas argues that to the extent that enlightenment is critique, Horkheimer and Adorno undercut their own *critical* project, as well as the 'modern' project at large—in other words, that *Dialectic of Enlightenment* is entoiled in what Habermas repeatedly calls a 'performative contradiction' (*Philosophical Discourse* 119, 127, 185) that vitiates the whole project.[8]

I am arguing the contrary here, that just this performative contradiction is what gives *Dialectic of Enlightenment* its force and its weird power. If Habermas puts the stress on the contradiction, I want to put it on the performativity, the book's ingenious enactment of what it stages as a historically specific social contradiction: a contradiction not merely incidental to a particular critical rhet-oric, but a contradiction 'objectively' there in the cultural predicament the cri-tique means, 'immanently', to take on, to suffer or 'repeat' as well as to negate or 'reliquify'. And an irony, or dialectic, that might seem to vindicate the book against Habermas is that Habermas's indictment itself can manage no better than to 'repeat' the offense it protests—for consider: according to *Dialectic of Enlightenment*, enlightenment denounces every precedent *episteme* as 'myth'.

Repeating that gesture, *Dialectic of Enlightenment* denounces enlightenment as 'myth'. And now, here is Habermas, denouncing *Dialectic of Enlightenment* as 'myth' (*Philosophical Discourse* 125, 127). Habermas usually makes Adorno and Horkheimer's unfortunate fall into myth sound unwitting, but not always—and indeed, he is never more indignant at the 'paradox' of *Dialectic of Enlightenment* than when acknowledging that it is deliberate: 'Adorno was quite aware of this performative contradiction' (*Philosophical Discourse* 119). What's further ironic is the question of Habermas's own awareness of his own implication in the tangle. It's like an Escher drawing, a fractal-recursive, self-replicating structure into which Habermas's reading has conducted itself despite itself. It would seem that *Dialectic of Enlightenment* has indeed tapped some 'objective' systemic 'virus', so to speak, or structural meme, so pervasive and self-activating in the sociocultural DNA of enlightenment—a.k.a. modernity, late capitalism, the administered world—that neither enlightenment, nor Horkheimer and Adorno's critique of enlightenment, nor Habermas's critique of their critique, can quarantine the infection 'inside' a boundary, nor secure itself safely 'outside' the zone of contamination. Thus the Horkheimer/Adorno QED: that there is no way to get 'outside' the ideological dilemmas of 'enlightenment' and/as 'myth'.

Pace Habermas, I would put it that *Dialectic of Enlightenment*'s brilliance is to have sustained a fertile and high-voltage rhetoric not *despite*, but precisely *because* of the contradictoriness of what seem initially quite ahistorical, un-dialectical (sc. 'mythical') conjunctions. The measure of its success is how effectually it manages to communicate those contradictions—understanding 'communicate' here to evoke not the model of transmission of message from sender to receiver, but the ambition of the text to make the pain of all this contradiction *common*, a kind of ideological *communion* of suffering that, Adorno insinuates, is as close to a legitimate solidarity as our alienated culture may allow. 'The need to lend a voice to suffering', again, 'is the condition of all truth' (*ND* 17–18). *Dialectic of Enlightenment* is a text in which diverse kinds of difficulty motivate, indeed, over-determine each other; hence the 'difficulty' of the text is irreducible, and by design: it cannot, it should not, be rendered lucid by any paraphrase or commentary. The un-lucidity conveys the 'textual effect' (or affect) of feeling, in the reading, always a direct function of the general apprehension of 'contradiction' as the motivation of the writing. It is the very point of Adorno's 'immanent critique' that we are not merely *shown* this contradiction or that, but that we *feel* what Adorno elsewhere calls the 'Objectivity of Contradiction' (*ND* 151–3) in the very experience of reading. Contradiction is realized, or concretized *in* its very concept, and *as* feeling: a model of the 'labor of conceptualization' and the 'labor of affectualization', as well as the *chorismos* of the ideological will to separate them, to diminish the force, to numb the pain, of each. Contradiction thus, *performed*, concretized in the medium of Adorno's writing practice, is 'performative contradiction' not as a critical lapse or deficit, but as the relevant designation of a fully achieved 'immanent critique'.

It's the potent contradictoriness of this effect that is dialectical despite appearances: a (so to speak) 'semblance'-undialecticalness. In his 'metacritique' of Husserl, Adorno insinuates, again, the functional convertibility of these terms:

> Dialectic's very procedure is immanent critique. It does not so much oppose [Husserlian] phenomenology with a position or 'model' external and alien to phenomenology, as it pushes the phenomenological model, with the latter's own force, to where the latter cannot afford to go. Dialectic exacts the truth from it through the confession of its own untruth (*AE* 5).

'Immanent critique', that is, 'repeats' Husserl's 'phenomenological model', *and* its 'untruth'—but with the effect of not merely 'repeating' the 'untruth', but forcing a critical 'confession' from the 'untruth' itself:

> Dialectics is the quest to see the new in the old instead of just the old in the new. As it mediates the new, so it also preserves the old as the mediated. If it were to proceed according to the schema of sheer flow and indiscriminate vitality (*Lebendigkeit*), then it would degrade itself to a replica of the amorphous structure of nature, which it should not sanction through mimicry, but surpass through cognition. Dialectic gives its own to the old as reified and consolidated, which dialectic can move only by releasing the force of its own weight (*AE* 38–9).

Dialectics, a.k.a. 'immanent critique', must 'not sanction through mimicry, but surpass through cognition': this usefully enlarges the 'repeat and reliquify' motif; more to the present point, it preempts the Lukács complaint in the warning lest critique 'degrade itself . . . to a replica of . . . nature' (this last the signifier here of the 'naturalizations' of the cultural that are the specific work and effect of ideology as such, the mystifying will to 'sanction through mimicry'). The cautionary point is the liability of 'immanent [or "dialectical"] critique' to such dangers: because it must 'repeat' in order to 'reliquify' or 'surpass' its ideological object, it must perforce risk approaching a 'replica[tion]' or 'mimicry' of it. It must risk appearing as an example or symptom, as Lukács charged, or as itself 'mythical', as Habermas warned. It may seem to confirm rather than contest what *Dialectic of Enlightenment* calls 'the power of repetition over reality' (Cumming 12); it cannot contest its object without risking the danger of succumbing to it, or at least of appearing to. Which, for critique 'as a kind of writing', means something in the realm of the critical like the property the German philosophical tradition ambiguously or polysemously denominates, in the realm of the aesthetic, as '*Schein*'—appearance or illusion: the artful contrivance, variously concealing its own art or, in more modern terms, critically baring its own device(s), whereby any 'composition', whether of art or of critique, hesitates between the aesthetic as ideology and (Adorno's theme in *Aesthetic Theory*) the aesthetic as bearer of 'truth'.

'Immanent Critique' as 'Dialectical Mimesis'

So 'immanent critique' must pursue, in the writing, and not as aesthetic flour-
ish but as inescapable burden, a strategy of something like what *Dialectic of
Enlightenment* seems, *prima fâcie*, to indict: 'mimesis'. This word signals one of
the most unstable, most conflicted—i.e., most 'dialectical'—motifs in the book.[9]
For many, the first association with 'mimesis' will be Aristotle on tragedy, assimilated in the long Western tradition to the 'copy' or 'mirror' theory of representation. For our generation, Derrida has done most to ascribe this 'copy' theory
rather to Plato—an argument *Dialectic of Enlightenment* anticipates, in reassign-
ing Aristotle's 'mimesis', in the *Poetics*, to the habitus of dramatic performance,
public symbolic occasions much closer, in Aristotle's Athens, to rituals of
collective morale-management ('catharsis' of pity and fear) persisting from
prehistory, than to the Platonically inflected 'logocentric' acceptation of representation and signification, art, artifice, 'the aesthetic' (etc.), familiar since the
Renaissance. In *Dialectic of Enlightenment*, 'mimesis' gathers the force of an
anthropological category, 'sympathetic magic', cognate rather with shamanism
and *mana* than with Logos and Idea. ('The magician imitates demons; in
order to frighten them or to appease them, he behaves frighteningly or makes
gestures of appeasement' [Cumming 9].) If Adorno's period psychologized
the human sciences generally, the Frankfurt School Freudianized materialist
critique in particular. 'Mimesis' as an anthropological category in chapter 1 of
Dialectic of Enlightenment becomes a psychological syndrome or diagnosis in the
'Anti-Semitism' chapter, where it helps explain the introjection of pathological
attitudes in imitation of idealized role-models.

Even a first-time reader of *Dialectic of Enlightenment* readily sees the ways in
which 'mimesis' is a bad thing, the marker of 'myth' in the senses that link *pen-
sée sauvage* with the 'political unconscious', with ideology, false consciousness,
and the uncritical repetition and naturalization of 'what is'. But Enlightenment's rigorous 'anti-mimesis' (another 'absolute negation') turns out to be
just as bad: the will to eliminate all metaphor and 'picture-thinking' in order to
achieve a thorough 'mathematization' of the world *'an Sich'*, an 'immediate'
apprehension of reality that would by-pass all the dilemmas of representation
and epistemology to open a transparent windowpane on naked, unmediated
reality 'in itself'—a delusional 'progress', on Horkheimer and Adorno's showing, in pursuit of which 'enlightenment' liquidates itself in an unwitting 'regression' to the very condition of 'mythical thinking' it had credited itself with
escaping:

   Like science, magic pursues aims, but seeks to achieve them by mimesis, not
   by progressively distancing itself from the object. . . . The 'unshakeable confidence in the possibility of world domination', which Freud anachronistically

ascribes to magic, corresponds to realistic world domination only in terms of a more skillful science (Cumming 11).

Against this pathology, 'mimesis' will prove to have some immanent-critical uses—or ruses: as we've seen, 'immanent critique' contrives to 'repeat' its object, incurs the risk of 'replicating' it or 'mimicking' it—or, to use the word Adorno often seems to valorize *against* the rhetoric of 'representation', 'immanent critique' must 'express' all of the contradictions, reifications, of what it would critique. And here, such terms as 'ruse', 'imaginary', 'false consciousness', and 'ideology' designate not obstacles critique must obviate, but rather the very most obdurate problematics of 'the matter at hand', precisely the predicament into which critique must plunge. To 'repeat' and 'reliquify' must be to 'express' the predicaments to which critique struggles to make itself 'immanent'. And that is precisely why 'mimesis' is critique's own most potent, if also most treacherous, device: why the potency and the treachery must be its very *condition*. If ideological 'mimesis' is the problem or danger, the solution or program involves a 'mimesis' that I will here call 'dialectical mimesis', on the model of Walter Benjamin's usage of 'image' as against, 'dialectical image'. With Peter Sloterdijk in mind, we might say that Adorno's 'dialectical mimesis' enacts a kind of satirical parody, but with affects of angst, rage, and sorrow rather than the Sloterdijkian 'kynical' or 'cheeky' (sc. Bergsonian) laughter of mockery that we usually associate with parody.[10]

Apropos 'dialectical mimesis', a few qualifications. To be explicit, the phrase is mine, not Adorno's. I propose it to encode a self-historicizing gesture, to distinguish a new, indeed a modern or even *modernist* and critical kind of mimesis, a marked departure from an archaic, compulsive practice of mimesis that is ideological insofar as it functions to 'repeat', not 'reliquify' the precedent state of things, to reinforce and even sanctify, rather than critique, 'what is'. Adorno accedes to the common view that in 'modern' times, with the rise of the bourgeoisie, the emancipation of the arts from noble and ecclesiastical patronage opened the potential for art to shed its ideological livery and refunction itself as a vehicle of critique. 'Dialectical mimesis' aims at a *critical* mimesis, as (again) Benjamin's 'dialectical image' aims at a critical deployment of the (otherwise ideological) image. To put it in the terms of the previous chapter, Adorno means to disencumber 'mimesis' of the baggage imposed on it under the rubric of 'representation', with all its metaphysical (ideological) criteria of *adaequatio*; he aims to elaborate it rather under the sign of 'negation', as an agency of critique.

Yet Adorno deploys no verbal cue to signal the distinction I am trying to make explicit, between a 'dialectical' and (call it) an 'ideological' mimesis: between a *critical* practice of mimesis and the imitative, regressive reflex of repetition that mimesis has usually been in Western culture, from the 'sympathetic magic' of primitive shamanism to its modern persistence in imitative 'introjection' of super-ego authority figures, not to mention the practices of wan 'imitation' of idealized models inherited from the past in the arts and other domains of what should be a 'tradition'. Adorno, in short, leaves strategically equivocal the 'equivocation'—the word/concept charged with 'antithetical' meanings—that I am trying to clarify. The equivocation is the more loaded for leaving what's at stake so obscure: elsewhere in Adorno the 'make-it-new' impulse is usually artic- ulated or structured on some implicit model of old versus new, of 'becoming modern'; with 'mimesis' it's as if Adorno wants the old/new binary itself to be 'sublated': as if, in the case of 'mimesis', more than with the other stale Hegelian-Marxist categories Adorno aims to 'make new', that it is indeed, pre- cisely, the *old*, the archaic, that is to be 'made new'—that here especially we should be on our guard against complacent self-congratulation about our modernity. Adorno's immanent critique turns to critical account the mimesis that remains implicated in (or immanent to) it, even as it grapples to surmount, to make conscious on the model of 'transference', all the pathological ruses by which 'mimesis' becomes compulsive, defensive, abreactive against the 'new' and the unknown: all the ways, in short, that resistance to the new becomes ideological.

But I don't want to conclude this section without recalling that other direc- tion in which *Dialectic of Enlightenment* tilts its construction and its distrust of 'mimesis': that is, against Enlightenment's own (very different) distrust of mimesis, its anti-mimetic biases, its literalist construction of facticity ('the con- cept of sugar is not sweet'). Horkheimer and Adorno deplore the Enlightenment aspiration to mathematicize everything, to do away with the problematic of representation, and the infinite regress of original and copy, the real and the appearance, in the 'abstract negation' of all quality to quantity—a motif that sits in highly charged tension with that of Judaism's *Bilderverbot*, the ban on images, on representations, that underwrites much of Horkheimer's and Adorno's (and Benjamin's) own reluctance to image or imagine utopia. On which, more later. For now, two sections demonstrating the diversely ingenious ways Adorno puts 'dialectical mimesis' to work.

The Use and the Ruse of 'Metacritique'

I said above that 'immanent critique' attests Adorno's conviction that all critique is 'immanent', from 'inside': that what calls itself 'external' or 'transcendent' critique is the dupe of ideological (false) appearance. In Adorno's 'dialectical' force-field, any such categorical statement seems fated to suffer qualification if not outright reversal; and some readers may at that point have remembered two instances in which Adorno uses the word 'metacritique'. Part Three, Section One of *Negative Dialectics*, entitled 'On the Metacritique of Practical Reason', treats Kant's 'critical' effort to find the limits or boundaries between cognitive domains, where, in Kant's terminology, they become mutually 'transcendent'; 'metacritique' in this context operates as synonym for Kant's 'transcendental critique', an effort that Adorno shows again and again to fail—most of all in the *Critique of Practical Reason*, in which what Kant constructs as

> the monadological structure of both will and freedom . . . is contradicted by the simplest of things: by way of what analytical psychologists call 'the test of reality', countless moments of external—notably social—reality invade the decisions designated by the words 'will' and 'freedom'; if the concept of rationality of the will means anything at all, it must refer precisely to that invasion, however obstinately [ideologically] this may be denied by Kant. . . . [I]n more Kantian terms, the empirical subject who makes those decisions (and only an empirical one can make them; the transcendentally pure I would be incapable of impulses) is itself a moment of the spatio-temporal 'external' world. This is why the attempt to localize the question of free will in the empirical subject must fail (*ND* 212–13).

A page further on, Adorno observes that 'The antinomics of freedom is an essential moment of Kant's philosophy, as the dialectics of freedom is an essential moment of Hegel's' (*ND* 214–15). Here the opposition of Kant's 'antinomics' (mutually exclusive, or 'transcending', oppositions) to Hegel's 'dialectics' (mutually qualifying, or 'immanent' oppositions), in effect, summarizes Adorno's whole critique of Kant. But the larger point is that the 'metacritique' in question is Kant's; and to the extent that we take this 90-page section of *Negative Dialectics* as Adorno's *own* 'metacritique' of Kant, the word connotes '[Adorno's immanent] critique of [Kant's transcendental] critique': a 'dialectical mimesis' of Kant's effort that will expose its failures.

Likewise the study of Husserl, *Against Epistemology: A Metacritique*. The German, incidentally, puts 'Metacritique' in the title, not the subtitle: *Zur Metakritik der Erkenntnistheorie: Studien über Husserl und die phänomenologischen Antinomien*. Titling a book '*Zur Metakritik*' quite suggests that Adorno intends a critique 'from outside', situating his critical operation 'meta-' to the object of his criticism. But the subtitle's adversion to 'Phenomenological Antinomies' signals Husserl's implication in the Kantian problematic we've just seen Adorno demolish. Adorno repeats Hegel's dissent from Kant, putting 'dialectic' and 'contradiction' where 'analytic' and 'antinomy' had been. Hence the 'Introduction', instead of explaining what Adorno means by 'Metacritique', announces instead (in a passage already quoted) that this 'metacritique' of Husserl will really be an 'immanent critique', contriving to 'repeat' Husserlian 'metacritique' by way of a 'dialectical mimesis':

> Dialectic's very procedure is immanent critique. It does not so much oppose [Husserlian] phenomenology with a position or 'model' external and alien to phenomenology, as it pushes the phenomenological model, with the latter's

own force, to where the latter cannot afford to go. Dialectic exacts the truth from it through the confession of its own untruth (*AE* 5).[11]

Adorno goes on to explain that it was Husserl's neo-Cartesian need for *certitudo* that led him to circumscribe his field of inquiry so stringently that a critic, i.e., Adorno himself, who tries to stay 'immanent' to Husserl's presuppositions 'seems to pander to the fruitless transcendent critique [sc. metacritique] which repays the empty claim to an overarching "standpoint" with being non-binding and with the fact that it never did enter into the controversy, but prejudged it "from above", as Husserl would have said' (*AE* 5). The very next thing on the page is the rubric, 'Immanent Critique', and the text continues with the quotations cited, repeating and reliquifying (so to speak) the quasi-Lukácsean/ Habermasian anxieties lest critique 'degrade itself to a replica . . . which it should not sanction through mimicry, but surpass through cognition' (*AE* 39).

The mere sequence implies that Husserl's 'fruitless' aspiration to 'metacritique' is to be answered with 'immanent critique'; but the book's title lends the point an ironic dilation, as '*Zur Metakritik*' turns out to mean not 'on' or 'toward' metacritique, but *against* it: the force of 'On [or Towards] the Metacritique of Epistemology' turns out to bear not on 'Epistemology' but on 'Metacritique', with the aim of showing that Husserl's effort to 'transcend' the phenomenological conditions he aimed to describe, his (near-Wittgensteinian) circumscription of the field of what he must attend to—his strategies of *epoché* and 'bracketing', his transcendental, eidetic, and other 'reductions'—has black-boxed so much of reality that the merest pinprick in the hermetic seals guarding the structure against contamination from without threatens to reverse the relation of 'meta-' to 'infra-', which is to say, of 'metacritique' to 'immanent critique'. An ancient Zen koan teases us to think of the shell of an egg not as we usually do, as separating the yolk and the white 'inside' from the rest of the cosmos outside, but as enclosing the cosmos, including ourselves, standing there egg in hand (or mind), 'inside' a boundedness that the yolk and white occupy the other side (sc. the 'outside') of. Adorno insinuates that Husserl's 'meta-' is so confining, excludes so much, that on the one hand, remaining 'immanent' to it is possible only at the cost of suffocation, and, on the other, that the merest whiff of what it excludes makes the exercise 'meta-' to Husserl's project willy nilly: the egg turns inside out the moment it is handled. Husserl's avowed 'meta-' is in practice so 'infra-' that merely to hint at what it would repress ('to push [it] . . . where it cannot afford to go') is already to have admitted immanences fatal to Husserl's program. Such an 'immanent critique' must so transcend Husserl's methods that its results actually *will* be 'meta-' to Husserl's findings. Hence Adorno's 'immanent critique' of Husserl is a 'metacritique' in an insidiously ironic way, such that (again) despite Husserl's fastidious attempt to 'bracket' dialectic, his system is 'dialectic in spite of itself' (*AE* 49–50). Inverting this irony, we might say that Husserl has provoked Adorno's critique to a (mock-)

'transcendence despite itself'. Adorno provokes a deliberate aporia (or performative contradiction), in which the binary of immanent critique versus meta- is shown to fail.[12]

Another equivocation that Adorno's 'dialectical mimesis' here exploits is that 'mimesis' cannot but connote a degree of resemblance between the original and the imitation. But the 'repetition' staged in Adorno's 'metacritique' of Husserl would seem a 'mimesis' *not* particularly *semblant* of the original. In Hegelian terms: 'dialectical mimesis' needn't be 'pictorial'; that is, like philosophy itself, it can sublate the 'pictorial' without lapsing back into the 'abstraction' of the pre-'pictorial', or what Hegel calls in the *Aesthetics* 'the symbolic'. (Hegel's strictures on 'the [pre-"aesthetic"] symbolic' anticipate Horkheimer and Adorno's on the 'anti-mimetic' [post-aesthetic] ideology of 'enlightenment' positivism.) To the formula 'dialectical mimesis', one might justifiably object that Adorno's 'metacritique' of Husserl is more 'dialectical' than 'mimetic', with the feel more of a witty conceptual-speculative ricochet than of a mirroring 'semblance', and to that extent not a 'mimesis' at all—except that Adorno *does* title the book 'A Metacritique', advancing his own 'immanent critique' under the rubric of its unlucky target: an ironic stroke instantiating a challenge Adorno's writing poses that I think has gone under-remarked, namely a volatility, a dialectical jiu-jitsu, of idea and expression that in English can only be called 'wit'. For often enough, the wit of a semblant, sc. parodic, critique is best measured in its *dis*-resemblance from the target or object it mocks: despite resemblances, Cervantes is not writing the sort of chivalric romances that have maddened Don Quixote; and ditto Jane Austen's send-up of Gothic in *Northanger Abbey*, Flaubert's of 'fiction for ladies' in *Madame Bovary*, Joyce's in the 'Nausicaa' episode of *Ulysses*. These examples remind us that literature has for some time put parody to 'critical' purposes; to the extent that Matthew Arnold's old saw about literature as 'a criticism of life' retains some investment in the Aristotelian notion of literature (and the other arts) as mimesis, we may adduce the increasing sense, as modernity advances, that 'life', too—especially 'life' as art imitates it—increasingly figures as itself an ensemble of representations. Art and critique increasingly represent precedent representations and representation itself—so that as archetype becomes cliché, mimesis becomes parody. That in modern conditions, art becomes criticism is a familiar idea; but the converse implications are oftenest left unsaid. Criticism may acknowledge its own artfulness; but criticism is less ready to renounce the methodological fiction of 'critical distance' between critique and its object: recall Lévi-Strauss's advisory that we take Freud's thesis of the Oedipus complex less as a second-degree *account* of the myth, than as another *version* of it (an irony whose import for Lévi-Strauss's own 'structural analysis' of the myth, Lévi-Strauss leaves hanging).

Adorno's 'metacritique' of Husserl instantiates how un-resembling Adorno's 'immanent critique' can be from its object. But I want now to turn to *Dialectic of Enlightenment* as an example in which the *resemblance* to the object of critique (our ideological condition in the West) is so close as to risk that its 'dialectical mimesis' might be mis-taken (as by Lukács and Habermas above) for a mere repetition or replication of that ideological pathology.[13] *Dialectic of Enlightenment* shares with *Against Epistemology* the root-thesis that enlightenment exempts itself from 'the labor of the concept' and of dialectical [self-] consciousness in the mistaken attempt to bargain for certainty at the expense of scope: to achieve a 'transcendant' standpoint 'meta-' to the problems (fewer and fewer) that its scientific method allows itself to treat. But whereas *Against Epistemology* puts itself at oppositional loggerheads with Husserl, *Dialectic of Enlightenment* presents itself as a simulacrum, a virtual mock-up, of the 'dialectic of enlightenment' it protests. The ideology of enlightenment is indicted as an ideological 'appearance' or 'illusion', but Horkheimer and Adorno make their case by 'repeating', by contriving a 'semblance' or re-semblance, of that 'appearance' or '*Schein*'. In so doing, they emulate a modernist or *avant-garde* practice, though in a domain—not literature, but critique, or philosophy—where such an achievement is usually not looked for: a 'mimesis', but of a 'dialectical' kind. But it is a method that exposes itself to risk:

> . . . critical thought risks becoming infected by what it criticizes. Critical thought must let itself be guided by the concrete forms of consciousness it opposes . . . Thought is not purely for itself: especially practical thought, so closely tied to the historical moment that in this regressive age it would become abstract and false were it to continue to evolve from its own élan regardless of the regression. [This is a diagnosis as much of Leninism as of 'infantile leftism'.] This alone is the bitter truth to the talk of 'the thinker in indigent times' [the reference here is to a phrase of Hölderlin's]: what he produces depends on the fact that in making it conscious he activates the moment of regression imposed upon him (*CM* 71).

Like psychoanalysis, 'immanent critique' involves a 'making conscious' achievable not by insight, but only experientially, by way of a 'transference' that must risk 'regression': must risk reactivating the disorder it would relieve. Adorno's critique, of course, addresses collective disorders whose link to our 'merely subjective' psychological miseries, our collective ideologies repress:

> In the open-air prison which the world is becoming . . . [a]ll phenomena rigidify, become insignias of the absolute rule of that which is. There are no more ideologies in the authentic sense of false consciousness [!], only advertisements for the world through its duplication and the provocative lie which does not seek belief but commands silence. . . . Of course, even the immanent method is eventually overtaken by this. It is dragged into the abyss by its object. The materialistic transparency of culture has not made it [culture] more honest, only more vulgar (*P* 34).

—and here we confront the further irony that on the one hand, Adorno urges that 'immanent critique' must take on all such perils deliberately, but on the other hand, the whole point of the exercise is that these perils cannot, in any event, be escaped: we suffer them, will we or nill we; and 'immanent critique' must enact this helplessness or impotence before 'the absolute rule of what is' as the condition of such critical power as it may bid for. In seeking to awaken the dread that ideology has numbed society against, critique must risk seeming to cry wolf. 'Immanent criticism' is, yes, 'dragged into the abyss', as if against its will; but in the writing, an 'immanent criticism' that somehow found itself stranded on the sunlit brink would oblige itself to jump.

So 'dialectical mimesis' is a risky program for critique as 'a kind of writing', as the strictures of Lukács and Habermas (and Lyotard) attest. Adorno bids defiance to the risks as knowingly as any of the great moderns defied the jeers of their earliest audiences. Picasso knew the squinting bourgeois would think his kindergartner could paint better, Schoenberg that his dissonances would be taken as artless pounding of the keyboard, Joyce that his 'stream of consciousness' would be likened to verbal diarrhea. Freud coolly cited the 'resistances' of his critics as confirmation of his outraging speculations—and I take it that Adorno (and Horkheimer) might similarly take the adverse reactions of Lukács or Habermas as a kind of credential: evidence that their salt has found the raw spot in the social wound. But reveling in the scorn of your adversaries can be a vanity; and the riskiness of the 'repeat/reliquify' operation—the danger that the 'repeat' will confirm itself without the critical follow-through of 'reliquify'; that critical negation will blur into ideological symptom; that analysis, through the affective disturbances reawakened in the 'transference', may actually worsen the condition—is real.

The 'Dialectic' of *Dialectic of Enlightenment*

I want now to consider *Dialectic of Enlightenment* by the light of the speculations above: 'constellation' as a device for compelling disjunct social materials into an agitated stasis, in which 'mediation' functions not to reconcile, harmonize, or resolve the contradictions between the 'constellated' terms, but rather as the conflicted result, when these contradictions have been so elicited, dramatized, 'exaggerated' as to work 'the power of the negative' on reconciliation and resolution as themselves ipso facto ideological. Such an 'immanent critique' engages social, cultural, and political predicaments from the *inside*, in a 'dialectical mimesis' that must 'repeat' what it would 'reliquify' or redeem, defying the danger of replicating the very conditions it would condemn and change: must risk resembling (reinforcing? becoming?) the very thing it means to critique. Such is the failure ascribed, again, by Lukács to modernism in general and to the Frankfurt School in particular, by Habermas to *Dialectic of Enlightenment*, by

Adorno himself to Benjamin's Baudelaire essay: clearly the risk is large, subtle, chronic, and treacherous—but also inextricable from the program of 'immanent critique' and of 'dialectic' as Adorno conceives it, as a strategy of setting concepts, methods, ideas, thought-instruments in conflict with themselves, 'driving thoughts with the utmost consequentiality to the point where they turn back on themselves' (*MM* 86). This dialectic of 'objective contradiction' turned mimetically inward cannot but generate effects of impulses mutually checked and stymied, especially when its declared target and object is 'dialectics at a standstill'. Lukács on modernism, Habermas on *Dialectic of Enlightenment*, Adorno on Benjamin's Baudelaire essay, are all worried about a loss or surrender of critical power.

Critique is, programmatically, polemical, and it's part of the generic 'sediment' of polemic that some deep structure of good/bad generates for-and-against arguments in and through binary pairs. But Adorno's 'dialectical' imperative is that such binaries as (here, in my own argument), kinesis/stasis, static/narrative, mediated/un-mediated, parataxis/synthesis, dialectical/mythical should operate not as sorting devices—this good, that bad—but rather as terms demarking the coordinates of particular conflicted problem-points, or better, force-fields within which the conflicting energies of crucial contradictions seethe and collide. In critical practice 'as usual', oppositional binaries, the two terms separated by the crisp marker of the slash, suggest black/white distinctions. The sheer polemical energy of Adorno's prose can *seem* to drive or be driven by such stark contrasts, but my own experience learning to read Adorno has been that he means his black and his white ('turned back on themselves') to stand revealed as exaggerations of grey. Adorno's writing means to stage an agon in which terms like 'enlightenment', 'science', 'philosophy', 'concept', and 'dialectic' appear as narrative actants, with characters differing according to circumstance and context: so that, for example, 'philosophy' is Adorno's critical target when (in the neo-Kantians) it acts as hand-maiden to positivism; it is the hero of the drama when it acts as Adorno thinks it should, mobilizing 'the power of the negative' against the willfully anti-intellectual premises of natural science.

A 'dialectical mimesis' of 'dialectic at a standstill' aims to 'repeat and reliquify' the predicament, and precisely that is what *Dialectic of Enlightenment* undertakes: what the ironies and double-, triple-, multiple-*entendres* of its very title already begin to dramatize, and with the effect of seeming to replicate the very miscarriage of 'dialectic' itself that is the crux of the book's indictment of 'enlightenment'. When a Lukács or a Habermas complain that *Dialectic of Enlightenment* is 'un-dialectical', they are not exactly wrong. Habermas at least perceives that at issue is a 'performative contradiction': what he misses is that the contradiction is deliberate, motivated. (For Lukács's generation, the formula was 'the fallacy of imitative form'; the presupposition of fallacy ruled out seeing any valid motivation in advance.)

This problem of 'dialectic', I recall from my own 'novice' first reading of *Dialectic of Enlightenment*, was the most baffling of the problems and 'difficulties' it presented for me. The book's narrative organization was readily legible as an ironic reversal of the Hegelian narrative—the story of *Geist* as not a triumphal progress to Enlightenment but rather that narrative's ghastly 'regression' to a nightmare of violence ('humanity, instead of entering into a truly human condition, is sinking into a new kind of barbarism' [Cumming xi]; 'The curse of irresistible progress is irresistible regression' [Cumming 36]). And the attenuation of narrative in modernist literature had accustomed me to the gesture of a story whose thematic burden of failure and waste would be enacted formally in the failure of the narrative to achieve not only any putative thematic telos, but the telos of narrativity itself. (On all which, more in the next chapter.) The thornier problem for me was the book's organization around binary pairs that defied my every presupposition concerning how an avowedly, and programmatically, historicizing and 'dialectical' presentation would or should proceed. 'Dialectic', I thought I knew, was about difference, about a refusal to homogenize, especially when the task was to 'historicize' difficult problems, which is to say, exorcize the mystifications of, for example, a constant 'human nature' by which historical 'problems' are rendered epiphenomenal, even as their 'solutions' are falsely universalized. But in *Dialectic of Enlightenment*, the governing binaries (Odysseus/bourgeois, myth/Enlightenment) seemed to collapse large and crucial historical differences, to homogenize them by, in effect, detemporalizing or dehistoricizing them—as if 'bourgeois', 'myth', 'Enlightenment', etc., were names for essentialized or essentializing trans-historical archetypes, permanent and immutable. And likewise for binaries whose aligned pairs were not from different historical periods, but contemporaneous, e.g., Kant and de Sade, or Hitler and Hollywood, whose nominal 'differences' the book startlingly homogenized, to incriminating effect. To expose as 'bourgeois' classical philology's idealization of Homer's 'universal' hero, as well as to root 'modern' bourgeois values in the primordial ('heroic') violences of self-preservation; to vandalize Enlightenment's self-constituting 'demythologizing' *difference* from the myth-mongering, archaic past; to elicit the unowned foundational commonalities between the categorical imperative and de Sade's monstrously reductive naturalism of the boudoir, or between Hitlerian anti-Semitism and the emerging culture industry: I could read in all this a strategy of protest and dissent and exposé—even, despite the extremity and alarums of the subject matter, something at moments oddly like satire—but not, within the terms of what I took 'critical theory' to be aiming at, a strategy of critique that could be called 'dialectical'. To expose Odysseus as 'bourgeois', or 'myth' and 'Enlightenment' as 'the same' seemed a homogenization that I only later (instructed by further immersion in *Dialectic of Enlightenment* itself) learned to see as exercises of 'absolute' [rather than 'determinate'] 'negation' meant to display the liabilities of that complacent miscarriage of the critical impulse, that facile all-or-nothing moralism masquerading as thought.

The critical uses of such a contravention of (received) principle are intimated in Adorno's first published book, *Kierkegaard: Construction of the Aesthetic.* The section called 'Mythical Content' protests the 'indifferentiation' of what *Dialectic of Enlightenment* will project as the binary of 'myth' versus 'enlightenment', 'history', 'dialectic'; the crucial term for us in the passage is 'image', in its association with 'myth', i.e., with eternalizing, reifying, essentializing miscarriages of thinking—which is why special interest attaches to the appearance here of the important modifier, the '*dialectical* image' (emphasis mine):

> Dialectic comes to a stop in the image and cites the mythical; in the historically most recent as the distant past: nature as proto-history. For this reason the images, which . . . bring dialectic and myth to the point of indifferentiation, are truly 'antediluvian fossils'. They may be called dialectical images, to use Benjamin's expression, whose compelling definition of 'allegory' also holds true for Kierkegaard's allegorical intention as a configuration [sc. 'constellation'] of historical dialectic and mythical nature. According to this definition 'in allegory the observer is confronted with the *facies hippocratica* of history, a petrified primordial landscape' (*KCA* 54; the Benjamin quotation is from *Origins* 166; Benjamin quotes *this* passage in *Arcades* 461).

'Dialectic comes to a stop'—i.e., to 'a standstill'; compare the theme later in the book of 'Intermittence' (*KCA* 100–2), when dialectic falters, becomes a stop-and-start affair—'and *cites* the mythical', the act of 'citation' here implying a self-consciously *critical* deployment of the given, *ideological* image, as if in quotation marks; or, on the analogy of the speech-act distinction, as (self-conscious) 'mention' rather than (naïve) 'use'—with the implication of some critical or 'negative' consequence or result. Crucial here is that the 'indifferentiation' of myth/dialectic equivocates, in the transit between the quoted passage's second sentence and the third, between the ideological sediment of the 'image' and the *critical* potential of the '*dialectical* image'. And, as sign, vehicle, 'motivation' of such 'indifferentiation', the implicit Medusa motif here appears in something like the inverted or (Freud) displaced form of the '*facies hippocratica*', Benjamin's image in the *Trauerspiel* of unhappy consciousness, an image drawn from Hippocrates (see Hullot-Kentor's note, *KCA* 151–2): a visage like the anguished mask of tragedy, or better, like the face of Medusa's victim, struck by the horror of a 'petrified primordial landscape'. Hence the analogously 'antithetical' (or 'dialectical' wobble in Adorno's own usage as regards 'dialectics at a standstill', which, again, figures sometimes as an ideological condition critique and art *protest*, at other times as an effect critique and art must try to *achieve*—the latter as critical (or 'dialectical') mimesis of the former.[14]

'Dialectics at a standstill', in these 'antithetical' senses (both ideological condition to be protested, and critical 'effect' to be achieved), is a formula especially apposite to *Dialectic of Enlightenment*. The book indicts positivism's refusal of dialectic, and (more daringly) the Soviet world's official Marxist-Leninist fetishization of dialectic as an orthodoxy, as equally deluded miscarriers or betrayers of dialectic (and/as 'the labor of the concept') itself. To that end the 'appearance' of such an un-'dialectical' pair as Odysseus/bourgeois, or myth/Enlightenment presents a 'dialectical image' aiming, with critical force, to 'bring dialectic and myth to the point of indifferentiation'—or an 'allegory' presenting a 'configuration [sc. "constellation"] of historical dialectic and mythical nature'. This 'appearance' of 'indifferentiation' (not to say 'identity') of dialectic and myth enacts what Horkheimer and Adorno regard as Enlightenment's fatal ideological false consciousness, its sacrifice of qualitative to quantitative thinking—and enacts it 'immanently', taking upon itself the full ideological burden of what it protests and would redeem. This gesture or ruse could be thought of as Adorno's self-conscious (in-)version of the situation he calls 'dialectic despite itself' (*AE* 49–50), which underlies his enthusiasm for thinkers avowedly critical of or indifferent to 'dialectic'; hence the affinities of Adorno's seemingly static and essentialized binaries with (say) Nietzsche's tragedy/Socrates, and *Übermensch*/priest, or Freud's Eros/Thanatos, or the antinomies of instinct and 'vicissitude' that in the late work on Moses seem to force on Freud a quasi-Lamarckian view of the heritability of acquired characteristics. Equally pertinent would be the great works of modernist music and literature with all their techniques of seeming 'im-mediation' or 'de-mediation': works that attempt to escape outworn habits of mediation, to conjure thereby an atmospherics of immediacy (whether nostalgic or anxious), and achieve a kind of re-mediation (new mediations) that it is no mere word-play to hope might also be remedy.

Again, 'dialectical mimesis' produces an immanent critique that can seem dismayingly (or 'homeopathically') 'infected' by the very ideologies supposedly under critique: can seem that way even to Adorno himself, as in the case of Benjamin's essay on Baudelaire. We've cited Adorno's criticisms as delimiting errors or lapses Adorno wanted to avoid; but they also index an effect Adorno wanted both to evoke ('repeat') and to redeem ('reliquify'). If Benjamin's 'disenchantment of the dialectical image leads directly to mythical thinking' (*CC* 107), *Dialectic of Enlightenment* means to enact enlightenment's own regression to myth 'transferentially', as prerequisite to its ('dialectical') 'making-conscious'. Adorno complains that 'your [Benjamin's] study is located at the crossroads of magic and positivism. The spot is bewitched. Only theory could break this spell' (*CC* 283)—but in *Dialectic of Enlightenment*, the aim isn't to circumvent that crossroads, but on the contrary to steer precisely at that X-marks-the-spot. Both the book and its reader are meant to suffer ('repeat') the bewitchment *and* break ('reliquify') the spell. To that extent *Dialectic of Enlightenment* is *hommage* to Benjamin and critique of him at the same time: the book's 'dialectical mimesis' of the predicament of the West aims to *enact*, rather than merely to *explain*, how 'enlightened' disenchantment and demythologization revert to 'myth' precisely in executing their 'absolute negation' of it. Horkheimer and Adorno aim to perform the process by which a positivism that eschews theory and dialectic and 'the labor of the concept' delivers itself inexorably into the seemingly paradoxical condition in which magic and positivism converge. 'Theory' here is evoked in the disaster of its absence: it 'breaks the spell' in seeming assent to it, in something like the way (or an inversion of the way) art keeps the 'promise of happiness' only negatively, by breaking, if not the promise, then the ideology that presents the promise as fulfilled or fulfillable.

All of which, I worry, must seem stratospherically (implausibly) speculative. But if the Kierkegaard book's account of 'indifferentiation' doesn't suffice, it happens there's a more (so to speak) colloquial confirmation that *Dialectic of Enlightenment* was deliberately written to enact some such 'dialectical mimesis' of modernity's failures as I've just described. In August 1942, with *Dialectic of Enlightenment* in prospect if not yet actually in progress, Max Horkheimer wrote to Paul Tillich to explain that he and Adorno intend no mere manifesto 'as usual' elaborating 'exotic theses'. No, the 'dialectics project', as they were then calling it, would rather proceed by a kind of mimicry, that would 'repeat' the enemy routines, defying the (what we might now call Girardian) risks, in order to 'reliquify' them:

> The style of the theory will become simpler. But this is only because the style will expose simplicity, consciously making simplicity a reflection of the process of barbarization. The style will assimilate itself to the racketeers in the strength of its hatred, and thus become their opposite. Its logic will become as summary as their justice, as crude as their lies, as unscrupulous as their agents—and in this contradiction to barbarism it will become specific, exact and scrupulous . . .

I don't find quite such hardboiledness—let alone such 'simplicity'!—in the finished product, but that last clause ('specific, exact and scrupulous') cogently concretizes the ethic (so to speak) of 'determinate negation', an ethic abrogated by mere philosophical hand-wringing; as Horkheimer continues, his language evokes the constellational writing practices we have been elaborating:

> . . . in its lack of detailed description of the apparatus, the absence of syntactic links giving the why, when and wherefore of the disaster, there becomes eloquent in philosophy the night of despair in which one victim is the same as any other. Science reaches for statistics; but for the understanding, one concentration camp is enough (qtd. Wiggershaus 317–18).

The passage conflates Hegel's ghastly 'night of the world' (qtd. Verene 7–8) with his famous figure of thinking so abstract that in it all difference is lost, as in the 'night in which all cows are black' (*Phenomenology* 9). But if Hegel evoked this metaphor *against* a kind of error his own work meant to evade, Horkheimer poses it as an effect the 'dialectics project' is aiming to *achieve*: by mimesis of the pathologies it diagnoses, to achieve a 'dialectical mimesis' of that very abstraction or 'absolute negation' itself, in which, 'during Auschwitz', all victims are the same—in which, indeed, all the living are victims—in which qualitative difference has been subjected to homogenizing abstraction, a 'negation' so 'absolute', so literal, as to make 'night' a pale metaphor for the carnage and murder engulfing the world. *Dialectic of Enlightenment* enacts the 'performative contradiction' of a critique of such abstraction, such abolition of difference, prosecuted, 'immanently', as a 'dialectical mimesis' of that very abstraction, that very denial of dialectic, that very liquidation of 'the labor of the concept', that very arrest of history itself, that 'dialectic at a standstill' in which 'civilization' lapses into barbarity, 'progress' reverses into 'regress'.

We have traced the 'antithetical' motif of 'standstill' as Adorno enacts or exploits it by way of such devices as the 'constellation', of his provocative, perverse-seeming reinvention of 'mediation', of his 'dialectical' (Benjaminian) sense of the 'image', and the ruse of his 'mimetic' sabotage of 'dialectic' itself— all of them, again, devices tending to de-narrativize, de-temporalize, even (seemingly) de-historicize critique's objects and critique itself. To render history as *image* rather than as *story*, as if to de-historicize history itself. In the next chapter we test this premise further, with respect to the most conflicted 'performative contradiction' of all in Adorno, and especially in *Dialectic of Enlightenment*, one that the de-temporalizing devices of 'constellation' at once contravene and heighten, that of narrative, or indeed the ideology of narrative—both as theory and as practice.

Chapter 4

Narrative and Its Discontents

. . . the art of storytelling is coming to an end. . . . It is as if something that seemed inalienable to us, the securest among our possessions, were taken from us: the ability to exchange experiences.

One reason for this phenomenon is obvious: experience has fallen in value. And it looks as if it is continuing to fall into bottomlessness. . . . Was it not noticeable at the end of the war that men returned from the battlefield grown silent—not richer, but poorer in communicable experience? . . . [N]ever has experience been contradicted more thoroughly than strategic experience by tactical warfare, economic experience by inflation, bodily experience by mechanical warfare, moral experience by those in power. A generation that had gone to school on a horse-drawn streetcar now stood under the open sky in a countryside in which nothing remained unchanged but the clouds, and beneath these clouds, in a field of force of destructive torrents and explosions, was the tiny, fragile human body.

—Benjamin, 'The Storyteller' (Illuminations *83*)

History decays into images, not into stories.

—Benjamin (Arcades *476*)

Narrative and Anti-Narrative

Dialectic of Enlightenment invites us to read it as a historical narrative, and therefore, like (presumably) any historical analysis or explanation, as a 'mimesis' of Western history or civilization itself. More concretely, it's my suggestion that we consider *Dialectic of Enlightenment* 'as if' it were what I've been calling a 'dialectical mimesis' of Hegel's *Phenomenology of Spirit*. Whether or not Adorno and Horkheimer 'intended' that, the resonances are there, 'objectively', as part of the vast social and historical fact Horkheimer and Adorno mean to confront, for *Dialectic of Enlightenment* enacts both a critique and a renewal of Hegel and of the uses that social power and social thought have found for Hegel in the modern period. *Dialectic of Enlightenment* enacts the critique of historicism Benjamin spells out in his 'Theses on the Philosophy of History'—indeed, considering that Benjamin's text had made its way from the suitcase in Port Bou to Adorno and Horkheimer by the time they started writing *Dialectic of Enlightenment* (Wiggershaus 311–12), it is no stretch to think of their book as a response, even a posthumous *hommage* to their dead friend and his last substantive piece of writing. Horkheimer and Adorno enact their repudiation of post-Hegelian historicism by way of an 'immanent critique' that produces a 'dialectical mimesis', a seeming-'repeat', of that historicism and of its dead-end—with the hope, or 'broken promise', that it may be 'reliquified', set back in motion, and not as the mere whirl of force and compulsion, but as a movement answering in some degree to the desires of human beings, re-empowered as subjects, not objects, of the agitation and turbulence of 'what is'.

The affinities of *Dialectic of Enlightenment* with *Phenomenology of Spirit* are numerous and suggestive: both were written in a moment of crisis perceived by their authors as world-historical, and both aim to diagnose and prescribe for the cultural pathologies of their respective cultural moments. The Table of Contents of *Dialectic of Enlightenment* discloses a narrative and historical arc broadly similar to Hegel's, orchestrating a passage from Greek antiquity to the period of the Enlightenment proper, and thence to the present-day moment of the authors' own period. The historicizing organization, the antique and modern instances chosen for elaboration, the proportions allotted to them, all invite us to take *Dialectic of Enlightenment* as a production, albeit on a smaller scale, on the model of Hegel's *Phenomenology of Spirit*. Horkheimer and Adorno renew Hegel's terminology, and supplement it with newer ones—Marxist, Nietzschean, Weberian, Freudian—that have emerged since Hegel; but their account of the devolution of 'philosophy' into a mere handmaiden of (positivist) 'science', and the attendant reification of thinking as instrumentalized to serve the purposes of scientific and technological 'rationalization' patently continue Hegel's story—if ironically, as a nightmare sequel to an overture (a terminal overture, Hegel had supposed) that, in Hegel's enthusiastic afflatus, had promised a considerably happier finale. Indeed, this issue—'optimism' versus 'pessimism' was the mid-century topos—marks the fundamental dissent or 'contradiction' or 'negation' that Horkheimer and Adorno's 'unhappy [critical] consciousness' operates on Hegel. Hegel diagnosed 'unhappy consciousness', and prescribed for it, in ways anticipating the morale-management counsels of Nietzsche and William James, in the faith that modernity would eventually enable a universal 'happy consciousness'. The textual effect or affect of *Dialectic of Enlightenment* joins the darker tone of Freud, Spengler, Mann, Eliot, and other moderns venting the anxieties of 1914-and-after. *Dialectic of Enlightenment* thereby contravenes the bien-pensant liberal hopes of the day, but also the 'official' party-line 'optimism' of the Stalinist Comintern of that period, in which 'defeatism' could be a capital [thought-] crime.

But *Dialectic of Enlightenment* enacts a more insidious 'dialectical mimesis' of Hegel-and-after on the level of narrative itself. The book organizes its argument around binary pairs that link disjunct historical phenomena—most saliently, 'myth'/'enlightenment' and 'Odysseus'/'bourgeois'. We've touched on these as instances of Adorno's de-temporalizing dialectical 'constellation'. Here we want to restore the temporalization: to interrogate the implicit narratives these binaries at once encode and subvert. These oppositions initially seem the conventional constituents of a familiar modernizing historicism; but they turn out to act in the book not as opposed (historical) pairs, but as virtual transhistorical equations or (to make the ideological baggage more explicit) 'identities': in the latter instance exposing nineteenth-century philology's fetishization of the Homeric protagonist as 'universal' hero; in the former 'deconstructing' (if you'll permit the anachronism) the binary terms of enlightenment's own self-constituting ancients/moderns narrative. Both work to activate the downside, as it were, of 'equivalence' or 'exchange' logic: in the one case offering a 'dialectical image/mimesis' of an equivalence bourgeois modernity wants to embrace (Odysseus = bourgeois), in the second enforcing an equivalence it seeks to disown (Enlightenment = myth). In both cases, as in many others *passim*, we get not the historical narrative that mediates the development from one to the other, but a sequence of non-narrative juxtapositions or 'constellations', enforcing the point that the narrative of progress has not only stalled, but now (1944) looks to have been a deception or 'ruse of history' all along, insofar as it has masked history's chronic steady-state or -cycle of 'repetition', blocking our recognition that the history we are living out is not the narrative of progress, reason and freedom we so desperately want to believe it is, but rather a stasis, indeed a regress, of violence and 'domination'. Recall here Walter Benjamin's aphorism that every document of civilization is also a document of barbarism. In *Dialectic of Enlightenment*, the progressive world-story becomes the failure of the narrative to realize not only its thematic or programmatic *telos*, human liberation, but more fundamentally, its generic or formal constitutive *sine qua non*, narrativity itself.

J. M. Bernstein (*Disenchantment and Ethics* 84–6; see especially 86n18) coolly scorns this way of reading *Dialectic of Enlightenment*. For Bernstein, the critical force of *Dialectic of Enlightenment* is trained not on Enlightenment's historicist narrative investments but rather on the 'conceptual dualism' underlying them. Of course Adorno critiques such dualism as undialectical; just as he critiques a mere inversion of an 'affirmative universal history' into a 'negative' one (even Walter Benjamin's [*H&F*89–98]) as undialectical. But that doesn't mean the latter possibility is so simply absent, or should be so quickly dismissed, from a reading of *Dialectic of Enlightenment*. Horkheimer and Adorno have indeed evoked this very error, mobilized it deliberately (just as, I've argued, they mobilize the apparently 'undialectical' pairs of 'enlightenment/myth' and 'Odysseus/bourgeois')—as 'performative contradiction', as '[dialectical] mimesis' enacting the very devolution of 'dialectic' as the enlightenment miscarried it.[1] This, indeed, is the book's central burden, the contradiction named in its very title. Let me cite here the brief but profound exchange between Bernstein and

Simon Jarvis over Adorno's 'conscious unhappiness'. For Jarvis, it's a symptom
of Adorno's hairshirt ethos that in *Dialectic of Enlightenment* 'the philosophy of
history becomes a dynamic more than a dialectic, and one by which Odysseus
is already proleptic of Auschwitz' (Browning 68). Jarvis is complaining that
Horkheimer and Adorno reduce history to a straight-ahead, linear, cause-and-
effect (sc. undialectical) mechanism. Bernstein rejoins:

> *Dialectic of Enlightenment* . . . does not possess a philosophy of history at all.
> Rather it contends that after Kant-Hegel, history itself becomes more a
> dynamic than [a] dialectic through the pursuance of Enlightenment demy-
> thologization. As a consequence, Enlightenment becomes mythical, i.e., a
> practice of the understanding not reason. The statement concerning myth
> (Odysseus) and Enlightenment is not historical but speculative, about their
> conceptual entwinement [cf. Bernstein's point quoted just above about
> 'conceptual dualisms']. If it presents a history, it is a history of the present
> (Browning 77n5).

Obviously I'm on Bernstein's side of this point; but the very gambit of 'dialectical mimesis' is to invite being mis-taken, at least initially, in exactly the way Jarvis
has just done. The aim is to enact that very error, not merely to analyze and
indict it, but to *display* it, as the flaw endemic to the 'dialectic of enlightenment'
itself: the 'semblance' that is the textual effect of the book is their 'dialectical
mimesis' of the ideological 'mass [*and* elite] deception' prevailing in the culture at large, a deception that has produced, in some sense simply *is*, the disen-
chanted and demoralized devolution of 'dialectic' into mere 'dynamic' that
Bernstein so shrewdly calls 'the history of the present'. To that extent, Jarvis's
mis-reading is on the track of something Bernstein might be missing. *Dialectic of
Enlightenment* stages its critique of the West's detemporalized, non-narrative
'conceptual dualism' by de-concealing the petrification or 'standstill' that dualism has wrought on its own narrative categories: to perform the ways in which
our culture's fundamental contradictions, and our ideological denial of them,
disclose themselves only in the condition—or the 'dialectical mimesis'—of
'dialectic at a standstill', in which we see and even *feel* the conceptual dualities
arresting, freezing, petrifying the very narrative progress and movement we'd
expected them to mobilize.

Earlier we suggested some of the ways in which *Dialectic of Enlightenment*
contravenes the theory-and-practice of dialectic 'as usual' and as orthodox in
the Soviet-dominated left culture in which *Dialectic of Enlightenment* was written;
this suppression of narrative is another. 'Dialectic' had been a term—indeed, a
piety, even a shibboleth—close to co-extensive, in social thought from Hegel-
and-Marx to Adorno's own day, with *narrative* as such and with the broad array
of historicist conceptions of 'progress' at stake in the contentions between
liberal- to left-critical traditions at large. Benjamin's locution, 'dialectics at a

standstill', handily registers the provocations Adorno is trying for, but such non-
or even anti-temporalizing terms as 'constellation' or 'dialectical image' similarly imply the affront Benjamin's 'Medusa-glance' and Adorno's 'immanent
critique' were meant to work upon received historicist (narrative) traditions
of culture-criticism. Adorno follows Hegel in prescribing that 'modern' philosophical (sc. critical, theoretical) consciousness must be self-conscious—which
means, since modernity understands itself chiefly in relation to the cultural past
against which it emerges or 'becomes', that it must be *historically* conscious.
Hegel's *Phenomenology* models the ways in which, even as it makes the arguments
why, 'modern' philosophical writing must be narrative, however sublimatedly
so: must narrate, moreover, not merely whatever precedent history is relevant
to the problem at hand, but its own process of becoming-conscious of that history and of its own place in relation to it—a self-consciousness to be implicit in
the text's composition, its writing, its labor of conceptualizing its history *and* its
place in that history. Hegel prescribes that the philosophical text must perform
the process of its own (self-) discovery, the eventuation, so to speak, of its own
'event'. ('The power of Spirit is only as great as its expression, its depth only as
deep as it dares to spread out and lose itself in its exposition' [*Phenomenology* 6].)
And 'dialectic', in Hegel's usage, was likewise, therefore, ineluctably narrative,
an affair of 'moments', of 'process', of actualization and event or result, as well
as of 'contradiction', 'mediation', 'negation', and 'sublation'—all transitive
actions occurring in a temporality (and, for Hegel, in a textuality) that they
punctuate as moments in a narrative unfolding.

This was new: in all the diverse forms in which philosophers since Socrates
have elaborated it, 'dialectic' was a method of thinking ideally applied in the
atemporal domain of Logos, of the noumenon, of (capital R) Reason. Hegel's
radical step was to project the procedures of reason onto the processes of
history, on the premise that the progress of reason was the historical unfolding
or 'becoming [self-] conscious' of the World-Spirit as such. Thus was dialectic
after Hegel historicized and narrativized. After Hegel, bourgeois historicism—
Michelet and Carlyle to Croce, Spengler, Toynbee, Wells—exhibits diversely
Hegel-esque visions of historical change, progressive or reactionary (or 'Abder-
itic', in Hayden White's coinage), according to the historian's beholding eye,
while mostly discounting, as futile philosophical fuss, 'dialectic' itself. The
left-Hegelian strain, from Marx to 'official' Marxism-Leninism, retained 'the
dialectic' but, by Horkheimer and Adorno's day, in debased form, as a *deus ex
machina* to guarantee the fore-ordained happy ending of its own providential
'grand narrative' (inevitable revolution, dictatorship of the proletariat, withering away of the state . . .).

But note that the *narrative* conventions operative across this putatively diverse
and conflicting spectrum of historicizing critique, Hegel to Spengler, are, functionally, 'the same'. I characterize the aims, the complex gesture, of *Dialectic of
Enlightenment* in these terms to foreground how very different is Horkheimer
and Adorno's (in)version of Hegel from Marx's. Marx claimed to have turned

Hegel right-side up, putting his great precursor's idealist headstand squarely back on its materialist feet—but Marx's figure owns that he and Hegel are talking about the same creature, the same orientation of posture (vertical) and mode of mobility (bipedal ambulation). In Marx as in Hegel we have a forward-moving story, a dynamic indisputably narrative; the coloration of particular episodes and themes varies between the two—the story of alienation, of *Aufhebung*, of human beings rendered thing-like, but achieving the self-consciousness of the '*für Sich*' in the end—but the happiness of the providential ending and the kinetic momentum of the progress to it are macrofeatures that Hegel and Marx share: a set of themes and (more fundamentally) of presuppositions regarding the use of historical narrative in works of social interpretation, explanation, diagnosis, and critique.

It is this unacknowledged (unconscious) ideology of *narrative*, no less than the de facto homogenization of 'dialectic', whether by bourgeois dismissal or by Soviet dogmatization, that Adorno's non- or anti-narrative practice of 'constellation' (like Benjamin's, of the 'dialectical image') means to expose. It is a gesture very much in line with the attenuation of narrative interest in the modernist novel's contraventions of pre-1914 fiction: for example—one that will evoke (again) Georg Lukács and his chronic 'debate' through the '30s with Brecht, Benjamin, and Adorno—the ways canons of nineteenth-century Realism are transgressed in Joyce, Kafka, Proust, and Woolf, pioneering techniques ('epiphany', 'montage', 'juxtaposition without copula') patently cognate with Adorno's 'constellation'. It's a constant presupposition of Lukács's indictment of 'the ideology of modernism' that the likes of Joyce and Proust are apostates to the imperative of narrative as such, to the Lukácsian maxim, as laid down in 'Art and Objective Truth', that 'only through plot can the dialectic of human existence and consciousness be expressed' (*Writer and Critic* 51). If Joyce et al., connote the habitus of bourgeois Europe and America, I invoke Lukács as reminder that Adorno's dissent from post-Hegelian or historicist story-telling 'as usual' was a heresy far more daringly directed against the 'official' Comintern or Stalinist orthodoxy of the Soviet bloc, in which 'optimism' was a dogma binding on the faithful and 'pessimism' (a.k.a. 'defeatism') like Benjamin's or Adorno's a marker of the 'class enemy'. We must remember that a work like *Dialectic of Enlightenment*, written in 1944, is witnessing the nightmare not only of the Hitlerian barbarism, but of the Stalinist gulags, murders, show trials, betrayals as well (and not only within the Soviet sphere of influence, as witness Trotsky's assassination in Mexico City in August 1940).

Discomposing Narrative: Affect (Again)

Dialectic of Enlightenment asserts its own place or moment in the historical process by way of a radical (and modernist) refunctioning of narrative itself—most tellingly, in the extent to which the Horkheimer/Adorno re-telling of the enlightenment/Hegelian/Marxist meta-narrative is so little narrative in its effect. Granted Marx's boast, that he had inverted Hegel's story (stood it on its head/feet), he still narrated it according to story-telling conventions recognizably of the same type, bearing marked family resemblances, to Hegel's own. Horkheimer and Adorno's narrative is much more ambiguously 'narrative'; it less *tells* the story than elaborates chosen moments, images, problems from it; it presupposes the reader's knowledge of the story's received outlines, and turns the energy thus released from narration to eliciting resonances and potencies undeveloped in more narratively invested versions. Though the narrative interest of the precedent 'story' necessarily prolongs itself in *Dialectic of Enlightenment*, the narrative impulse is clearly subordinate to the interpretive; and to that extent the book stands to Hegel-and-Marx in a relation in some ways like that of Midrash to Torah. But that analogy needs qualification, to the extent that both scripture and commentary minimize affect: the Biblical narratives are terse as if precisely to purge affective or aesthetic power, 'textual effect' or affect. (On the theory that the Torah narratives are prose synopses of originally much longer, and more libidinally cathected, oral narratives, and that the minimalist Biblical précis was intended precisely to deprive those bardic narratives of the affective power pagans associated with divine inspiration [the Muses], we might speculate that Biblical narrative's estrangements of narrative effects or affects anticipates the *Republic*'s expulsion of the poets.)

By contrast, the affective program I've ascribed to *Dialectic of Enlightenment*— to arouse enlightenment to its chronically suppressed 'fear', to disturb enlightenment's 'tranquility of mind', to arouse enlightenment's 'bad conscience'—adds to the mode of Midrashic exposition an emotionalism, a 'labor of affectualization', absent in the precursor text(s); here the analogy that comes to mind is Aeschylus's sensationalizing reconstitution of Homeric epos, in which (again) the familiar epic 'story' need not be re-told—the audience already knows the plot—so that the hypnogogic work of the choral song can instead work a stroboscopic activation of the story's most horrific associations, as when the Chorus in the *Agamemnon* is beset by images from the curse-of-Atreus story (a boiling pot of infant limbs! a mighty fleet becalmed at sea! a princess's lovely neck bared to the sacrificial knife!). Aeschylus contrives to agitate this imagery so elliptically, but also so obsessively, as to motivate the elision of their collectively known narrative context as a collective effort to repress anxieties that are recurring with the force of nightmare. (Compare the cognate impulse in a more contemporary instance, Christopher Logue's operatic workouts on the *Iliad*.) The 'nobility' of the Homeric grand style, idealized since antiquity, has much to do with what Horkheimer and Adorno indict as its 'narrative composure' (Cumming 78–80); Aeschylus's rescript (and Logue's) represses the narrative the better to distill from its imageries the panic Homer's 'composure' composes—and however deliberately, Horkheimer and Adorno seem to me to stand in some such relation to Hegel, or at least to that side of him they most deplore, his Panglossian, happy-consciousness, theodicy-mongering 'optimism'. The intrusion, into the quasi- or even mock-Hegelian habitus of *Dialectic of Enlightenment*, of de Sade and Nietzsche, anti-Semitism and Hollywood, 'motivates' this gesture.

In doing so, *Dialectic of Enlightenment* (again) projects a panorama of catastrophe that mobilizes Marx as readily as Hegel, and without mitigating the force of its anti-enlightenment indictments against either. But particular or 'party' ideological provocations aside, *Dialectic of Enlightenment* means to present a vision of global cultural catastrophe that challenges the competing received partisan scenarios. It is addressed to readers of good will of, at least, potentially, all ideological stripes: to loyal communists, it says that their party-line optimism is fraudulent—that the revolution under Stalin partakes of a barbarism every bit as savage as the alternatives. To rightwingers short of outright fascism, conservatives like, say, Spengler, it offers something like a 'dialectical mimesis' of *The Decline of the West*, but one in which the catastrophe appears as present, not future, and is attended by anguish rather than the paradoxically anodyne knowingness typical of early-modern 'cultural despair' reactionaries of the Spengler type. Most complicatedly it addresses liberals and non-Stalinist leftists, inheritors and stewards of the Enlightenment tradition, whose received view of the catastrophe—that the bad guys, the forces of darkness, are winning—they affront by diagnosing the failures and shortcomings of the good guys themselves, of Enlightenment itself. In their account of Enlightenment's devolution or regression into barbarism, via positivism, scientism, 'identity-thinking', anti-theorism and literal-mindedness of all kinds, they enact the Enlightenment narrative's failure not only to achieve its narrative telos, but also to maintain its 'dialectical' ethos—whether or not it's still telling itself that progressive or revolutionary story, or (as in the USSR) fetishizing the word 'dialectic' itself. They narrate the failure of the Enlightenment narrative to achieve narrativity, as well as the failure of Enlightenment 'dialectic' to be dialectical. As if 'dialectic' itself could be subject to 'negation'—and not '*determinate* negation', the kind that alters quality, but '*absolute* negation': an annihilation, that is reduction *ad nihil*, to zero, that, in the terms of Horkheimer and Adorno's indictment of enlightenment, liquidates 'quality' altogether, and therefore 'dialectic' itself, leaving only the 'bad infinity' of the merely quantitative, the domain in which the logic of equivalence/exchange has its limited but lethal validity. This, as *Dialectic of Enlightenment* projects it, is the irony, or indeed the peculiar 'dialectic', of the 'dialectic of enlightenment'.

Horkheimer and Adorno's evocation of the failure is, in my view, the most potent such book of the mid-century period, a period peculiarly rich in efforts at cultural diagnosis—and I include here everything from pre-war works like Freud's *Civilization and its Discontents* and Spengler's *Decline of the West* to such post-war productions as Norman O. Brown's *Life Against Death*, Herbert Marcuse's *Eros and Civilization*, and Erich Fromm's *Flight From Freedom*. *Dialectic of Enlightenment* remains an epitome of critical 'unhappy consciousness', fully answering to the angst, rage, and despair of the 'during-Auschwitz' ordeal and, prophetically, to the 'after-Auschwitz' prolongation in which the shutdown of the ovens at Auschwitz offered so little comfort in view of the prospect of global murder opened by the nuclear attacks against Hiroshima and Nagasaki. In the 1944 'Introduction', Horkheimer and Adorno explain that all rhetorics of 'affirmation' are by now so compromised as to make affirmation itself a lie—a premise that all but forecloses any possibility of the utopian in the book itself. Yet the book has its hints of utopian hope—a hope indissociable from a sense of the 'dialectic' simply as the historically unforeseeable, but capable of horror as well as blessings. Against all optimisms from Hegel to Stalin and beyond, Horkheimer and Adorno de-conceal a historical dialectic leading to catastrophe rather than reconciliation, an Absolute of despair rather than exaltation, a Golgotha of the Spirit or 'slaughterbench of history' more literal and more atrocious than any Hegel could ever have imagined, projected as the apparent liquidation of dialectic—or as Marxists liked to say, '*the* dialectic'—itself.

Which returns us to the 'performative contradiction' of 'dialectics at a standstill' enacted in a seemingly *narrative* form.

The Poetics of 'Standstill'

In his 1964 essay, 'Progress', Adorno spells out, in terms extending those of *Dialectic of Enlightenment*, an implicit rationale for the anti- or non-narrative habitus of his work: that the quantification and commodification of all of life on the model of the fungible medium of money, and the attendant psychology or ideology of 'equivalence exchange' effectively aborts the forward motion or unfolding of historical time itself, so that the very motif of 'progress' increasingly functions as an ideological deceit:

> In bourgeois society, which created the concept of total progress, the convergence of this concept with the negation of progress originates in this society's principle: exchange. Exchange is the rational form of mythical ever-sameness. In the like-for-like of every act of exchange, the one act revokes the other, the balance of accounts is null. If the exchange was just, then nothing should really have happened, and everything stays the same. At the same time, the assertion of progress, which conflicts with this principle, is true to the extent that the doctrine of like-for-like is a lie. . . . But this injustice [i.e., capital's expropriation of surplus value from labor] is . . . also the condition for possible justice. The fulfillment of the repeatedly broken exchange contract would converge with its abolition; exchange would disappear if truly equal things were exchanged; true progress would be not merely an Other in relation to exchange, but rather exchange that has been brought to itself. Thus thought both Marx and Nietzsche, antipodes of each other; Zarathustra postulates

that man will be redeemed from revenge. For revenge is the mythical prototype of exchange; as long as domination persists through exchange, myth will
dominate as well (*CM* 159).

'Exchange is the rational form of mythical ever-sameness' asserts, again, the
theme of *Dialectic of Enlightenment*, the persistence within 'enlightenment' of
what enlightenment constitutes itself by repudiating, 'myth'; and the theme of
exchange as revenge (attested by Marx and Nietzsche, even across the antipo-
dean opposition between them) similarly suggests the persistence in our 'rationalized' modernity of the most primordial and atavistic violences. I have alluded
above to the way *Dialectic of Enlightenment* treats as functionally convertible terms
(e.g., 'myth'/'enlightenment', 'Odysseus'/'bourgeois') whose opposition is
fundamental to enlightened, historicizing modernity's self-conception, a gesture the passage helps us see as a 'dialectical mimesis' of bourgeois civilization's
'law of exchange'. The passage continues, tellingly evoking Benjamin, and
especially the atmospherics of the *Arcades Project*:

> The life-process itself ossifies in the expression of the ever-same: hence the
> shock of photographs from the nineteenth century and even the early twenti-
> eth century. The absurdity explodes: that something happens where the
> phenomenon says that nothing more could happen; its attitude becomes ter-
> rifying. In this experience of terror, the terror of the system expands, the
> more it hardens into what it has always been. What Benjamin called 'dialec-
> tics at a standstill' is surely less a Platonizing residue than the attempt to raise
> such paradoxes to philosophical consciousness. Dialectical images: these are
> the historically-objective archetypes of that antagonistic unity of standstill
> and movement that defines the most universal bourgeois concept of progress
> (*CM* 160).

The passage goes on to acknowledge that not just the 'bourgeois' concept of
progress, but the 'dialectical' one too, 'needs correction', as 'Hegel as well as
Marx bore witness'. Our look, in an earlier chapter, at the 'Epistemo-Critical
Prologue' to the *Trauerspiel* acknowledged that Benjamin's usages ('idea', 'beauty',
'saving the appearances') do indeed bear 'Platonizing residues'; Adorno here
redescribes these as themselves 'dialectical' reinventions of ideological reifications Benjamin's practice yearned to 'redeem'.

But of course, no more than Benjamin's is Adorno's repudiation of historicism a call for ahistorical consciousness. Elsewhere, referring to post-1945
historical amnesia in Germany, and Henry Ford's 'History is bunk', Adorno
evokes

> the nightmare of a humanity without memory. It is no mere phenomenon of
> decline, not a reaction of a humanity that . . . is flooded with stimuli and can-
> not cope with them. Rather it is necessarily connected to the advancement of

the bourgeois principle . . . [i.e.,] the law of exchange, of the like-for-like accounts that match and that leave no remainder.

The loss of historical memory is not only a symptom of our period's 'nightmare', but also an ideological effect specific to a culture founded on the 'law of exchange':

> In its very essence exchange is something timeless; like ratio itself, like the operations of mathematics . . . they [sic] remove the aspect of time. Similarly, concrete time vanishes from industrial production. It transpires more and more in identical and spasmodic, potentially simultaneous cycles . . . [Weber's and Sombart's contrast of 'traditionalism' with capitalist 'rationalization'] means nothing less than that recollection, time, memory is being liquidated by advancing bourgeois society itself, as a kind of irrational residue . . . (*CM* 339n11).

This 'remov[al of] the aspect of time' recalls Benjamin's alarums against the ideological conception of 'homogeneous, empty time' (*Illuminations* 261) that sustains *but also* neutralizes the historicist conception of progress itself. ('Homogeneous, empty time' as the quantifiable time measured by clocks and registered in history books by timelines and dates represents the making-fungible of time, as well as instantiating what Horkheimer and Adorno indict as positivism's forfeiture of 'quality' for 'quantity'.) Against positivist homogenization of time and of history, Benjamin avows that 'History is a structure whose site is not homogeneous, empty time, but time filled by the presence of the now [*Jetztzeit*]' (*Illuminations* 261). Benjamin goes on, in references (Robespierre and ancient Rome) that evoke Marx's *Eighteenth Brumaire*, to contrast bourgeois historicism's sense of history as a 'continuum' with a very different, discontinuous, ruptured and rupturing, revolutionary and Messianic consciousness of history that 'blasts' its saving insights *out* of the continuum of history as bourgeois historicism conceives it:

> Historicism rightly culminates in universal history . . . [which] has no theoretical armature. Its method is additive; it musters a mass of data to fill the homogeneous, empty time. Materialistic historiography, on the other hand, is based on a constructive principle. Thinking involves not only the flow of thoughts, but their arrest as well. Where thinking suddenly stops in a configuration pregnant with tensions, it gives that configuration a shock, by which it crystallizes into a monad. . . . In this structure [the historical materialist] recognizes the sign of a Messianic cessation of happening, or, put differently, a revolutionary chance in the fight for an oppressed past. He takes cognizance of it in order to blast a specific era out of the homogeneous course of history (*Illuminations* 263).

The concern, then, is to break or 'blast' free of a fatalistic, self-enforcing ('scientific') ideology of cause-and-effect:

> Historicism contents itself with establishing a causal connection between various moments in history. But no fact that is a cause is for that reason historical. It became historical posthumously, as it were, through events that may be separated by thousands of years. A historian who takes this as his point of departure stops telling the sequence of events like the beads of a rosary. Instead, he grasps the constellation which his own era has formed with an earlier one. Thus he establishes a conception of the present as the 'time of the now' which is shot through with chips of Messianic time (*Illuminations* 263).

These passages sound many notes suggestive of Benjamin's critical poetics of standstill: critique involves 'the flow of thoughts', but 'their arrest as well'; as with Medusa's glance, this arrest is at once a 'symptom' critique attacks, and an effect critique seeks to produce: thinking can 'shock' a numbed world into awareness only when the 'flow'—of historicist narrative, ritually rehearsed like 'the beads of a rosary'—has been 'arrested', constellated, into a 'monad'. Here the technique of 'constellation' is quite explicitly posed *against* narrative historicizing, not as a mere alternative but as its critique.[2]

All this in a passage whose rhetoric of discontinuity—'blasting' new revolutionary insight out of the linear continuum of homogeneous historical consciousness—lends a feeling of something like movement quite unusual in Benjamin's work. Which, I suspect, is partly why 'Theses on the Philosophy of History' moves so many as a crucial text in Benjamin's oeuvre: the theme of the '*Jetztzeit*', stated with a force felt nowhere else in Benjamin, here releases a potency sufficiently invigorating to excuse (even for secularizing moderns like us) the evocation of 'the Messianic'. (Not that the *Jetztzeit* motif, recapitulating the thematics of *kerygma* and *khairos* from existentialist theology, could have been dissociated from religion in any event.) But the norm of Benjamin's work is more static than that—recall Adorno's figuration of Medusa, of petrifications, of taxidermy, of feigned death—and I've quoted Benjamin at such length to underline the recurring tension that Adorno's 'constellation' is (again) a non-narrative device, and would seem to import for Adorno's work something of the ethos of Benjamin's static, petrifying method and/or effect. But as we've seen, for all his reverence for Benjamin, Adorno feels considerable misgiving about Benjamin's method ('it swears loyalty to reification instead of flatly rejecting it' [*P* 233]), lest the petrifaction Benjamin's Medusa-gaze wreaks on its object should indeed merely confirm or even reinforce the stony rigor mortis of a society already too fatally in thrall to reification. (Again, Adorno's reservations about Benjamin's methods coincide with Lukács's against Adorno.) At issue here are less conceptual differences than matters of textual and indeed critical effect or effectivity—an anxiety motivating, I argue, the jumpy agitation of Adorno's writing, in sharp contrast with the *facies hippocratica* of Benjamin's laconic, funereal, Saturnine, 'playing possum' prose.

Marx and 'Constellation'

I have frequently cited Marx as an exemplar of the historicist story-telling style of critical exposition that Adorno and Benjamin repudiate: they, as modernists, do to the narrative historicizing of nineteenth-century critique (Hegel and Marx) something like what Proust and Joyce do to the realist novel. But Marx can occasionally anticipate their non-narrative model of revolutionary time. Marx's 'first time as tragedy, second time as farce' in the *Eighteenth Brumaire* has become one of his most familiar quotations; and its point, of course, is the *failure* of a revolution; but just a few paragraphs further on, Marx attempts to model successful revolution—and, within the terms he's already started with, he characterizes an authentically revolutionary 'repetition' that escapes declension into farce and achieves 'true tragedy': in other words, first time as tragedy, and in the case of authentic revolutions (1871, as against 1851), the second time as tragedy as well. Adorno quotes the passage (twice [*B* 79, 190]):

> Absorbed in money-making and in the peaceful warfare of competition, it [bourgeois society] forgot that the shades of ancient Rome had sat beside its cradle. Nevertheless, unheroic though bourgeois society may seem, heroism had been needed to bring it into being—heroism, self-sacrifice, the Reign of Terror, civil war and the slaughter of the battle-fields. In the stern classical tradition of the Roman Republic, its gladiators found the ideals and the forms, the means of self-deception they needed, that they might hide from themselves the bourgeois limitations of the struggle in which they were engaged, and might sustain their passion at the level appropriate to a great historic tragedy. In like manner, more than a century earlier, and in another phase of development, Cromwell and the English people had borrowed the phraseology, the emotions, and the illusions of the Old Testament as trappings for their own bourgeois revolution. As soon as they had reached the goal, as soon as the bourgeois transformation of English society had been effected, Locke supplanted Habakkuk (I transcribe here the 1926 translation of Eden and Cedar Paul as given at B 79; the passage appears in a different, uncredited translation in *Marx-Engels Reader* 595–6).

Adorno comments:

> This passage has the most far-reaching implication, not for a critique of the heroic posture but for the category of totality itself—in Beethoven as in

Hegel—as a *transfiguration* of mere existence. And just as, from this stand-point, the Hegelian transition to the whole seems questionable in all its stages, so, too, does the superiority of the 'objective' Beethoven over the 'private' and as it were empirical Schubert. However much more truth there may be in the former, there is as much more untruth as well. The whole as truth is always also a lie. But were not the 'stern classical traditions' of the Roman Republic *themselves* already a lie—the Roman as a bourgeois in fancy dress? Cicero no less than Cato? Was not Marx, in this part of his construction of history, too *naive*? (*B* 79)

Marx too naive? Naively cynical, perhaps—as witness his patent discomfort conceding the heroism of bourgeois revolutions, and that final reversal, Locke supplanting Habakkuk: second time as tragedy, but only for a moment, before farcical, unheroic 'last man' *Bürgertum* reasserts itself. (Locke! And for that matter, coming from the author of 'The Jewish Question', Habakkuk risks making the 'first time' farcical as well. For affective/ideological co-ordinates, compare Yeats: 'Locke sank into a swoon; / The garden died; / God took the spinning-jenny / Out of his side'.) Marx's diagnosis of the 'self-deception' by which revolutionary actors 'hide from themselves the bourgeois limitations of the struggle in which they were engaged, and [so] sustain their passion at the level appropriate to a great historic tragedy' refuses any credit to the Nietzschean 'redemption by illusion' the passage so nearly anticipates. Yet Marx concludes with a summary paragraph that could be mistaken for Benjamin:

> The awakening of the dead in those revolutions therefore served the purpose of glorifying the new struggles, not of parodying the old; of magnifying the given tasks in imagination, not of taking flight from their solution in reality; of finding once more the spirit of revolution, not of making its ghost walk again (*Marx-Engels Reader* 596).

But if, in these passages, successful revolution is 'tragic', we may recall that the earlier Marx had thought of historical transformation as 'comic', meaning not laughs, but happy endings—as here, from the 1844 'Contribution to the Critique of Hegel's *Philosophy of Right*: Introduction':

> The modern *ancien régime* is the comedian of a world order whose real heroes are dead. History is thorough, and it goes through many stages when it conducts an ancient formation to its grave. The last stage of a world-historical formation is comedy. The Greek gods, already once mortally wounded in Aeschylus's tragedy *Prometheus Bound,* had to endure a second death, a comic death, in Lucian's dialogues. Why should history proceed in this way? So that mankind shall separate itself *gladly* from its past. We claim this joyful destiny for the political powers of Germany (*Marx-Engels Reader* 57).

Marx's 'joyful' sarcasm here is in service to what Nietzsche would have regarded as a Socratic-Euripidean debasement of 'the tragic'; still, the resemblance to Nietzsche's own 'gay science' of cheerful vandalism against all powers that be is a telling symptom. Marx's satirical costume metaphor resonates with one of Nietzsche's sneers at modernity: 'we are the first age that has truly *studied* "costumes" . . . Perhaps this is where we can still discover the realm of our *invention*, this realm in which we, too, can still be original, say, as parodists of world history and God's buffoons . . .' (*Beyond Good and Evil,* # 223) 'Original parodists'! In the older Marx, though—after 1848, 1851, and 1871—the sarcasm is part of the coloration of the tragedy, and thus much closer in mood to Benjamin and Adorno: revolution as *not* 'comedy' in the happy-ending sense, but as sobering cataclysm *despite* whatever putatively 'happy' (revolutionary) outcomes. We would be grateful if history could boast even one example of a 'happy ending' revolution, one that vouchsafed, at least, the baby *with* the blood-bath. Here— *successful* revolution as tragedy—compare Marx's chastened tone with the younger Niezsche's swaggering evocation, in *The Birth of Tragedy,* of primordial 'terror'.

It seems proleptic of various modern or postmodern 'linguistic turns' that Marx characterizes the possible outcomes in literary-generic terms: 'tragedy', 'comedy', 'farce'. Compare Adorno: 'It would not be difficult to read something like a theory of universal history from the *Phenomenology of Spirit* . . . These ideas are roughly equivalent to the conception of world literature which was of such great importance at around the same time, as we can see from Goethe. . . [and] throughout the Romantic movement . . .' (*H&F* 80). But cognate attempts to reimagine the relation of past and present are pervasive in the twentieth century—Eliot's 'mythical method', Pound's 'make it new'; two generations of Joyce criticism pondering the question whether *Ulysses* is 'epic' or 'mock-epic'—in short, whether, vis à vis Homer, *Ulysses* is or isn't an instance of 'second time as farce'. And clearly, 'farce' would never do for any work of Adorno's, least of all *Dialectic of Enlightenment,* the one (precisely) most 'second-time' in its conception. Even granting the Panglossian view of the *Phenomenology,* which would make Hegel's 'first-time' a 'comedy' rather than 'tragedy', I don't see how the Adorno/Horkheimer repetition can be read otherwise than as 'tragedy'—except to the extent that tragedy, like comedy, might seem an ineluctably *narrative* category. Farce has shown itself well able to accommodate visions of bleak and desperate 'standstill' throughout the twentieth century, from Eliot and Brecht and Capek and Beckett on (Döblin, Pynchon, Terry Gilliam . . .)—evidence enough that we badly need some 'other' of 'farce', that would stand in relation to it as tragedy does to comedy, to evoke the peculiarly operatic, not at all 'farcical' (or 'cynical') effect of *Dialectic of Enlightenment.*

Marx's 'tragic' inflection of revolution—his nod, if you will, to Hegel's 'slaughterbench of history'—owns his chastened recognition that the violence of historical change ('the Reign of Terror, civil war and the slaughter of the battle-fields') comes at an exorbitant price, indeed at a cost that makes the language of 'price', as if it could be calculated—as if it could be refused—obscene. When Adorno calls Marx 'too naive', I take him to be indicting Marx's attempt to discriminate *moral* value in particular historical moments—as if 'truth' and 'lie' could be reliably sorted, assigned unmixed, between one totality and the other. One would like to pause over the question this implies for Benjamin's 'Theses', where we *feel* investments that cry out to be called moral, though they eschew the too-obvious handles Marx provides. But what of Adorno himself? in whom no such cathexis of privilege and judgment—good/bad, tragic/farcical—ever appears, at least not attaching to historical 'totalities'. Adorno nowhere displays anything like Marx's richly contradictory 'attitudes toward history' (Kenneth Burke's phrase). Marx is too committed to a historical—i.e., again, *narrative*, and progressive—sense of the human condition to figure revolution as an apparition *de novo*, as if *ex nihil*; Marx's usual impulse is to project it, narratively, as *event*, an outcome complicatedly (over-?) determined by an antecedent past. The passages above, drawn from every phase of his career, are aberrant in imagining revolutionary history not narrated as events in sequence but 'constellated' as cognate moments brought together in revolutionary (sometimes in mock-, or failed-revolutionary) consciousness—as if, in that consciousness, at least, all the mediating historical narrative producing (determining) one event from the other is suspended, by-passed. This evasion of narrative, however aberrant in Marx, is a constant motivation in Benjamin and Adorno.

Nietzschean 'Uses of History'

In a 1963 lecture, Adorno remarked that 'of all the so-called great philosophers, I owe [Nietzsche] the greatest debt, more even than to Hegel . . .' (*PMP* 172)—so, having posed Benjamin and Marx as foils to Adorno's anti-historicist, anti-narrative practice, it would be remiss to leave Nietzsche out of the account.[3] Adorno's is a Nietzsche very much against the grain, insofar as Adorno sees more of Hegel in Nietzsche than Nietzsche himself did. But Nietzsche's refusal of historical narration underwrites Adorno's anti-narrative practice; likewise his refusal of the Hegelian 'mediation', corollary for Nietzsche to a refusal of dialectic wholesale. Adorno concedes Nietzsche's disdain of Hegel, but argues that there's a method in Nietzsche's contradictoriness that qualifies as 'dialectical despite itself':

> There can be no doubt that [Nietzsche] was as acutely aware of the so-called contradictions as the worthy professors of philosophy . . . who have given him bad marks because of them. They undoubtedly originate in one of his very well-founded theses that nothing that we know actually obeys the laws of logic, but that we employ logic to organize the world in a particular manner.

In the light of this Nietzsche represents the conscious attempt to heal knowledge, to rescue it from the process of organization, from the illusion of its own logicality, but he uses the methods of logic to achieve this. Incidentally, there is a profound agreement between Hegel and Nietzsche on this point—even though Nietzsche knew very little about Hegel. Despite this, the affinity between them leads me to conclude that this healing of thought from the wounds that it inflicts on its own objects is in actual fact the true task of philosophical reflection (*KCPR* 84).

This assimilation of Nietzsche to Hegel makes, at the very least, a 'constellation' suggestive of what is most provocative about *Dialectic of Enlightenment*—for instance, a possibility I have held in abeyance for too long, namely that of reading Hegel's *Phenomenology* itself 'constellationally' rather than narratively, a heuristic Adorno would endorse, and for more reasons than simply that 'Nietzsche was one of the few after Hegel who recognized the dialectic of enlightenment' (Cumming 44). It seems more than implicit, for example, in his constant yoking of Hegel and Beethoven[4]—to the extent that for Adorno (as we'll see) Beethoven epitomizes 'composition' as a non-narrative, quasi-'constellational' process. ('In the equidistance of all elements from the centre [in Beethoven] . . . dialectic comes to a standstill' [*B* 16].)

Reading Hegel through the lens of Nietzsche: we may recall the David Lodge joke about 'the influence of Joyce on Shakespeare', the point of which is, more or less, Nietzsche's point in 'The Use and Abuse of History': that because the historical past only lives 'for us', it's our vital prerogative to reimagine it as willfully, as 'strongly', as we can. The influence of Nietzsche—or Beethoven—on Hegel scorns any question of what Hegel was 'really'; the question is what we (or Adorno) make of Hegel now. Hence Nietzsche's alternative to historicism, 'genealogy':

> . . . the whole history of a thing, an organ, a custom, becomes a continuous *chain* of reinterpretations and rearrangements, which need not be causally connected among themselves, which may simply follow one another. The 'evolution' of a thing, a custom, an organ is not a *progressus* towards a goal, let alone the most logical and shortest *progressus*, requiring the least energy and expenditure. Rather, it is a sequence of more or less profound, more or less independent processes of appropriation, including the resistances used in each instance, the attempted transformations for purposes of defense or reaction, as well as the results of successful counterattacks. . . . partial desuetude, atrophy and degeneration, the loss of meaning and purpose—in short, death—must be numbered among the conditions of any true *progressus*, which latter appears always in the form of the will and means to greater power and is achieved at the expense of lesser powers. The scope of any 'progress' is measured by all that must be sacrificed for its sake (*Genealogy of Morals* 210 [II, xii]).

Nietzsche in this vein is conventionally taken as profoundly, and cannily, anti-Hegelian: but this description readily tunes with the experience of what the *Phenomenology* is actually like *to read*, in which the chaotic intrusions of the 'night of the world' motif *passim* quite contest Hegel's 'official' thematic of 'the Absolute'. (Put it that Hegel was of the Devil's party without most of his readers knowing it.) Nor, for that matter, does Hegel's story of *Geistlich* interpretation and counter-interpretation—what Hegel meant by 'contradiction'—imply anything like the positivist 'causality' Nietzsche is attacking here. Read by the lights of Adorno, Benjamin, and Nietzsche, the *Phenomenology* seems quite susceptible to a non-'historicist' reading—as presenting, à la Nietzsche, 'a continuous *chain* of reinterpretations and rearrangements, which need not be causally connected'; or, à la Benjamin, constellations of crisis-moments or—images between which Hegel 'blasts' a continuum of Messianic/revolutionary meaning that outleaps the merely chronological (homogenous) continuum of historicist time.

Historicism at a Standstill

I want to clinch the foregoing excursus on Adorno's 'poetics of standstill'—its motivations in the 'Progress' essay and its antecedents in the theory-and-practice of Benjamin, Marx, and Nietzsche—with another detailed reading from the first chapter of *Dialectic of Enlightenment*. I've argued that the most devious and subversive (and 'modernist') of that book's many transgressions against the practice of critique 'as usual' is its 'immanent critique', its 'dialectical mimesis', of the chief ideological presupposition of enlightenment, progress, historicism and the rest, namely that of *narrative* or *narrativity* itself as the *sine qua non*, the necessary condition, the mental form or format indispensable to any account of human progress, insofar as the very idea of 'progress' must involve a before-and-after, perforce, a *narrative* understanding of human history. We have rehearsed the ways, and the reasons, that Adorno's method, typically, eschews narrative in favor of alternative, non-narrative ways to 'constellate' his materials; in various places Adorno 'motivates' this method by appeal to the failure of progress itself, as 'dialectical mimesis' of the 'dialectics at a standstill' characterizing the predicament of the early twentieth century at large. But *Dialectic of Enlightenment* is, again, exceptional—and recall here my speculations in the 'Introduction' as to the importance of Horkheimer's more conventionally narrative mode of critique in producing, in tension with Adorno's non- or anti-narrative critical *gestus*, the peculiarly potent performative contradiction of *Dialectic of Enlightenment*, which is to *perform* the failure, the 'standstill' of enlightened, progressive 'grand narrative' in what seems at first glance a version of that narrative, obeying the generic imperatives and conventions of narrative itself, but which proves on closer inspection to subvert them utterly, using their own 'logics' against them, to subvert not only 'the grand narrative' they are conventionally mobilized to tell, but narrativity itself.

Let's consider a passage that puts this performative contradiction on display. The premise is, again, one of the fundamental gestures of *Dialectic of Enlightenment*, namely the identification of Enlightenment with what Enlightenment itself disowns, the 'other' against which it defines itself, with which it refuses identification, namely *myth*. *Dialectic of Enlightenment* appeared in a polemical milieu in which the word 'dialectical' retained crucial force as a shibboleth of Soviet orthodoxy, so the identification of these supposed polar terms risked, or defied, grave ideological peril on the order of defeatism, bourgeois deviation, Trotskyism, and the like. In redescribing 'enlightenment' *as* 'myth', Horkheimer and Adorno expose the Enlightenment imperative of demythologization as myth by other means, myth unwittingly prolonged or 'preserved', under the very sign of its having been 'cancelled'—*Aufhebung* (so to speak) in if not reverse, than in a recursive oscillation between the poles of 'preserve' and 'cancel' such that the object becomes *Aufhebung* itself. (One could read this as a variation on the theme of the 'Intermittence' of dialectic Adorno elaborated in his book on Kierkegaard [*KCA* 100–2].) Adorno and Horkheimer thus risk or defy, again, the devolution of their own critique (as Lukács and Habermas warn) into an undialectical 'mythical thinking' in which the trope of Odysseus-as-bourgeois can be taken to project the enterprise of the Homeric hero as 'the same' as the bourgeois acquisitiveness and instrumentalism of a very different age—as if 'myth', 'bourgeois', 'Enlightenment', and the book's other key terms, were transhistorical categories, recurrent or chronic (sc. 'eternal') features of (at least Western) civilization from Homer to Hitler and presumably on into the foreseeable future: as if historical development can have counted for nothing, can have made no change, no difference, at all; as if the dialectic of Enlightenment were no dialectic, but a transhistorical antinomy on the model of Kant's—i.e., insoluble, and by reason of the very insolubility setting absolute limits—but projected not merely onto the categories constitutive of reason or 'human understanding', but onto history itself.

All of which would seem to contravene these authors' constant injunctions to historicize ('the core of truth is historical, rather than an unchanging constant to be set against the movement of history', they advise in the 1969 'Preface to the New Edition'; they add that 'Our conception of history does not presume any dispensation from it' [*Dialectic of Enlightenment* ix–x]); moreover it would quite reverse any sense of dialectic germane to the narrativizing or historicizing premises constitutive for the Hegelian tradition, including, signally, its Marxist version, in both of which narrative history is indissociable from the dialectic itself. The question is the more urgent to the extent that historicism was itself an Enlightenment invention, and in its own self-historicizing, Enlightenment idealizes itself as having transcended what Horkheimer and Adorno project as its original sin, the homogenizing will-to-mastery, the constant reinscription of the new as 'the same', the domesticating introjection of what is 'outside' in order to undo the unknown's 'outsideness as the source of fear' (Cumming 16).

For the inaugural motive of Enlightenment historicism is precisely to assert its *difference* from all the backwardness and superstition, the 'darkness', of the past. Most immediately, *Dialectic of Enlightenment*'s apparently transhistorical yoking together of disjunct things (e.g., 'myth' and 'Enlightenment', 'Odysseus' and 'bourgeois') means to affront this vanity (so to speak) of Enlightenment: to reproach its fantasies of historical novelty and difference with evidence of its reversion to the supposedly superceded fear-conditioned reflexes of the deep past; here we glimpse what I take to be the most comprehensive and consequential of Horkheimer and Adorno's estrangements of 'dialectic', namely, as we will see, a model of 'dialectic' as driving (or driven) backwards as well as forwards.

A fitting instance of the 'dialectical' undoing of Enlightenment historicism's official story—the more conflicted, again, in being itself a (quasi-? faux-?) *narrative*—is *Dialectic of Enlightenment*'s evocation of the birth of historical awareness itself, as allegorized in the Horkheimer/Adorno reading of the Sirens episode in Homer:[5]

> Their allurement [i.e., that of the Sirens] is that of losing oneself in the past. But the hero to whom the temptation is offered [i.e., Odysseus] has reached maturity through suffering. Throughout the many mortal perils he has had to endure, the unity of his own life, the identity of the individual, has been confirmed for him. The regions of time part for him as do water, earth, and air. For him the flood of that-which-was has retreated from the rock of the present, and the future lies cloudy on the horizon. What Odysseus left behind him entered into the nether world; for the self is still so close to prehistoric myth, from whose womb it tore itself, that its very own experienced past becomes mythic prehistory. And it seeks to encounter that myth through the fixed order of time. The three-fold schema is intended to free the present moment from the power of the past by referring that power behind the absolute barrier of the unrepeatable and placing it at the disposal of the present as practicable knowledge (Cumming 32).

Here Horkheimer and Adorno sketch the emergence, even the institution of a 'fixed order of time', the kernel from which will grow that 'homogeneous time' underpinning the historicism protested in Benjamin's 'Theses on the Philosophy of History'. From the cyclical repetition of the mythical ever-same emerges the 'three-fold schema' of past-present-future: a development explicitly linked to an instrumentalization of affective experience that is also a historicization of it, the conversion of 'allurement' (pleasure, what will become, further instrumentalized and segregated from lived experience in the bourgeois age, 'art') into a dispassionate, disciplined, de-affectualized 'practicable knowledge'. The allurement of the past had threatened grave dangers, chronic in the eternal present of mythic time; and it is this danger that is (enlightenment wants to believe) firmly sequestered behind an 'absolute barrier', relegated to what in a linear (no longer cyclical or recurring) temporality, has thereby been rendered an 'unrepeatable' past—so that the present has delivered itself, by dint of sheer consciousness and will (the Odyssean cunning includes self-management), from dangers that had once seemed chronic, cyclical, inescapable, the very figure of repetition, or indeed, the very thing itself. This instrumentalization institutes the *chorismos* of 'art' (pleasure) from history, narratively conceived, as 'practicable knowledge':

> So long as art declines to pass as cognition and is thus separated from practice, social practice tolerates it as it tolerates pleasure. But the Sirens' song has not yet [i.e., in the epic time or consciousness of the *Odyssey*] been rendered powerless by reduction to the condition of art. The Sirens know 'everything that ever happened on this so fruitful earth', including the events in which Odysseus himself took part, 'all those things that Argos' sons and the Trojans suffered by the will of the gods on the plains of Troy'. While they directly evoke the recent past, with the irresistible praise of pleasure as which their song is heard, they threaten the patriarchal order which renders to each man his life only in return for his full measure of time. Whoever falls for their trickery must perish, whereas only perpetual presence of mind forces an existence from nature. Even though the Sirens know all that has happened, they demand the future as the price of that knowledge, and the promise of the happy return is the deception with which the past ensnares the one who longs for it (Cumming 32–3).

Here we see how the 'broken promise' of art got broken, such that today 'Neutralization is the social price of aesthetic autonomy' (*AT* 228). We see also how the coming to consciousness of epic narrativity encodes the dynamic that will eventuate in the 'ideas of history' (to recall Collingwood) as 'enlightened' ('demythologized', 'demythologizing') cultural self-expression and self-idealization, but also the individual 'case history' that will eventually culminate (and diagnose, in making the unconscious conscious, in recovering the 'irrecoverable') the price of that culture's construction of subjectivity: 'Men had to do fearful things to themselves before the self, the identical, purposive, and virile nature of man, was formed, and something of that recurs in every childhood' (Cumming 33).

Hence the irony that the instrumentalizing story-telling meant to secure survival, projected in terms of narrative event and deliverance, should regress— 'dialectic of enlightenment' with a vengeance—to the cyclical, recurrent repetitions of domination and exploitation that the West's supposedly 'linear' (progressive) history prides itself on having overcome. By way of a quote from the master/slave section of the *Phenomenology*, the conspectus dilates to encompass labor, and the less-heroic context of Odysseus in his relations with his vassals:

Just as he [Odysseus] cannot yield to the temptation of self-abandonment, so, as proprietor, he finally renounces even participation in labor, and ultimately even its management, whereas his men—despite their closeness to things—cannot enjoy their labor because it is performed under pressure, in desperation, with senses stopped by force. The servant remains enslaved in body and soul; the master regresses. No authority has yet been able to escape paying this price, and the apparent cyclical nature of the advance of history is partly explained by this debilitation. . . . adaptation to the power of progress involves the progress of power, and each time anew brings about those degenerations which show not unsuccessful but successful progress to be its contrary. The curse of irresistible progress is irresistible regression (Cumming 35–6).

The language of psychoanalysis here (the fixation of instincts [*die Fixierung der Instinkte*], repression [*Unterdrückung*], regression [*Regression*]) brings explicitly into view a subtext implicit from the mention of the 'irrecoverable past', associating the mythic foretime, the Sirens' promise of pleasure, the descent to Hades, etc., with renunciation, the unconscious, the repressed. With, in other words, that which will return, either as neurosis to torment us, or as new consciousness bearing, Horkheimer and Adorno imply, utopian potential, when repression can be lifted, the instincts unfixed, when the *chorismos* of affect from cognition can be reversed, when to follow the phantasmagoria of the Sirens might be gain, not loss.

But such utopian imaginings are ideological in a milieu in which, as we've just read, 'The curse of irresistible progress is irresistible regression' (Cumming 36). In the concluding paragraph of the 'Progress' essay, Adorno retrojects this bleak vision back onto Hegel and Marx, two dialecticians often chided for their (supposed) Panglossian 'optimism':

Hegel as well as Marx bore witness to the fact that even the dialectical view of progress needs correction. The dynamic they taught is conceived not as a simple dynamic per se, but on the contrary as one unified with its opposite, with something steadfast, in which alone a dynamic first becomes legible at all. Marx . . . likewise rejected . . . the absolutization of the dynamic in the doctrine of labor as the single source of societal wealth, and he conceded the possibility of a relapse into barbarism. . . . [T]he dialectical taboo on concept-fetishes . . . extends even to the category that used to soften up reification: progress, which deceives as soon as it—as a single aspect—usurps the whole. The fetishization of progress reinforces its particularity, its restrictedness to techniques. If progress were truly master of the whole, the concept of which bears the marks of its violence, then progress would no longer be totalitarian. Progress is not a conclusive category. It wants to cuts short the triumph of radical evil, not to triumph as such itself. A situation is conceivable in which the category would lose its meaning, and yet which is not the situation of universal regression that allies itself with progress today. In this case, progress would transform itself into the resistance to the perpetual danger of relapse. Progress is this resistance at all stages, not the surrender to their steady ascent (*CM* 160).

The irony of that last sentence—resistance to 'steady ascent'—means, for Adorno, resistance to narrative itself, and to the meanings, the whole imaginary of 'progress', that narrative has sustained so ineluctably and, so far, so illusorily—so ideologically. 'Resistance', though, sounds chronic: altogether different, the 'other' indeed, of those 'Messianic' moments 'blasted out' of the 'continuum' of 'homogeneous time'. Such moments of breakthrough might attractively posit themselves as moments of liberation *from* narrative, but resistance? What would resistance without narrative look like? Stoic, presumably: resolute—a kind of hardened and enduring *durée*. 'Duration', Adorno advises in the Mahler book, 'is in itself the imago of meaning . . .' (*MMP* 73). Perhaps this is the suggestion to conclude with here, the model or figure for the agitated-but-static condition performed or enacted in *Dialectic of Enlightenment*'s strangely narrative antinarrative, in which pseudo-narrative gestures perform a 'dialectical mimesis' not only of the progressive tradition and of its great Hegelian founding document, the *Phenomenology*, but also of the failure of that tradition, the failure of history and of narrativity as such.

'Music'

. . . the essay approaches the logic of music, that stringent and yet aconceptual art of transition, in order to appropriate for verbal language something it forfeited under the domination of discursive logic—although that logic cannot be set aside but only outwitted within its own forms by dint of incisive subjective expression.

(NL1 22)

The 'poetics of standstill' we've been tracing operates in *Dialectic of Enlightenment* to great and stirringly dystopian effect. I want now to turn to a very different kind of 'model' for Adorno's non- or anti-narrative practice of critique: the model or models Adorno generates for himself in his engagement with music. The kinesis and volatility of Adorno's agitated prose has long invited the figuration of music, so much so, indeed, that Fredric Jameson has recommended a moratorium on the 'musical analogies that have become virtually a convention of Adorno criticism' (*Late Marxism* 60–2). If what I attempt here cannot evade the taint of mere analogy, I take comfort from Adorno's own extravagant ambition for the unfinished Beethoven project:

> The Beethoven study must also yield a philosophy of music, that is, it must decisively establish the relation of music to conceptual logic. Only then will the comparison [of Beethoven's oeuvre] with Hegel's *Logic*, and therefore the interpretation of Beethoven, be not just an analogy but the thing itself (*B* 11).

Of course, my aim here must be considerably more modest: to draw from Adorno's writings on music some models that seem suggestive, although Adorno resists making the connection more than implicit, for the methods and ambitions of Adorno's own writing or 'compositional' labor and practice. But this theme is sufficiently pervasive in Adorno to have surfaced in every chapter of this study so far—progressive and critical Schoenberg versus reactionary, ideological Stravinsky in *Philosophy of New Music*; the fact, and the interpretive consequences, of the 'musical quality' of Hegel's style (*HTS* 122); the assimilation of Hölderlin's music-like parataxis to Beethoven's 'technique of [proto-Schoenbergian] seriation' (*NL2* 135). But it is more than pervasive; it is programmatic, and the grand unfinished project of a 'philosophy of music' was surely Adorno's ruling intellectual ambition or passion lifelong.[6]

We've seen the conflicted motif of 'standstill'—at once an ideological condition to be protested *and* a strategy of 'dialectical mimesis' to be dared—in Adorno's practice-and-theory of a non- or anti-narrative narrativity; his music criticism similarly resists 'narrative' as a category applicable to music, and recurs chronically to the cognate problematic of music's atemporal temporality. In his last decade Adorno found in music models that suggested ways to loosen the dystopian strictures of his own 'poetics of standstill', the imperative by which 'the unhappy consciousness of critique' must scrupulously refuse hope, lest such conjurings offer a false consolation, 'an imaginary resolution to a real contradiction'. But our starting-point here must be, again, Adorno's refusal of any 'ideology of the aesthetic' that would disjoin art from critique (theory, philosophy)—and we might note here that in this ideology throughout the nineteenth century, 'music' plays a salient role, displacing poetry from its immemorial place at the apex of the hierarchy of the arts. The reason for this elevation, from Kierkegaard to Pater and beyond, was precisely music's non-verbal, therefore non-discursive character. If all the arts 'aspire to the condition of music', as Pater thought, it's because music's escape from the cognitive and the conceptual unavoidably attaching to language provided an ideal for the other arts to emulate. Adorno's lifelong project of a 'philosophy of music' (the never-finished Beethoven book was to be the realization) was but a special case of his effort to rejoin what the *chorismos* of the several humanities had so drastically sundered. As we have seen, Adorno asserts a 'critical' force for music in the early (1932) essay, 'On the Social Situation of Music':

> Music will be better, the more deeply it is able to express—in the antinomies of its own formal language—the exigency of the social condition and to call for change through the coded language of suffering. . . . The task of music as art thus enters into a parallel relationship to the task of social theory. . . . solutions offered by music in this process stand equal to theories (*EM* 393).

But I'm not proposing here to test the symmetrical possibility that Adorno's writing practice means to perform its 'theories' in ways we might usefully think of as 'musical'. Rather, I want to identify some tensions in Adorno's writings on music that seem to me to illuminate tensions in Adorno's own critical theory and practice—and particularly in connection with this chapter's theme, *narrative*.

The tension between narrative and anti-narrative manifests throughout Adorno's writings on music, because music is, on Adorno's showing, a temporal art, but a non-narrative one: it develops or unfolds in time, yet Adorno resists any formulation that would assign or allow its trajectory—in the received vocabulary, its 'variation' or 'development'—a *narrative* significance or interest. That said, I'd better caution here that Adorno's writing on music frequently has a crypto-narrative spin, an effect (so to speak) of 'narrative despite itself', because Adorno deploys—or 'constellates'—historical examples (Bach, Haydn, Beethoven, Schubert, Wagner, Schoenberg) in which a received historical narrative is already implicit, a narrative Adorno must acknowledge, will he or nill he, and which, therefore, he had better, when he can, exploit, and critique. Hence Adorno's aspiration to a 'philosophy of music' entails, as we'll see, a 'philosophy of history of music' as well. Adorno conjures this spectral narrativity in ways that acknowledge that his own anti-narrative sensibility produces the tension of anachronism with respect to past eras—call it a kind of 'presentism' that can recall how Benjamin's Messianic historian 'grasps the constellation which his own era has formed with an earlier one' (*Illuminations* 263). But however a given composer or composition stands in the history of music, Adorno tends to regard any musical composition as a structure that, though it can realize itself only temporally, in performance, has its meaning and significance in some sense outside of time.

I want now to assemble some of Adorno's fragments on Beethoven that will summon and 'constellate' the relevant issues—the 'standstill' of art and its relation, via the 'fungibility' or 'exchange' motif, to the 'dialectics at a standstill' of bourgeois ('enlightenment') society, the structural atemporality of a work of music as opposed to its quasi-narrative temporality in performance:

> The history of great bourgeois music at least since Haydn is the history of the interchangeable, or fungible: that no individual thing exists 'in itself', and

everything only in relation to the whole. The truth and untruth of this music can be determined from the solution it offers to the question of fungibility— which has both a progressive and a regressive tendency. The question in all music is: How can a whole exist without doing violence to the individual part? (*B* 34)

The motif of 'fungibility' here dovetails with that of 'exchange' and the 'removal of time' that we saw above from the essay explaining or exposing the false consciousness inscribed in the (narrative) ideology of 'progress'. In music, 'story' tends to function as 'program', an externality given in advance that distorts both the labor of composition and the process of listening. To have evaded this pitfall is the genius of Beethoven:

Beethoven's achievement lies in the fact that in his work—and in his alone— the whole is never external to the particular but emerges solely from its move- ment, or rather, is this movement. In Beethoven there is no mediation between themes, but, as in Hegel, the whole, as pure becoming, is itself the concrete mediation. (NB: In Beethoven there are really no transitional ele- ments, and the inventive richness of, especially, the young Beethoven has the essential purpose of dissolving the topological existence of individual themes. There are so many that none can make itself autonomous . . .) This achieve- ment becomes impossible if the development of the *material as a whole* . . . if its increasing richness, enforces an emancipation of melodies. To the eman- cipated melody the whole is no longer immanent. But it remains a task con- fronting this bad individuality. In this way the whole does violence to the particular (*B* 24–5).

For Adorno, narrative would be an epitome of 'totalization', in which 'the whole does violence to the particular', the details selected, shaped, subordinated, to the needs of 'the story'. A subtler provocation here is the suggestion that the relation of part and whole manifested in 'pure becoming' is not mediated, but 'is itself the concrete mediation': hence in Hegel as in Beethoven what is conventionally taken as a narrative process, one characterizable indeed as the emergence (and 'emancipation') of 'individual themes' or 'melodies', is not really narrative at all—so that a narrative acceptation of it would be an ideologi- cal appearance or delusion—because the condition of immanence is only illusorily breached. In other words, Adorno prizes Hegel and Beethoven not as offering models of 'emancipation', but as enacting the immanence within which every seeming-'emancipation' can be only a symptom of false conscious- ness—'an imaginary solution to a real contradiction'. ('Music withstands doom', Adorno advises, 'by being it' [*B* 166].) For Adorno, the relation of whole to part is not, as many Hegelians (and often enough Hegel himself can seem to) avow, one of narrative mediation moving ineluctably to resolution, but of immanent contradiction, 'dialectic at a standstill', for which 'concrete mediation' would be not the resolution, but rather a more shocking and heart-breaking name: no mere model, but rather an enactment or instantiation of 'the thing itself', of 'the way the whole does violence to the particular'.

As in the passage above from the 'Progress' essay, 'exchange equivalence' (a.k.a., 'fungibility') is the locus of the contradiction between an emergent (false?) consciousness of individuality and an ideology of reification and commodification which, as precondition for the valuation of everything in terms of exchange value, reduces all quality to quantity:

> [In music after Beethoven] it is worth noting the paradox whereby the tendency towards fungibility (or interchangeability)—as the organizing principle of a musical whole—increases together with the impossibility of fungibility, that is, with the uniqueness of the particular detail. This paradox circumscribes the whole recent history of music up to Schoenberg. The twelve-tone technique is probably its totalitarian resolution—hence my misgivings about this technique.
>
> Wagner knew of this paradox in his own production. His music is an attempt to resolve it by reducing the particular to fungible basic forms—fanfares and chromatic elements. But the historical state of the material gave him the lie. The fanfares merely impersonate aridity. Not even poverty can be reinstated—what in Beethoven was bare but significant in the sense used by Goethe can look merely threadbare even in Schubert; in Wagner it has become theatre and in Strauss kitsch (*B* 25).

The 'misgivings' about Schoenberg's 'totalitarian' technique are evidently the downside (as with the petrifications of Benjamin's Medusa-gaze) of what, in 'Schoenberg and Progress', Adorno commends as Schoenberg's achievement: that, as 'As an artist, he wins back freedom for mankind. The dialectical composer brings the dialectic to a halt' (*PNM* 96; cf. 50 and *B* 16, 21). More readily intelligible are the comments on Wagner, whose deployment of the *leitmotiv* attests an imagination predicated on the persistence of a Schopenhauerian steady-state (not to say 'identity') to which all the futile *Schwärmerei* of 'the will' must periodically—'ultimately'—default. Adorno goes on to argue that it is not a matter of Beethoven's volatility devolving into Wagner's stasis; rather Wagner's 'standstill' exposes as illusion what is normatively taken to be Beethoven's prowess in musical 'development':

> . . . in Wagner the elaboration of the model [sc. the 'development'], as expression, takes on the character of a fruitless, compulsive circling. In this, Wagner revealed something of the nature of musical development itself: that the futility which he made explicit is objectively implicit in development as such. This . . . is linked to the *social* nature of work, which is both 'productive', in that it keeps society alive, yet also fruitless, in its blind marking of time

(the tendency to regress to mere reproduction). If the change in the principle of development between Beethoven and Wagner reflects a developmental tendency of the bourgeoisie as a whole, the later phase also tells us something about the earlier one: that development was always inherently impossible, and could succeed only by a momentary paradox (*B* 37).

This fragment, dated by Rolf Tiedemann to 1944, the year *Dialectic of Enlightenment* was completed, evinces the progress/regress 'standstill' so characteristic of that text.

Music and/as 'Composition'

In the writings quoted above, musical 'composition' figures as a rigorously comprehensive labor, 'systematic' in the sense not of obeying an *a priori* mechanism of practice, a 'method' or technique adopted in advance, but of constant attendance on the tension between part and whole. I have often enough spoken of Adorno's 'writing practice'; here we might evoke something of Adorno's own actual labor of writing, the work of 'composition' through which his own texts achieved themselves. The 'Editors' Afterword' to *Aesthetic Theory* quotes some letters of Adorno's describing the process of composition, which, Adorno writes, doesn't really begin until an initial draft has gathered the relevant materials:

> Only then [in revising the first draft] does the real task begin, that is, the final revision; for me the second drafts [note the plural] are always the decisive effort, the first only assembles the raw material. . . : They are an organized self-deception by which I maneuver myself into the position of the critic of my own work, the position that for me is always the most productive (*AT* 363).

Adorno's contrivance of a 'critical' (sc. 'dialectical') relation to his own work *as he writes it* is of course telling, but in the case of *Aesthetic Theory*, the editors explain that the second draft 'was itself only a provisional version' (*AT* 363); and they go on to detail the pains Adorno took over the project:

> First he critically annotated the entire text as a preliminary to the actual revision. This consisted in a detailed handwritten reformulation of the typescript of the dictated material, a reformulation in which no sentence remained unchanged and scarcely one remained where it stood; innumerable passages were added and not a few, some of them lengthy, were rigorously deleted. . . . the division into chapters was relinquished. It was superseded by a continuous text that was to be articulated only spatially . . . (*AT* 363).

Other of Adorno's letters attest the half-expected exigencies that make composition so prodigious a labor, the labor of keeping in productive tension with 'form'—and here is one of the places where Adorno makes explicit the applicability of what he's observing in musical composition to the devices of his own composition:

> It is interesting that in working there obtrudes from the *content* [*Inhalt*] various implications for the form that I long expected but that now indeed astonish me. It is simply that from my theorem that there is no philosophical first principle, it now also results that one cannot build an argumentative structure that follows the usual progressive succession of steps, but rather that one must assemble the whole out of a series of partial complexes that are, so to speak, of equal weight and concentrically arranged all on the same level; their constellation, not their succession, must yield the idea (*AT* 364).

This passage confirms that what Adorno elsewhere calls 'the agency of form' (*NL1* 114) is a dynamic that he means to mobilize for his own work; the opposition of 'constellation' to 'succession' attests the self-consciousness of Adorno's effort, in the temporal medium of writing-and-reading, to resist the temporality of 'succession' in favor of the very different habitus suggested by 'constellation'. In yet another letter, Adorno puts the case negatively: in terms not of what he wants to achieve, but of a formally, quasi-syllogistic 'ineluctable movement from antecedent to consequence' that he must toil to evade or defeat, namely that of (generically speaking) 'the book' as such:

> These difficulties consist in . . . this, that a book's almost ineluctable movement from antecedent to consequence proved so incompatible with the content that for this reason any organization in the traditional sense—which up till now I have continued to follow (even in *Negative Dialectics*)—proved impracticable. The book must, so to speak, be written in equally weighted, paratactical parts that are arranged around a midpoint that they express through their constellation (*AT* 364).

—with which compare a formulation from years earlier (1950): 'In the equidistance of all elements from the centre which I have claimed to be a characteristic of modern music, the dialectic comes to a standstill' (*B* 16), in which again the 'standstill' effect is conditioned upon evading 'succession', temporality, narrative. The announced program of 'paratactical' composition recalls Adorno's late essay on Hölderlin, in which, as we've seen, 'parataxis' encoded (as here) the ambition to evade or circumvent the dynamic whereby the sequential or temporal character of a text begins ('ineluctably') to connote something like a cause-and-effect ordering of the material. Such an effect is an 'agency of [received] form' which it is the subversive aim of Adorno's 'composition' to try to undo or escape via the 'agency of [alternative deployments of] form'.

The 'agency of form' is uniquely instantiated in music, by reason of its non-conceptuality: 'form' is the only agency music has. In the Wagner book (in which 'myth' already connotes ideology, repetition, acquiescence to 'what is' as blind fate, etc.) Adorno allows himself the 'exaggeration' that 'symphonic form'—not any symphony in particular, but simply the form itself —'is the anti-mythological principle par excellence' (*ISW* 125/114). The 'agency of form' undertakes an agon with pre-given elements—in music, inherited formal schemata; in critique, ditto, but also a received repertoire (or history) of problems and responses to them—meant both to evoke ('repeat') them 'immanently' *and* to 'reliquify' them: to render them in all their obduracy, but also to render them plastic to critical and utopian will:

> A main concern of an interpretation of Beethoven is to understand his forms as the product of a combining of pre-ordained schemata with the specific formal idea of each particular work. This is a true synthesis. The schema is not just an abstract framework 'within' which the specific formal concept is realized; the latter arises from the collision between the act of composing and the pre-existing schema. It both stems from the schema and alters, abolishes or 'cancels' it. In this precise sense, Beethoven is dialectical . . . But the reconciliation of these demands, in showing up a contradiction *objectively* contained within the form, finally abolishes the prescribed order. The subject-object relationship in music, therefore, is a dialectic in the *strictest* sense; it is not a tugging at each end of a rope by subject and object, but an *objective* dialectic disconnected from the logic of form as such. It is the actual movement of the concept within the subject matter, which needs the subject only as an agent who complies with necessity out of freedom (but only the free subject can perform this function) (*B* 60–2).

In the locution 'disconnected from the logic of form', the thrust is on 'logic', as implying a compositional *a priori*, pre-given, reified and reifying, that is 'applied' externally—as conceptions of 'form' in criticism typically are. Adorno wants rather, a sense of form as active, as agonistic, as achieving itself *in* the agon with content, rather than as a prescribed shape, given before the fact, into which content will be decanted and thereby shaped, domesticated, pacified. The 'movement' characterized in the next sentence—'the actual movement of the concept within the subject matter'—virtually *is* this 'form':

> In Beethoven's procedures the most profound features of Hegelian philosophy will be discerned, such as the twofold position of 'mind' in the *Phenomenology* as both subject and object. As the latter it is merely observed in its movement; as the former, through observing, it brings the movement about (*B* 62).

Society's stalled dialectic finds its 'dialectical mimesis', I've argued, in a constellational 'stasis' that arrests narrative, or narrativity, itself. Adorno credits

Beethoven with achieving the compositional concomitant of this structural, anti-narrative impulse, so adapting inherited forms and codes to new musical materials that the whole and the part do each other no violence. But at moments Adorno discerns the threat of a dialectical backfire, and of a type we have seen before, in which Beethoven's rigor of 'totalization' seems to impel a dynamic in which 'dialectic at a standstill', as a critical-aesthetic desideratum (because it enacts a 'dialectical mimesis' of ideological stasis in the culture at large, a feat it takes a Beethoven or a Schoenberg to achieve), risks succumbing to the 'frozen', petrified stasis it meant to reliquify, as if Prometheus's agon were to leave him at last muscle-bound and rigid, cramped and stiffened by his long ordeal into an adamantine emanation, like Medusa's own mirror-image in Perseus's shield, of the rock he is chained to. We have seen above Adorno's worry that Schoenberg's serialism may less reliquify the 'fungibility' problem than deliver itself to a 'totalitarian resolution' of it (*B* 12). Nor is Beethoven himself immune from this liability: 'Hitler and the Ninth Symphony: Be encircled, O ye millions' (*B* 77). In earlier chapters we have noted the danger in 'immanent critique'—the crux of the debate between Lukács and Adorno—of the volatility by which critical negation becomes ideological symptom:

> The connection [in Beethoven] of the parts to the whole, their annihilation in it, and therefore their relation to something infinite in the movement of their finitude, is a representation of metaphysical transcendence, not as its 'image' but as its real enactment, which only partly succeeds—or is it mastered?—because it is *performed* by human beings. This is where the connection between technique and metaphysics—however ill formulated at this stage—is located. Beethoven's art achieves its metaphysical substantiality because he uses technique to manufacture transcendence. This is the deepest meaning of the Promethean, voluntarist, Fichtean element in him, and also of its untruth: the manipulation of transcendence, the *coercion*, the violence (*B* 77–8).

'This', Adorno concludes, 'is probably the deepest insight I have achieved into Beethoven'.

We may ascribe this despair—'Hitler and the Ninth Symphony'—to the date (1942). How the post-war years qualified that despair is too long a story to tell here, but a turning point would be the 1961 essay, 'Vers Une Musique Informelle', which loosens the rigors of 'composition' very much as the nearly contemporaneous 1958 'Essay as Form' tried to loosen those of 'system' and 'method'. But we find Adorno's 'happiest' resolution in his late writings on Mahler, especially the short book, *Mahler: A Musical Physiognomy*, which actually stages a (by Adorno's standards) daringly utopian renewal of narrative.

Return of the (Narrative) Repressed: Adorno's *Mahler*

Adorno's *Mahler: A Musical Physiognomy* reverses the non- or anti-narrative rule of Adorno's practice: not only embracing narrative as a critical category, but practicing narrativity as a Promethean textual potential. Narrative unbound! As we've seen, Adorno usually characterizes what he calls 'great music'—Beethoven, Schoenberg—as an affair of rigorous 'composition', in which whole and part (universal and particular, totality and fragment) are in continual dialectical interaction, and structural determinants loom largest, in an agon 'alien to time'. In *Dialectic of Enlightenment*, a compromised narrativity enacted the failure, the ideological delusion, of narrative as such. But in *Mahler: A Musical Physiognomy*, Adorno celebrates the Mahler corpus as essentially *narrative*—and makes the case, moreover, in an argument that is itself narrative. The ambivalent problematic (and poetics) of 'standstill' is gone. Here Adorno posits as the 'essential genres in [Mahler's] idea of form' the fundamentally *narrative* (and utopian) categories of 'breakthrough', 'suspension', and 'fulfillment' (*MMP* 41) in agon with their dystopian inversions ('outbreak', 'decay', and 'collapse' [*MMP* 51ff., 122ff., 45]). It is in these terms that Adorno valorizes Mahler's achievement.

But the surprise of *Mahler* is less its theoretical rehabilitation of narrative than the book's own *practice* of narrative. This 'late' work is unique in Adorno's corpus in staging itself explicitly as narrative, with all the baggage I have made that term bear above. In it, most tellingly, the return of what we might call a *narrative* repressed entails as well the return of a *utopian* repressed. The book projects Mahler's oeuvre as itself a development to be narrated, and as an oeuvre enacting problems in a *narrative* way; accordingly, Adorno's discussion must also conduct itself *narratively*—and dramatically, at that. Its first chapter is called 'Curtain and Fanfare', quite as if, in this opening movement, the book itself appropriates the quickening and excitement of the moment when house lights go down, and the orchestra begins to play as the curtain rises. And so forth as the chapter continues: scene one (so to speak) opens on the opening of Mahler's First Symphony, and narrates the development to 'the height of the movement', when suddenly, what had been a distantly heard fanfare 'explodes'.

> It is not so much that this crescendo has reached a climax as that the music has expanded with a physical jolt. The rupture originates beyond the music's intrinsic movement, intervening from outside. For a few moments the symphony imagines that something has become reality that for a lifetime the gaze from the earth has fearfully yearned for in the sky. With it Mahler's music has kept faith . . . If all music, with its first note, promises that which is different, the rending of the veil, [Mahler's] symphonies attempt to withhold it no longer, to place it literally before our eyes (*MMP* 5).

Adorno evidently means 'the symphony' to evoke the whole genre and its history, not merely Mahler's First—indeed, that the whole of art, and of non-art too, feels the force of this transfiguration, since Adorno dares to evoke it in terms ('beyond the music's intrinsic movement, intervening from outside') that clearly make this utopian 'rupture' more than merely aesthetic. At issue is not some mere evocation or mimesis or representation or expression of that 'rending of the veil' that the earth has been 'fearfully yearning' for: no, Adorno insists, Mahler has here managed 'to place it literally before our eyes'. Mahler's art achieves a 'rupture', a 'breakthrough', to something 'beyond' mere art, even 'inimical to art'. But, of course, there's a 'but'; there always is:

> But Mahler's primary experience, inimical to art, needs art in order to manifest itself, and indeed must heighten art from its own inner necessity. For the image corresponding to breakthrough is damaged because the breakthrough has failed, like the Messiah, to come into the world. To realize it musically would be at the same time to attest its failure in reality. It is in music's nature to overreach itself. Utopia finds refuge in no man's land. . . . In the entrapment that music would breach, it is itself entangled as art . . . Music as art transgresses against its truth; but it offends no less if, violating art, it negates its own idea. Mahler's symphonies progressively seek to elude this fate (*MMP* 6).

The second of these two quotations puts the predicament of art (and of critique: of *Geist* at large) in terms any reader of Adorno will find familiar. The novelty is in the first quotation. If the second passage rehearses the thematics of the 'broken promise', the first, quite daringly, limns something of what the promise in its unbroken form would deliver. Or never mind 'would', as if the promise were conditional or contrafactual: Adorno asserts unequivocally that Mahler has 'kept faith'; and hence the success, genuine however short-lived, of the 'breakthrough' this symphony vouchsafes; as Adorno later puts it:

> . . . because Mahler's music keeps the promise, because it is truly consummated where other music . . . attains its climaxes and then, disappointed and disappointing, starts again from below, a yearning is fulfilled with which the unfettered spirit really approaches all music and to which the fettered one only believes itself superior as taste because it has again and again been cheated of it, and most of all in the greatest works of art (*MMP* 43–4).

But back in 'Curtain and Fanfare', Adorno foreshadows the story of how Mahler 'gradually concretizes' the dialectic of his utopia with the ideological condition surrounding and compromising it:

> Aware at the musical level of the crude abstractness of the antithesis between the world's course and the breakthrough, Mahler gradually concretizes it,

and so mediates it, through the internal structure of his compositions (*MMP* 9).

This is the story Adorno's opening chapter tells, the story of Mahler's oeuvre as it develops from symphony to symphony, a story that begins in hope that redemptive powers—of art, of affect, of sympathy with the downtrodden and the impotent—can achieve a 'breakthrough' that will intervene in 'the course of the world' (i.e., ideology, repetition, 'fate') in 'Messianic' fashion (*MMP* 6). This hope animates Mahler's first four symphonies; but with the Fifth, a new sense of fatality and despair—of the futility and the limitations of musical mastery itself—enter Mahler's dialectic (*MMP* 11), and the hopes of the younger Mahler's work now commence to take on the tinctures of Adorno's chronic thematization of 'the broken promise'. In Adorno's telling, this story turns on the Fifth Symphony, in which a crucial 'breakthrough' fanfare, rather than renewing the (so to speak) *naive* 'breakthrough' so potent in the earlier symphonies, enacts, as if conscious of it for the first time, the becoming-aesthetic—*merely* 'aesthetic'—of what had begun to offer so much more-than-aesthetic promise. Here the attempted breakthrough only

> reveals the impossibility of the possible even in the midst of mastery. The apparition is marred by appearances. What ought to be entirely itself bears the mark of consolation and exhortation: reassurance from something not present. Impotence attends manifested power; were it the promised and no longer the promise it would not need to assert itself as power. . . .

Nevertheless, symphonies Five through Nine do not *altogether* despair: Adorno finds in them, and praises, accents of hope that persist despite, and beside, full acknowledgment that 'the course of the world' stands in antithesis to the ethos of 'breakthrough'—and so, in the Fifth Symphony, and prophetically for the rest of Mahler's work,

> The end has not been achieved. The utopian identity of art and reality has foundered. But it is to this failure that Mahler's music henceforth addresses itself, no less earnestly in its technical progress than in its disenchanting experience. The artistic obligation that occasioned his aversion to the program constrains him to elaborate the breakthrough in strictly musical terms, to shed his naïve hostility to art, until the breakthrough itself becomes an intrinsic element of form. However, his concept is not inviolable. It is in the logic of composition to criticize what it seeks to represent; the more achieved the work, the poorer grows hope, for hope seeks to transcend the finitude of the harmoniously self-sufficient work. Something of this dialectic is present in all that is called maturity, unqualified praise of which is always corruptible by resignation. This is the affliction of aesthetic judgment. Through the insufficiency of the

successful work the insufficient one, condemned by that judgment, becomes significant (*MMP* 11–12).

Adorno's chronic dialectic of the aesthetic: to the extent that the aesthetic will-to-'harmonious self-sufficiency' succeeds, the aesthetic becomes a 'finitude' that will require a 'breakthrough' to transcend, except that by then 'break-through' itself will have been aestheticized—routinized, familiarized, domesti-cated, which is to say instrumentalized for ideological purposes—into a 'strictly musical' effect, a mere 'intrinsic element of form'. Aesthetic 'success' becomes a kind of failure, to be achieved only by a renunciation of artistic mastery that must then appear as a failure to be redeemed, if at all, only in the failure's having been deliberate: a protest against the familiarizations of 'aesthetic judgment'.

But, as in *Dialectic of Enlightenment*, what the thesis argues, the form qualifies: for Adorno stages all of this *narratively*, as a story that he has here appointed himself to tell, this very story we are reading, in which *narrative* figures as both a principle theme *and* as, itself, a narrative actant. This is emphatically *not* a half-conscious default to a storytelling mode. In *Mahler* Adorno explicitly 'makes thematic' the issue and the stakes of narrative and its 'agency of form' (*NL2* 114). Again, Adorno forgrounds as 'essential genres in [Mahler's] idea of form' (*MMP* 41) the narrative, and narrative-making 'categories' (41, 44) of 'break-through', 'suspension', and 'fulfillment'; elsewhere in the book, further elabo-rations of these basic 'categories' (e.g., 'rupture' [5], 'collapse' [45], 'intervening from outside' [5]) abound. And frequently the various *actants* of the story Adorno tells act as subjects of the verb par excellence of narrative, 'become'— e.g., in the book's first paragraph: 'Instead of illustrating ideas, [Mahler's sym-phonies] are destined concretely to become the idea' (4). The book's third chapter, called 'Characters', urges that Mahler's musical forms be seen as just such *actants*—'characters'—conferring on musical 'form' itself a (narrative) 'agency'. The next chapter of the book, called 'Novel', argues that Mahler's work is novel-like in making itself from the bottom up, rather than on the top-down model of the compositional practice of Beethoven. In this, Adorno suggests, Mahler seized an opportunity opened by a certain decadence in the symphonic form itself:

> Immediate and mediated elements are coupled because the symphonic form no longer guarantees musical meaning, both as a compelling set of relation-ships and as a repository of truth, and because the form must seek that mean-ing. From a kind of basic musical existence, popular music, are to be derived the mediations by which alone existence is justified as meaningful.

Mahler's brilliance was to achieve a liberty from precedent conventions of sonata form akin to that of the breakout of the novel from the stylized conventions of romance; and his refusal to assume any (merely formal) 'justification' *a priori* aligns him with materialism: 'Thus, in historical-philosophical terms, Mahler's form approaches that of the novel' (*MMP* 61). Adorno promptly adduces 'the novel of novels, Flaubert's *Madame Bovary*'—a first indication that Adorno here restores to the novel as a genre all the heroic (and utopian) credit of the golden age of nineteenth-century realism, and in terms that Lukács himself could endorse. The novel figures here as the genre that escapes genre, the literary vehicle for explorations whose findings aren't given in advance. This commitment to discovering the *novum*, the not-already-known, is, so to speak, *meta-* to mere narration 'as usual':

> It is not that the music wants to narrate, but that the composer wants to make music in the way that others narrate. By analogy with philosophical terminology this attitude would be called nominalist. The movement of the philosophical concepts begins from the bottom . . . with the facts of experience . . . instead of composing from above, from an ontology of forms [as does, e.g., Beethoven]. To this extent Mahler works decisively toward the abolition of tradition. At the bottom of the musical novel form lies an aversion that must have been felt long before Mahler, but that he was the first not to repress. It is an aversion to knowing in advance how the music continues. Knowing it offends musical intelligence, spiritual nervosity, Mahlerian impatience (*MMP* 62).

In short, 'knowing in advance how the music continues' rules out the *novum*, the 'new', the not already known: that which can be reached only through 'breakthrough' and 'rupture', which is to say, everything whose advent or event can be conceptualized, let alone realized, only *narratively*, in before-and-after terms. Per contra, the passage to that future *novum* is opened in Mahler's Utopian 'breakthrough'. Adorno asserts this 'progressiveness' as Mahler's exploration of 'the question of the possibility of a kind of musical novel in several volumes', to which Mahler 'responded with inexorable construction' (79). Adorno casts Mahler's achievement of a novelistic musical *oeuvre* as a self-consciousness, or even self-authorship, that manifests also as self-critique—with the caveat that the reflexive 'self' here is that of the unfolding work, not of the composer's private subjectivity:

> That each of Mahler's works criticizes its predecessor makes him the developing composer par excellence; if anyone, it is in Mahler's far from copious oeuvre that one can speak of progress. . . . Mahler's hard developmental line, like that of major exponents of the New Music, writes musical history as the composer progresses from work to work (*MMP* 84).

Here is a 'progress' that really progresses: gets somewhere, develops, unfolds, changes. It is not, as in the 'Progress' essay, mere shuffling of 'fungibilities', leaving the 'ever-same' in place.

An index of Adorno's enthusiasm for Mahler is that it can make him seem to derogate from two of his 'classical' idols, Beethoven and Schoenberg. But the chronology is telling here: Mahler, as a 'materialist' composer of what Adorno calls 'novel symphonies' is both preceded *and* followed by 'classical' composers, Beethoven and Schoenberg, whose work is (as we'll see in a moment) 'incapable' of Mahler's drama of 'breakthrough' and 'rupture' because their 'classical' ethos of composition obeys the 'economic principle' of bourgeois 'equivalence exchange'. That reified and reifying 'classicist' musical practice, writes Adorno, 'is consigned to the past by Mahler' (*MMP* 14)—but only temporarily, it seems, since the sequel is the great modernist 'classicist', Schoenberg. The twentieth century 'progressed' to utter regression, in ways the non-narrative faux-narrativity of *Dialectic of Enlightenment* affects to enact. As would, in Adorno's account, the compositional closed systems of Schoenberg, the 'dialectical composer', Adorno calls him, whose achievement is that 'he brings the dialectic to a halt' (*PNM* 96). Schoenberg epitomizes that *non-* or *anti-*narrative ethos Adorno poses as the only possible response to the steady-state nightmare of modernity: 'dialectics at a standstill' as an ideological condition to be at once protested and re-enacted, 'repeated' and 'reliquified' in a 'dialectical mimesis'.

Narrative, Music, Philosophy of History

Mahler's 'novel symphonies', in short, intervene between the closed (non-narrative) compositional systems of Beethoven before him, and of Schoenberg after him. In *Mahler*, Adorno improvises a 'historical-philosophical' scheme—a narrative constellation, we might say—that sets Mahler in relation not only to these 'classicist' composers, but also aligns the resulting array with masters and master themes in philosophy and the philosophy of history, in which Beethoven is assimilated rather to Kant and 'philosophical idealism' than to Hegel. When Adorno says that 'In historical-philosophical terms, Mahler's form approaches that of the novel' (*MMP* 61), he intimates a 'historical-philosophical' constellation—Kant, Beethoven, the novel, Schoenberg—in whose arrangement each element stands in fructive tension with all the others. Speaking as a non-philosopher, I will admit that among the very most difficult parts of Adorno's project for me to digest is his career-long attempt to coordinate or constellate philosophy and music. His effort to find the ozone where the two domains interfuse produces some of his most stratospheric and impenetrable writing, and I often simply cannot follow his impassioned pursuit of the senses in which each of these two activities could be said to be the other by other means. In *Mahler*, Adorno's efforts in this regard yield to my understanding as almost none of his other such efforts do—perhaps because, again, of the book's narrative habitus: here, the dialectic of music and philosophy is rendered as a story, integrating the philosophy with the more familiar (perhaps familiarizing) art form, the novel. These passages offer a historical-philosophical motivation for

Adorno's own practice at large, as well as themselves enacting a narrative illustrating Adorno's historical-philosophical particular point in this book.

The first of the two principle passages I will consider comes early, in the book's
first chapter. Adorno is explaining that even as early as the First Symphony,
Mahler's art 'reveals but does not resolve the tensions' within the music—a
practice that departs from the totalizing compositional habitus of Beethoven
in which all elements are integrated, reconciled, 'harmonized'. Beethoven
thus elaborates a *structure*; his 'development' is not a *narrative* development.
Beethoven's compositions are temporal, but (so to speak) 'as if' synchronic.
Mahler's musical unfoldings *are* narrative, and Mahler thus achieves a *novum*
whose novelty—whose 'breakthrough'—enacts itself diachronically, in the
unfoldment of something unforeseen at the outset, something not a compositional *donnée* from the start:

> The recapitulation after the breakthrough cannot be the simple recapitula-
> tion formally required. The return that breakthrough evokes must be its
> result: something new. To prepare for this musically, a new theme is evolved
> in the development . . . and then . . . it dominates the later development to
> emerge retrospectively, as it were, at the return of the tonic, as the main
> theme which, at the time, it never was. . . .
>
> Viennese classicism was incapable of this antithesis, as was any musical
> attitude to which the concept of philosophical idealism could be applied.
> For Beethoven's mighty logic, music composed itself as a seamless identity, an
> analytical judgment. The philosophy informing such music began, at its
> Hegelian apogee, to feel the spur of the new idea. In a note . . . in [Hegel's]
> *Science of Logic*, the grounds of scientific thought . . . are criticized for not
> moving 'off the spot', amounting to tautologies [cf. this theme in *Dialectic of
> Enlightenment*] . . . If music indeed has more in common with dialectical than
> with discursive logic it seeks in [Mahler] to attain what philosophy [i.e., Kant,
> and more successfully, more narratively, Hegel] strives with Sisyphean labors
> to wrest from traditional thought, from concepts hardened to a rigid identity.
> [Mahler's] Utopia is the forward motion of the past and the not-yet-past in
> becoming. As it was for Hegel in his critique of the principle of identity, truth
> for Mahler is the Other [i.e., the non-identical] . . . To be is to have become,
> as against merely becoming. The economic principle of traditional music,
> however, its kind of determination, exhausts itself in exchanging one thing
> for another, leaving nothing behind. It 'comes out' but has no outcome.
> Anything new that it cannot assimilate it shuns. Seen in this way even great
> music before Mahler [i.e., even Beethoven] was tautological. Its correctness
> was that of a system without contradictions. It is consigned to the past by
> Mahler (*MMP* 13–14).

Just as Hegel broaches the 'new idea' by narrativizing Kant, and moving 'dialectically' beyond his 'analytic judgments', Mahler achieves a dynamic that departs

from Beethoven insofar as the development of the whole is not inscribed in advance, implicit in the opening themes, but achieves breakthrough and rupture, such that new themes incite a reevaluation, well into the piece, of just what it was the opening movements portended in the first place. 'Philosophical idealism', in making mind the origin of everything, reinvents the apparatus of Platonic 'realism' so as to reinscribe its 'discursive' or 'analytic' (not 'dialectical') 'logic' in which the law of non-contradiction reigns supreme, in which the *novum* that cannot be assimilated is shunned, tensions or contradictions are repressed or falsely resolved, and the labor of thought devolves into tautology. If the mind originates all, then all development is in some sense 'known' (if only to God) in advance. Hegel's historicized inversion of all this, in which Absolute knowledge is not the *arché* but the *telos*—by which Hegel means a *result*—models a process in which there is scope for the genuinely 'new' to appear, in successive unfoldings.

Hegel thus anticipates, and Mahler enacts in music, the particular World-historical mission whose principle agent or actant is the novel, the narrative art form par excellence. As we have seen, Mahler composes 'from the bottom . . . instead of composing from above, from an ontology of forms'; like the novel itself, Mahler's 'musical novel form' evinces a 'nominalism, which no longer permits any harmonious synthesis with a preconceived totality' (*MMP* 62). Beethoven's compositional practice of 'development'—an epitome of 'composing from above, from an ontology of forms'—enacts sheer structure ('discursive logic'), setting whole and part, universal and particular, in necessary relations that are temporal, but without being narrative. (The argument of the Mahler book thus reverses the valences of the central premise running through the Beethoven fragments.) Adorno does suggest, however, that at the very end of his career, in the late quartets, Beethoven anticipates something like the 'nominalist' and 'materialist' narrative temporality of the novel and of Mahler's 'musical novel form'; Adorno passes directly from that observation to a 'historical-philosophical' assimilation of the novel to Mahler and to Nietzsche:

What induced [Beethoven], after the grandiosely retrospective first movement of the ninth Symphony, to write the last quartets may not have been entirely different from the obscure instinct that motivated Mahler long before the years of his mastery: he was clearly profoundly impressed by the late Beethoven, above all by op. 135. Since Kant and Beethoven, German philosophy and music had been a single system. What it could not embrace, its corrective, took refuge in literature: the novel . . . until the category of life, etiolated as *Bildung* and usually reactionary, also became assimilable to philosophy around the turn of the century. In contrast, the originality of Mahler's music takes up Nietzsche's insight that the system and its seamless unity, its appearance of reconciliation, is dishonest. His music takes issue with extensive life, plunges with closed eyes into time, yet without installing life as a substitute metaphysics [as in Schopenhauer and Wagner], in parallel to the objective tendency of the novel. His potential to do so derived from the partly prebourgeois feudal, partly Josephinistically skeptical Austrian air, untouched by German idealism, while symphonic integrity was still present enough to protect him from an attitude to form that made concessions to a weakly atomistic mode of listening. . . . In the productive conflict of the contradictory elements his art flourishes. That is why it is so foolish to patronize him as a composer caught between ages (*MMP* 64–5).

A few pages on Adorno remembers Mahler's investment in Dostoevsky (*MMP* 69); cites Balzac and Scott as pioneers of the nominalist/materialist ethos Mahler shares with the novel (*MMP* 71); and in a dozen or so scattered references *passim*, some explicit, some implicit, Adorno assimilates Mahler to his other great utopian favorite, that 'martyr to happiness' (*NL2* 317), Proust (see especially *MMP* 145–7, where Mahler stands to music much as Proust stands to the novel). But the 'classicist' ethos of composition returns—Schoenberg as Beethoven *redivivus*—and Mahler's Dostoevskian, Nietzschean, Proustian experiment is left behind, as if a mere interlude in a still-prevailing Cartesian stasis:

> The classical idea of the symphony takes for granted a definite closed multiplicity just as Aristotelian poetics assumes the three unities. A theme appearing as absolutely new offends its economic principle, that of reducing all elements to a minimum of postulates, an axiom of completeness that music has made as much its own as have systems of knowledge since Descartes's *Discours de la méthode*. Unforeseen thematic components destroy the fiction that music is a pure tissue of deductions, in which everything that happens follows with unambiguous necessity. In this, too, Schoenberg and his school were truer to the classical ideal . . . than was Mahler. . . . [Whereas in the 'classical'] the precedence of the whole over the parts is the uncontested priority of becoming over being . . . in Mahler, conversely, the thematic figure is no more indifferent to the symphonic flow than are the characters in a novel to the dimension of time within which they act. . . . Time passes into [Mahler's] characters and changes them as empirical time alters faces. . . . [whereas the classical symphony] beguiles time by converting it into spirit . . . [*MMP* 71–2]).

Adorno here elaborates, too lengthily to quote, a rich meditation on time, narrative, and 'duration' versus non-narrative temporality. ('[Mahler's novel symphony] enjoys time to the full, abandons itself to it, seeks to make physically measurable time into living duration. Duration is in itself the imago of meaning . . .' [*MMP* 73]) But our point here was to exhibit Adorno easing his ban on the utopian, noting its coincidence with his easing of the ban on narrative. The point about Schoenberg isn't of course, that Schoenberg should have composed in Mahler's fashion; it is that in Schoenberg's historical moment, the utopian possibility had passed, and now composers must seek new ways to make the devices and usages of 'classical' composition enact a (critical) 'dialectical mimesis' of bourgeois culture's 'dialectics at a standstill'. (This view of Schoenberg is consistent from *Philosophy of Modern Music* to *Mahler*.) Schoenberg's example is of course exemplary for Adorno himself; his unique resort to narrative gestures in *Mahler* constitutes its own kind of homage to what he regards as Mahler's great 'breakthrough' achievement, comparable and contemporaneous with that of Proust. After Auschwitz and Hiroshima, evocations of 'utopia' seem especially questionable, especially liable to pose 'false consolations', 'imaginary solutions to real contradictions'. Adorno's homage, late in life, to Mahler, however, implicitly dares to conjure utopian hope as at least a memory, and a still-stirring image of what might yet be: at once an acknowledgment, one more time, of the taboo against utopia, and a renewal of a still-credible instance of its transgression.

And in this (weak) *Aufhebung*—negotiation? conciliation? propiatiation?—of the 'taboo against utopia', we discern too some cognate relief of the 'taboo on narrative'. And hence we can conclude by turning this excursus on music back on the younger Adorno's anti-narrative poetics of standstill. As we've seen, Adorno not only concedes a kind of narrativity to Mahler's *oeuvre*; he stages his own account of Mahler as a kind narrative. This restoration or revival of narrativity is the condition of the utopian hopes late Adorno pins on Mahler, in whose work he allows that 'art's broken promise' comes something like 'true':

> . . . because Mahler's music keeps the promise, because it is truly consummated where other music . . . attains its climaxes and then, disappointed and disappointing, starts again from below, a yearning is fulfilled with which the unfettered spirit really approaches all music and to which the fettered one only believes itself superior as taste because it has again and again been cheated of it, and most of all in the greatest works of art (*MMP* 43–4).

Is it too much to say that Adorno's 'breakthrough' here takes fire from Mahler's own?—to attest that the longing for the utopian persists, that we must not let despair make the promise's 'failure in reality' a foregone conclusion.

A cognate readiness to hope also animates Adorno's late writings on Proust, in whose great novel a kind of narrativity persists or reinvents itself, a narrativity held in suspension within the achronological temporality of Proust's plotting or sequencing of the operations of memory—and we might here recall that among Benjamin's models of the heterogeneous Messianic time evoked in the 'Theses on the Philosophy of History' was Proust's model of how the '*mémoire involontaire*' sublates and relieves the drearier resignations of the (sc. homogeneous) '*mémoire volontaire*' (sections II and III of 'Some Motifs in Baudelaire' [*Illuminations* 157–62; *Baudelaire* 111–17]). In 'late Adorno', these reinscriptions—of utopia, of narrative—dare to conjure the 'promise' evoked by Hegel in the serene tone of his prose, and attested as 'broken promise' in the very different tone of Adorno's more usual 'unhappy consciousness of critique':

> Proust's fidelity to childhood is a fidelity to the idea of happiness, which he would not let himself be talked out of for anything in the world. . . . But because he is not satisfied with any happiness other than complete happiness, his need for happiness becomes a need for the full truth, unimpeded by conventionality. Such truth, however, is pain, disappointment, knowledge of the false life. The story Proust tells is that of happiness unattained or endangered. . . . To the question of the possibility of happiness Proust responds by depicting the impossibility of love. . . . The polarity of happiness and transience directs him to memory. Undamaged experience is produced only in memory . . . and through memory aging and death seem to be overcome in the aesthetic image. But this happiness achieved through the rescue of experience, a happiness that will not let anything be taken from it, represents an unconditional renunciation of consolation. Rather the whole of life be sacrificed for complete happiness than one bit of it be accepted that does not meet the criterion of utmost fulfillment. This is the inner story of *Remembrance of Things Past.* Total remembrance is the response to total transience, and hope lies only in the strength to become aware of transience and preserve it in writing. Proust is a martyr to happiness (*NL2* 316–17).

'A martyr to happiness': an apt formula for Adorno himself, as well as for his image of suffering humanity. This is an 'unhappy consciousness' that remembers what happiness would and should be, and for everybody (not the least of reasons for rejecting the customary sneer at Adorno's 'mandarinism'). If *Dialectic of Enlightenment* enacted the 'performative contradiction' or 'dialectical mimesis' of narrating the failure of narrativity, and of the ideologies of progress in which narrativity is implicated, Adorno's late writings on Mahler and Proust renew the utopian promise (however 'broken') of narrative's critical potential in the historical 'labor of affect and concept', a potential whose activation in (for Adorno's generation) the recent past—indeed, in the high-bourgeois age of the turn of the nineteenth into what would prove the most horrible century yet in human history—allows the hope of its reactivation in some, at present, barely imaginable future. In such a future, Adorno apparently dares to hope, 'the use of history' may narrativize Beethoven, Hegel, and Mahler, as well as Nietzsche and Benjamin and Adorno himself, in ways to 'reliquify' the 'dialectic of enlightenment'. If—or when?—such a future comes, *Dialectic of Enlightenment* itself may for the first time be legible not only as a 'dialectical image' of 'dialectics at a standstill', but also as itself a moment in the narrative of that now unimaginable future's coming to be.

Notes

Introduction: Adorno's Poetics of Critique

[1] To My mind, the best evocations of Adorno's writerly carriage are those of Gillian Rose and Fredric Jameson; but Rose's introduction to Adorno confines discussion of Adorno's 'style' to one chapter (*Melancholy Science* 11–26) of a book otherwise aiming to 'reconstruct his ideas in standard expository format' (*Melancholy Science* x). In Jameson's expansive commentaries, suggestive observations might turn up in any passage about Adorno (but see especially *Marxism and Form* 3–11, 53–8; *Late Marxism* 25–34, 63–72). For Jameson, Adorno epitomizes preoccupation with the style/content problematic, both on the level of theory (where it instances the antagonism of universal and particular, whole and part, abstract and concrete, transcendence and immanence, realism and nominalism), and on the level of writing practice, the level at which Adorno wrestled onto the page those Protean, writhing, 'self-consuming' but also self-multiplying 'dialectical sentences' in which he labored to dramatize the contradictions of his age. After Jameson, Shierry Weber Nicholsen comes closest to considering how Adorno actually writes, but as in Jameson, the interest of the writing practice is tributary to that of the critical theory. In a very different way, Robert Hullot-Kentor honors Adorno's writerly brilliance by taking it, as it were, massively and even aggressively for granted, as a *sine qua non* for any discussion of Adorno. The Adorno-esque vigor of Hullot-Kentor's own prose is itself a kind of *hommage* that becomes the most valuable kind of service in Hullot-Kentor's translations of Adorno.

  The premise of Adorno's brilliant writing, however, has not been universally shared, from such distinguished contemporaries of Adorno's as Karl Popper (see his pages in *PDGS, passim*) and Isaiah Berlin (*Conversations* 49) to the petty 'bad writing' awards of the '90s culture wars (for amusing examples, see Plass 1–6). Alex Thomson voices a reservation more compelling: 'In some ways Adorno's style is his great curse, and his highly condensed formulae can be easily missed as soundbites to be extracted from his texts. Because of their difficulty, knowledge of these gnomic sayings has often substituted for a reading of his works as a whole' (Thomson 122).

[2] But on the authorship of *Dialectic of Enlightenment*, see the 'Afterword' by the German text's most recent editor, Gunzelin Schmid Noerr (translated in Jephcott 217–47; see especially 219–24). Since my focus is on chapter 1 of the book, it is with some chagrin that I report Noerr's conclusion (based on whose filing cabinets contained which typescripts, bolstered by Habermas's report of Gretel Adorno's

memories) that chapter 1 was mostly Horkheimer's work. It's daunting to disagree with a Habermas on such a question, but Habermas's own eye is for 'content', not 'style'—his own writing is devoid of the interest I'm ascribing to Adorno—so my dissent here anticipates dissents from Habermas elsewhere in this study. I agree with Robert Hullot-Kentor in 'Back to Adorno' that Adorno's is the prevailing intelligence on display in the finished chapter (and indeed throughout the book) as we have it; and I'm pleased to cite Gillian Rose's agreement as well (*Judaism and Modernity* 59n18). Martin Jay's chapter on 'The Genesis of Critical Theory' (*Dialectical Imagination* 41–85) presents Horkheimer as the crucial thinker, the idea-source, of the Frankfurt group, but when it comes to the composition of *Dialectic of Enlightenment*, Jay contrasts Horkheimer's near-writer's block with the prolixity of Adorno, 'who continued to write at his characteristically furious pace' (*Dialectical Imagination* 255–6). Adorno's letters to his parents more than confirm this view: much of Horkheimer's own output of this period looks to have been ghost-written (to put it no more strongly) by Adorno, acting as unacknowledged co-author (*LHP* 5, 6, 37, 38n6, 43, 61n1, 71, 72n10, 86, 87n2, 170, 302–3n1). But again, my aim here is to give Horkheimer his due: that *Dialectic of Enlightenment* would not be the brilliant thing it is had it been up to Adorno to write it alone. (For purposes of comparison: contemporaneously with *Dialectic of Enlightenment*, Adorno wrote two texts solo, *Minima Moralia* and *Philosophy of New Music*, both revert to Adorno's customary non-narrative default; and it's no derogation to observe that they lack the drama and tension of *Dialectic of Enlightenment*.) After the *Dialectic*, Horkheimer and Adorno projected a major book on 'dialectical logic' that was never written. *Negative Dialectics* is presumably Adorno's single-handed shot at it; but my point is that Horkheimer's participation would have produced a very different book. Of all Adorno's never-executed projects, this collaboration with Horkheimer is the one I most regret.

Chapter 1: Cathecting Philosophy

[1] Adorno's attempt to validate the 'truth-claim' of the aesthetic is an accepted premise in Adorno commentary (Jay, Jameson, Nicholsen, Wellmer, Zuidervaart et al.), though, as noted in the 'Introduction', opinions differ on the success or failure of Adorno's attempt. The principle dissenter is Rüdiger Bubner, in 'Concerning the Central Idea of Adorno's Philosophy' (in Huhn and Zuidervaart 147–75; Bubner's original [German] title—'Can Theory Be [or Become] Aesthetic?'—had been a rhetorical question to be answered firmly in the negative). Sympathetic commentators tend to paraphrase Adorno's argument; J. M. Bernstein, in *The Fate of Art*, does much more: 'historicizes' it, arguing that against Kant's intention, the 3rd *Critique*'s categories of 'genius', 'the sublime', and '*sensus communis*', fatally compromised the autonomy (the putative up-side of *chorismos*) of the three clearly bounded domains of the true, the good, and the beautiful that Kant had intended the three critiques to establish. Bernstein sees Heidegger, Derrida, and Adorno as converging toward a 'post-aesthetic' appropriation of Kant's own thinking against Kant, a reworking of Kant aimed at restoring to each of the three domains, or at least turning to good account, the losses—the 'aesthetic alienation'—that the

impoverishing privilege of Kantian autonomy has entailed. The book's ambitious thesis is that Adorno, more consequentially than Heidegger or Derrida, engages the aesthetic predicaments Kant set for modernity.

2 For Hegel as a philosopher of happiness, see Forster 11–125. For incisive discussions, see Jarvis, 'The "Unhappy Consciousness" and Conscious Unhappiness' and Bernstein's 'Reply to Simon Jarvis' (both in Browning 57–77); as well as Rose, 'The Comedy of Hegel' and Jarvis's 'Response to Gillian Rose' (both in Browning 105–17). Bernstein extends his argument in 'Negative Dialectic as Fate: Adorno and Hegel' (Huhn 19–50).

3 Adorno's usual code for this condition is 'ego weakness'; particularly relevant here: *H&F* 6, and the speculation, *ibid.*, 206–8, that in current conditions, neither 'responsible subjectivity' nor 'radical evil' are any longer possible.

4 For Adorno's anticipation of this Lacanian-Zizekian take, see *H&F* 209–18.

5 For all those who 'did not know' about the Shoah till afterwards, Adorno treats it as established fact as early as March 1943 (*LHP* 131).

6 An example, in an interestingly similar context, of the usual, becoming-conscious sense: 'The concept of the individual becomes radical in the modern world, the bourgeois world, only when the economy, that is to say, the way in which the lives of human beings are reproduced, is determined by initiative, by labour, a sense of responsibility, the autonomy of individual human beings standing in a relationship built on exchange. "Radical" here means that for centuries, right down to the threshold of our own age, the individual has proved to be the figure through which the universal, that is, the reproduction of the human world, is mediated. Modern history begins with the discovery [the becoming self-conscious] of the individual . . .' (*H&F* 86).

7 For the most psychoanalytically loaded part of the indictment, see 'The Psychotic Aspect' and the sequence 'Depersonalization', 'Hebephrenia', and 'Catatonia' (*PNM* 125–6 and 124–34).

Chapter 2: Rewriting the Dialectic

1 See, e.g., Nicholsen's chapter on 'Configurational [sc. "Constellational"] Form' (*Exact Imagination* 103–36; see especially 105–13, 123–30).

2 Apart from a few asides, Nicholsen considers 'Skoteinos' only briefly (*Exact Imagination* 91–3; *HTS* xxv–xxxiii). J. M. Bernstein (Huhn 19–50) cites 'Skoteinos' for what it implies about Adorno's sense of the limits of 'the concept'; Samuel Weber adduces 'Skoteinos' in connection with how Adorno conceives 'the task of reading' (Weber 86–9); for 'Skoteinos' as a *literary* essay, see Plass 37–41.

3 For Jean-Luc Nancy on this passage, see *Speculative Remark* 10–19; on 'the proposition', see 73–101. For Hamacher's reading, see *Pleroma* 5–8, 78.

4 For a lucid exposition of this aspect of the Kant-Adorno relation and its relevance to Adorno's socio-political concerns, see Huhn, 'Kant, Adorno, and the Social Opacity of the Aesthetic' (Huhn and Zuidervaart 237–57). For a provocative elaboration, see Robert Kaufman, 'Red Kant'.

[5] Cf. Rose's audacious essay, 'From Speculative to Dialectical Thinking: Hegel and Adorno', which turns Adorno's critique of Hegel back on Adorno himself: 'Adorno reduces [Hegel's] *speculative* to *dialectical* thinking, replacing recollections of the whole by judged oppositions' (54)—for Rose, that is, it's not Hegel who betrays the dialectic by making it serve 'identity', but Adorno who betrays 'the speculative' by confusing it with, and confining it to, a reflexively antinomic thought-tic that reifies what Hegel aimed to loosen. Rose goes against the grain in defending Hegel against his detractors from Nietzsche on; see also her brief for (in effect) 'happy consciousness', 'The Comedy of Hegel and the *Trauerspiel* of Modern Philosophy'.

[6] The German: '*Die dialektische Methode, und gerade die vom Kopf auf die Füße gestellte, kann nicht darin bestehen, die einzelnen Phänomene als Illustrationen oder Exempel eines bereits Feststehenden und von der Bewegung des Begriffs selber Dispensierten abzuhandeln; so entartete die Dialektik zur Staatsreligion*' (*GS12* 32–3).

[7] Other passages in which 'becoming dialectical' figures as 'becoming writing': 'In artworks, nothing is literal, least of all their words; spirit is their ether, what speaks through them, or, more precisely, what makes artworks become script' (*AT* 87); 'all artworks are writing, not just those that are obviously such; they are hieroglyphs for which the code has been lost, a loss which plays into their content. Artworks are language only as writing' (*AT* 124); on film's potential to overcome its 'bad immediacy': 'It is [only] in the discontinuity of that movement'—i.e., the making static, slideshow-like, of the screen image—'that the images of the interior monologue resemble the phenomenon of writing . . . [and] may become art' (*CI* 180).

Chapter 3: Writing It New

[1] Still indispensable on 'constellation' as on so much else about Adorno is Susan Buck-Morss, *Origin*; on constellation see especially 90–110. See also Fredric Jameson, *Late Marxism* 54–60; elsewhere Jameson assimilates 'constellation' to 'model' (68); and if I opened by evoking Eisenstein and Pound, Jameson observes that the affinity of 'constellation' with Althusser's '*conjuncture*' makes Adorno 'Althusserian *avant la lettre*' (244). Nicholsen, in *Exact Imagination*, treats 'constellation' under the broader rubric of 'configurational form' (*passim*, but especially 103–36)—a useful reminder that the thematics of 'constellation' can often attach to such cognate terms as 'configuration', 'complex', even 'ensemble' or 'juxtaposition'. For a stimulating mobilization, as opposed to a mere discussion, of 'constellation'—a 'use' rather than a 'mention', if you will—see Bernstein *Fate of Art* 188–224, especially 206. Two rich and audacious recent discussions are Kaufman, 'Lyric Constellation' and Düttmann 88–139. Also useful on Adorno's aesthetics generally is Wolin, 62–79; Paddison has a lengthy chapter called 'Constellations'; see especially 35–7; more specific is Zuidervaart 45–8, 60–4.

[2] See Richard Wolin, 'Benjamin, Adorno, Surrealism' (Huhn and Zuidevaart 93–122).

[3] See also Adorno's first, withdrawn *Habilitation* written under Cornelius at Frankfurt (1927) and as yet unavailable in English, *Der Begriff des Unbewußten in der*

transzendentalen Seelenlehre (*GS1* 79–322); for an account, see Müller-Doohm, 103–6, 510n41; for background, see Claussen 96–8.

4 Adorno writes to Thomas Mann (June 3, 1950) that reading Lukács's *The Young Hegel* is 'among my most depressing recent experiences. One can hardly credit such reification of consciousness in the very man who coined this concept in the first place. Heidegger's essay in "Holzwege" on the *Phenomenology of Spirit* is almost dialectical by comparison. You may count yourself fortunate to be spared this kind of thing' (*AMC* 47). Mann had rendered a pen-portrait of Lukács in the character of Napthta in *The Magic Mountain* (1924).

5 For more on this episode, see Jay, *Dialectical Imagination* 180–1, 202–3, 207–11; Buck-Morss, *Dialectics of Seeing* 73–4; Wiggershaus 210–18; Claussen 236–7.

6 Adorno most movingly sounds this motif in his 1930 essay, 'Mahler Today': see especially *EM* 605, where Mahler's project sounds strikingly like Benjamin's; and cf. 608, where Adorno contrasts Mahler and Schoenberg in ways that suggest an analogy with his sense of the differences between Benjamin and himself.

7 Most valuable for my purposes have been Buck-Morss, *Origins* 66–9 (especially useful in delimiting some crucial differences between Adorno and Horkheimer); Hullot-Kentor, 'Introduction' 105–7; and Bernstein, *Disenchantment and Ethics* 87–90. For a specialized argument for immanent critique as a method at once of interpretation and of aesthetic evaluation, see Menke 136–43. See also Zuidervaart xvii–xx.

8 A similar exasperation drives Lyotard's 'Adorno as the Devil'. Commentators, however, have mostly favored Adorno (though see Hoy in Hoy and McCarthy 158–213). For Fredric Jameson's reaction, see *Late Marxism* 108. For the most thorough study of the Habermas-Adorno standoff, see Morris *passim*; on performative contradiction in particular, see 95–141, especially 118–41. Whitebook makes the Adorno-Habermas impasse the launch point for his thesis that the engagement of psychoanalysis (and aesthetic modernism) with reason's 'other' (Whitebook's titular 'perversion') opens accesses to 'utopia' foreclosed in Habermas's too-formal conception of 'reason', and his 'domestication' and 'deradicalization' of Critical Theory (*Perversion and Utopia* 1–17; see also Whitebook's 'From Schoenberg to Odysseus' 57–64). For an attempt to reconcile Habermas and Adorno, see Honneth. Martin Jay, in 'The Debate over Performative Contradiction: Habermas versus the Poststructuralists' (Honneth et al., 261–79), similarly begins with Habermas's critique of *Dialectic of Enlightenment*, but the essay's main interest is the contrast between Habermas and three poststructuralist thinkers, Michel Foucault, Rodolphe Gasché, and Paul de Man.

9 The richest discussions of Adorno's 'mimesis' are those of Fredric Jameson, who productively assimilates Adorno's problematic binaries—from subject-object to signifier-signified—to the dyad implicit in the relation of 'mimesis', thus at a stroke freeing them, on the model of Benjaminian 'allegory', from the metaphysics attaching to questions of identity, representation (*adaequatio*), substitution, affinity, *Schein* and the like (see Jameson, *Late Marxism* 63–9, 101–5, 167–9, 256n37; and cf. Hullot-Kentor, 'Introduction' 107–8). On relevant psychological usages of 'mimesis', especially its implication in 'compulsion(s) to repeat' resulting from the frustration of mimesis's 'cathartic' aim, see Jay, *Dialectical Imagination* 269–73, and Morgan, linking Adorno with Winnicott (91–4). On the sense in which

'mimesis' can play a (perversely) 'healthy' role in circumstances of social patho-logy—the sense in which harassing Jews can be 'cathartic' for anti-Semites—see Adorno's remarks on the work of Ernst Simmel (*CM* 98, 266, 341n23, 380n13; cf. 91, 111, 139, 301).

[10] Readers familiar with Michael Cahn's 'Subversive Mimesis' will recognize a family resemblance between his refunctioning of Adorno's 'mimesis' and my dis-tinction of 'dialectical mimesis' from the ideological kind. Fredric Jameson evokes something similar—a 'pseudo-totality'—at work in *Negative Dialectics*: 'It is as though . . . these totalizing dilemmas of a systematizing philosophy . . . were to be disarmed by the acting out (or the mimesis) of a kind of pseudo-totality (the shamanistic overtones of this formulation are authorized by the Frazerian tribal speculations included in *Dialectic of Enlightenment*' [*Late Marxism* 50]); likewise Robert Kaufman elicits a 'semblance'-commodification operant in Adorno and Benjamin's thinking about 'lyric' (Kaufman, 'Lyric Commodity Critique'). Lambert Zuidervaart cites (and implicitly endorses) Martin Lüdke's analogous distinction of 'mimesis' from 'mimicry' (Zuidervaart 111); but although 'mimicry' regularly connotes unthinking repetition in Adorno, 'mimesis' is not reliably its opposite.

[11] To Thomas Mann Adorno explained that the Husserl book 'is an attempt to break with idealism in an immanent way precisely by pursuing the consequences of its own dialectic. Basically the task is not to confront philosophy with dialecti-cal materialism in an external and dogmatic fashion, but rather to grasp this materialism as the very truth of philosophy in its objectivity. That this has never properly been done before, I am convinced, is in large part responsible for what has become of Marxism. If you read the book with these thoughts in mind, you may be able to forgive the terminological armour-plating on the outside and dis-cover a Brünhilde within—who was also originally conceived as a liberating figure of course' (*AMC* 62).

[12] '[I]mmanent critique . . . has a metacritical intent. Where the text shows itself inadequate by its own criteria, these criteria become problematic . . . Immanent critique becomes metacritique—a combination, often precarious, of dependence upon, and transcendence of, the object of criticism. . . . [and thus] the process of transcending the object takes on the character of self-criticism' (Zuidervaart xx).

[13] Slavoj Zizek similarly reads *Dialectic of Enlightenment* as lapsing into 'idealist' reifi-cations in a provocatively *political* essay, 'From *History and Class Consciousness* to *The Dialectic of Enlightenment* and Back Again'.

[14] Other instances abound; see, e.g., *B* 16, 21; *PNM* 50, 80, 91, 96; *NL1* 16; *CM* 160; *AT* 23, 30, 84, 196, 199, 236, 292.

Chapter 4: Narrative and Its Discontents

[1] I am citing Bernstein where my difference with him is most telling and useful; I hope it goes without saying that there's no question here of which of us is 'right' and which 'wrong': the question is, what lights can our differing approaches shed? Bernstein amplifies his argument in *The Fate of Art* (226–33) and 'Negative Dialectic as Fate' (Huhn 19–51; see especially 21–30).

² For a dazzling account of Benjamin's poetics or historiography of standstill in the 'Theses on the Philosophy of History', see Zizek, *Sublime Object* 136–45.

³ Despite her title, Karin Bauer in *Adorno's Nietzschean Narratives* is little concerned with narrative as such. She sees Adorno as 'Nietzschean' in offering 'counter-narratives' to the received ones, rather than, as I do here, enacting a critical contravention of the conventions (ideologies) of narrative itself. She does not link Adorno's practice to his and Benjamin's critique of historicism.

⁴ 'In a similar sense to that in which there is only Hegelian philosophy, in the history of Western music there is only Beethoven' (*B* 10); [Beethoven's music] 'expressed the same experiences which inspired Hegel's concept of the World-spirit' (*B* 32); 'In Beethoven's procedures the most profound features of Hegelian philosophy will be discerned . . .' (*B* 62); 'Beethoven's music is Hegelian philosophy' (*B* 14); Beethoven's music is 'comparable in power only to the philosophy of Hegel' (*B* 142); Beethoven 'is really more Hegelian than Hegel . . .' (*B* 160).

⁵ The passage of course bears other narratives as well; Albrecht Wellmer's 'The Death of the Sirens' proposes three of them, as well as a way of reading them 'stereoscopically'. See also Comay, Love.

⁶ For a discussion linking Adorno's 'philosophy of music' not only to his ambitions for 'immanent critique', but to his actual writing, see Plass 41–8. On the 'new music' as a model for Adorno's 'dissonant' critique, see Jay, *Adorno* 56–81; Hullot-Kentor, *Things Beyond Resemblance* 67–76; Savage, 'Dissonant Conjunctions'; and White-book, 'From Schoenberg to Odysseus'. Michael Spitzer tests a reader's expertise in musicology as well as in philosophy, but with special reference to *Dialectic of Enlightenment*, see 262–80.

Works Cited

Works by Adorno

(Abbreviations key)

'Adequacy': 'On the Historical Adequacy of Consciousness', *Telos* 56 (Summer 1983), 97–103.

AE: *Against Epistemology: A Metacritique*, trans. Willis Domingo. Oxford: Blackwell, 1982.

AMC: With Thomas Mann. *Correspondence 1943–1955*, ed. Christoph Gödde and Thomas Sprecher; trans. Nicholas Walker. Cambridge UK: Polity, 2006.

AR: *The Adorno Reader*, ed. Brian O'Connor. Blackwell: Oxford, UK; Malden, MA, 2000.

AT: *Aesthetic Theory*, trans. Robert Hullot-Kentor. Minneapolis: U of Minnesota P, 1997.

B: *Beethoven: The Philosophy of Music*, ed. Rolf Tiedemann; trans. Edmund Jephcott. Stanford: Stanford UP, 1998.

CC: With Walter Benjamin, *The Complete Correspondence, 1928–1940*, ed. Henri Lonitz; trans. Nicholas Walker. Cambridge, MA: Harvard UP, 1999.

CI: *The Culture Industry: Selected Essays on Mass Culture*, ed. J. M. Bernstein. London and New York: Routledge, 2006.

CM: *Critical Models: Interventions and Catchwords*, trans. Henry W. Pickford. New York: Columbia UP, 1998.

Cumming: With Max Horkheimer, *Dialectic of Enlightenment*, trans. John Cumming. New York: Continuum, 1988.

EM: *Essays on Music*, ed. Richard Leppert. U of California P: Berkeley, Los Angeles, London, 2002.

GS1: *Philosophische Frühschriften*, in Adorno, Theodor W., *Gesammelte Schriften, Band 1*, ed. Rolf Tiedemann. Frankfurt: Suhrkamp, 1996.

GS3: With Max Horkheimer, *Dialektik der Aufklärung*, in Adorno, Theodor W., *Gesammelte Schriften, Band 3*, ed. Rolf Tiedemann. Frankfurt: Suhrkamp, 1996.

GS11: *Noten Zu Literatur*, in Adorno, Theodor W., *Gesammelte Schriften, Band 11*, ed. Rolf Tiedemann. Frankfurt: Suhrkamp, 1996.

GS12: *Philosophie der neuen Musik*, in Adorno, Theodor W., *Gesammelte Schriften, Band 12*, ed. Rolf Tiedemann. Frankfurt: Suhrkamp, 1990.

H&F: *History and Freedom: Lectures 1964–1965*, ed. Rolf Tiedemann; trans. Rodney Livingstone. Cambridge UK: Polity, 2006.

HTS: Hegel: Three Studies, trans. Shierry Weber Nicholsen. Cambridge, MA: MIT, 1994.

'Idea': 'The Idea of Natural History', trans. Bob [a.k.a. Robert] Hullot-Kentor, *Telos* 60 (1984), 110–24. Reprinted in Hullot-Kentor, *Things Beyond Resemblance* 252–69.

IS: Introduction to Sociology, trans. Edmund Jephcott. Stanford: Stanford UP, 2000.

ISW: In Search of Wagner, trans. Rodney Livingstone. London: NLB, 1981; rpt. with different pagination, London and New York: Verso, 2005. Page references in the text are to both editions, separated by a slash.

Jephcott: With Max Horkheimer, *Dialectic of Enlightenment*, trans. Edmund Jephcott. Stanford CA: Stanford UP, 2002.

KCA: Kierkegaard: Construction of the Aesthetic, trans. Robert Hullot-Kentor. Minneapolis: U of Minnesota P, 1989.

KCPR: Kant's Critique of Pure Reason, ed. Rolf Tiedemann; trans. Rodney Livingstone. Stanford: Stanford UP, 2001.

LHP: Letters to His Parents: 1939–1951, ed. Christoph Gödde and Henri Lonitz; trans. Wieland Hoban. Cambridge UK: Polity, 2006.

MCP: Metaphysics: Concept and Problems, ed. Rolf Tiedemann; trans. Edmund Jephcott. Stanford: Stanford UP, 2000.

MM: Minima Moralia: Reflections from Damaged Life, trans. E. F. N. Jephcott. London: Verso, 1974.

MMP: Mahler: A Musical Physiognomy, trans. Edmund Jephcott. Chicago: U of Chicago P, 1992.

ND: Negative Dialectics, trans. E. B. Ashton. New York: Continuum, 1973.

NL1 and *NL2: Notes on Literature*, 2 volumes, trans. Shierry Weber Nicholsen. New York: Columbia UP, 1992.

P. Prisms, trans. Samuel and Shierry Weber. Cambridge, MA: MIT, 1981.

PDGS: With Hans Albert, Ralf Dahrendorf, Jürgen Hambermas, Harald Pilot, and Karl Popper. *The Positivist Dispute in German Sociology*, trans. Glyn Adey and David Frisby. London: Heinemann, 1977.

PMM: Philosophy of Modern Music, trans. Anne G. Mitchell and Wesley V. Blomster. New York: Continuum, 1994.

PMP: Problems of Moral Philosophy, ed. Thomas Schröder; trans. Rodney Livingstone. Stanford: Stanford UP, 2001.

PNM: Philosophy of New Music, trans. Robert Hullot-Kentor. Minneapolis: U of Minnesota P, 2006.

QUF. Quasi Una Fantasia: Essays on Modern Music, trans. Rodney Livingstone. London and New York: Verso, 1998.

Works by Others

Bauer, Karin (1999), *Adorno's Nietzschean Narratives: Critiques of Ideology, Readings of Wagner*. Albany, NY: SUNY.

Benjamin, Walter (1969), *Illuminations*, ed. Hannah Arendt; trans. Harry Zohn. New York: Schocken.

— (1983), *Charles Baudelaire: The Lyric Poet in the Era of High Capitalism*, trans. Harry Zohn. New York: Verso.

— (1998), *The Origin of German Tragic Drama*, trans. John Osborne. New York: Verso.

— (1999), *The Arcades Project*, ed. Rolf Tiedemann; trans. Howard Eiland and Kevin McLaughlin. Cambridge, MA: Belknap/Harvard UP.

Berlin, Isaiah and Ramin Jahanbegloo (1992), *Conversations with Isaiah Berlin.* London: Peter Halban.

Bernstein, J. M. (1992), *The Fate of Art: Aesthetic Alienation from Kant to Derrida and Adorno.* Oxford: Polity.

— (2001), *Adorno: Disenchantment and Ethics.* Cambridge UK: Cambridge UP.

Bloom, Harold (1973), *The Anxiety of Influence.* New York: Oxford UP.

Browning, Gary K., ed. (1997), *Hegel's* Phenomenology of Spirit: *A Reappraisal.* Dordrecht, Boston, and London: Kluwer Academic Publishers.

Buck-Morss, Susan (1977), *The Origin of Negative Dialectics: Theodor W. Adorno, Walter Benjamin, and the Frankfurt Institute.* Sussex: Harvester P.

— (1989), *The Dialectics of Seeing: Walter Benjamin and the Arcades Project.* Cambridge, MA and London: MIT.

Bürger, Peter (1991), 'Adorno's Anti-Avant-Gardism', *Telos* 86, 49–60.

Cahn, Michael (1984), 'Subversive Mimesis: Theodor W. Adorno and the Modern Impasse of Critique', in Spariosu, Mihai, ed., *Mimesis in Contemporary Theory: Volume I: The Literary and Philosophical Debate.* Philadelphia and Amsterdam: John Benjamins, 27–64.

Comay, Rebecca (2000), 'Adorno's Siren Song', *New German Critique* 81, 21–48.

De Man, Paul (1982), 'Sign and Symbol in Hegel's *Aesthetics*', *Critical Inquiry* 8(4), 761–75.

— (1983), 'Hegel on the Sublime', in *Displacement: Derrida and After*, ed. Mark Krupnik. Bloomington: Indiana University Press, 139–53.

Detlev Claussen (2008), *Theodor W. Adorno: One Last Genius*, trans. Rodney Livingstone. Cambridge, MA and London: Harvard UP.

Derrida, Jacques (1976), *Of Grammatology*, trans. Gayatri Chakravorty Spivak. Baltimore and London: Johns Hopkins UP.

— (1982), *Glas*, trans. John P. Leavey, Jr., and Richard Rand. Lincoln: U of Nebraska P.

— (1982), *Margins of Philosophy*, trans. Alan Bass. Chicago: U of Chicago P.

Düttmann, Alexander Garcia (2002), *The Memory of Thought: An Essay on Heidegger and Adorno*, trans. Nicholas Walker. London and New York: Continuum.

Eagleton, Terry (1990), *The Ideology of the Aesthetic.* Oxford: Blackwell.

Forster, Michael N. (1998), *Hegel's Idea of a Phenomenology of Spirit.* Chicago and London: U of Illinois P.

Freud, Sigmund (1960), *The Ego and the Id*, trans. James Strachey. New York: W. W. Norton.

— (1961), *Beyond the Pleasure Principle*, trans. James Strachey. New York: W. W. Norton.

— (1962), *Civilization and Its Discontents*, trans. James Strachey. New York: W. W. Norton.

— (1963), *General Psychological Theory*, ed. Philip Rieff. New York: Collier.

— (1965), *The Interpretation of Dreams*, ed. and trans. James Strachey. New York: Avon.

— (1967), *Moses and Monotheism*, trans. Katherine Jones. New York: Vintage.

— (1977), *Introductory Lectures on Psychoanalysis*, trans. James Strachey. New York: W. W. Norton.

Habermas, Jürgen (1986), *Autonomy and Solidarity: Interviews*, ed. Peter Dews. London: Verso.

— (1987), *The Philosophical Discourse of Modernity*, trans. Frederick G. Lawrence. Cambridge, MA: MIT.

Hamacher, Werner (1998), *Pleroma: Reading in Hegel*, trans. Nicholas Walker and Simon Jarvis. Stanford: Stanford UP.

Hegel, G. W. F. (1952), *Philosophy of Right*, trans. T. M. Knox. London, New York: Oxford UP.

— (1977), *Phenomenology of Spirit*, trans. A. V. Wallace. Oxford: Oxford UP.

— (1984), *The Letters*, trans. Clark Butler and Christine Seiler. Bloomington: Indiana UP.

— (1989), *Science of Logic*, trans. A. V. Miller. Atlantic Highlands, NJ: Humanities Press International.

— (1991), *The Encyclopedia Logic: Part I*, trans. T. F. Geraets, W. A. Suchting, and H. S. Harris. Indianapolis: Hackett.

— (1991), *Philosophy of History*, trans. J. Sibree. Buffalo, NY: Prometheus Books.

— (1998), *The Aesthetics*, trans. T. M. Knox. Oxford: Oxford UP.

Honneth, Axel (2000), 'The Possibility of a Disclosing Critique of Society: the *Dialectic of Enlightenment* in Light of Current Debates in Social Criticism', *Constellations* 7(1), 116–27.

Honneth, Axel, Thomas McCarthy, Claus Offe, and Albrecht Wellmer, ed. (1992), *Philosophical Interventions in the Unfinished Project of Enlightenment*. Cambridge, MA and London: MIT.

Horkheimer, Max (1999), *Critical Theory: Selected Essays*, trans. Matthew J. O'Connell et al. New York: Continuum.

— (1999), *The Eclipse of Reason*. New York: Continuum.

Hoy, David Couzens and Thomas McCarthy (1994), *Critical Theory*. Oxford UK and Cambridge MA: Blackwell.

Huhn, Tom, ed. (2004), *The Cambridge Companion to Adorno*. Cambridge UK and New York: Cambridge UP.

— and Lambert Zuidervaart, ed. (1997), *The Semblance of Subjectivity: Essays in Adorno's Aesthetic Theory*. Cambridge, MA and London: MIT.

Hullot-Kentor, Robert 'Introduction to Adorno's "Idea of Natural History"' (1984), *Telos* 60, 97–110. Reprinted in Hullot-Kentor, *Things Beyond Resemblance* 234–51.

— (1989), 'Back to Adorno', *Telos* 81, 5–29. Reprinted in Hullot-Kentor, *Things Beyond Resemblance* 23–44.

— (2006), *Things Beyond Resemblance: Collected Essays on Theodor Adorno*. New York: Columbia UP.

Hyppolite, Jean (1972), 'The Structure of Philosophic Language According to the "Preface" to Hegel's *Phenomenology of the Mind*' [sic] and 'Discussion', in *The Structuralist Controversy*, ed. Richard Macksey and Eugenio Donato. Baltimore: Johns Hopkins UP, 157–85.

— (1974), *Genesis and Structure of Hegel's* Phenomenology of Spirit, trans. Samuel Cherniak and John Heckman. Evanston IL: Northwestern UP.

Jameson, Fredric (1971), *Marxism and Form*. Princeton: Princeton UP.

— (1989), 'Regarding Postmodernism': Interview with Anders Stephanson, in *Postmodernism, Jameson, Critique*, ed. Douglas Kellner. Washington DC: Institute for Advanced Cultural Studies/Maisonneuve Press, 43–74.

— (1990), *Late Marxism: Adorno, or, the Persistence of the Dialectic*. London and New York: Verso.

— (1990), *Postmodernism, Or, The Cultural Logic of Capitalism*. Durham, NC: Duke UP.

— (2007), *The Modernist Papers*. London and New York: Verso.

Jarvis, Simon (1998), *Adorno: A Critical Introduction*. New York: Routledge.

Jay, Martin (1973), *The Dialectical Imagination: A History of the Frankfurt School and the Institute of Social Research, 1923–1950*. Boston and Toronto: Little, Brown.

— (1984), *Adorno*. Cambridge, MA: Harvard UP.

— (1984), *Marxism and Totality: The Adventures of a Concept from Lukács to Habermas*. Berkeley CA: U of California P.

Kaufman, Robert (2000), 'Red Kant, or the Persistence of the Third *Critique* in Adorno and Jameson', *Critical Inquiry* 26(4), 682–724.

— (2005), 'Lyric's Constellation, Poetry's Radical Privilege', *Modernist Cultures* 1(2), 209–34.

— (2006), 'Poetry's Ethics? Theodor W. Adorno and Robert Duncan on Aesthetic Illusion and Sociopolitical Delusion', *New German Critique*, 97, 73–118.

— (2008), 'Lyric Commodity Critique, Benjamin Adorno Marx, Baudelaire Baudelaire Baudelaire', *PMLA* 123(1), 207–15.

Kaufmann, Walter (1965), *Hegel: Reinterpretation, Texts, Commentary*. Doubleday: Garden City, NY.

Kojève, Alexandre (1980), *Introduction to the Reading of Hegel*, trans. Raymond Queneau. Ithaca: Cornell UP.

Lacoue-Labarthe, Philippe and Jean-Luc Nancy (1988), *The Literary Absolute: The Theory of Literature in German Romanticism*, trans. Philip Barnard and Cheryl Lester. Albany: SUNY.

Lévi-Strauss, Claude (1969), *The Elementary Structures of Kinship*, trans. James Harle Bell, John Richard von Sturmer, and Rodney Needham. Boston: Beacon P, 1969.

Love, Nancy S. (1999), 'Why Do the Sirens Sing?: Figuring the Feminine in *Dialectic of Enlightenment*', *Theory and Event* 3(1).

Lukács, Georg (1971), 'Art and Objective Truth', in *Writer and Critic and Other Essays*, ed. Arthur D. Kahn. New York: Grosset and Dunlop, 25–60.

— (1971), 'Healthy or Sick Art?', in *Writer and Critic* 103–9.

— *History and Class Consciousness* (1971), trans. Rodney Livingstone. Cambridge, MA: MIT.

— (1971), 'Narrate or Describe?', in *Writer and Critic* 110–48.

— (1971), 'What is Orthodox Marxism?', in *History and Class Consciousness* 1–26. Reprinted in *Marxism and Human Liberation* 20–48.

— (1973), 'The Ideology of Modernism', in *Marxism and Human Liberation*, ed. E. San Juan, Jr. New York: Delta, 277–307.

— (1980), 'Realism in the Balance', in *Aesthetics and Politics*, ed. Ronald Taylor. New York: Verso, 28–59.

Lyotard, Jean-François (1974), trans. Robert Hurley, 'Adorno as the Devil', *Telos* 9, 127–37.

Mallarmé, Stéphane (1985), 'Crise de Vers', in *Oeuvres*, ed. Yves-Alain Favre. Paris: Garnier, 269–79.

Marx, Karl and Friedrich Engels (1978), *The Marx-Engels Reader*, 2nd ed., ed. Robert C. Tucker. W. W. Norton: New York.

Menke, Christopher (1998), *The Sovereignty of Art: Aesthetic Negativity in Adorno and Derrida.* Cambridge, MA: MIT.

Morgan, Ben (2001), 'The Project of the Frankfurt School', *Telos* 119, 75–98.

Morris, Martin (2001), *Rethinking the Communicative Turn: Adorno, Habermas, and the Problem of Communicative Freedom.* Albany, NY: SUNY.

Müller-Doohm, Stephan (2005), *Adorno: A Biography*, trans. Rodney Livingstone. Cambridge UK: Polity.

Nancy, Jean-Luc (2001), *The Speculative Remark (One of Hegel's Bon Mots)*, trans. Céline Surprenant. Stanford CA: Stanford UP.

Nicholsen, Shierry Weber (1997), *Exact Imagination, Late Work: On Adorno's Aesthetics.* Cambridge, MA: MIT, 1997.

Niethammer, Lutz (1992), *Posthistoire*, trans. Patrick Camiller. New York: Verso.

Nietzsche, Friedrich (1954), *The Portable Nietzsche*, ed. and trans. Walter Kaufmann. New York: Viking.

— (1956), *The Birth of Tragedy and The Genealogy of Morals*, trans. Francis Golffing. Doubleday Anchor: Garden City, NY.

— (1966), *Beyond Good and Evil*, trans. Walter Kaufmann. Random House/Vintage: New York.

Noerr, Gunzelin Schmid (2002), 'Editorial Afterword'. In Horkheimer, Max and Theodor W. Adorno, *Dialectic of Enlightenment*, trans. Edmund Jephcott. Stanford: Stanford UP, 217–47.

Paddison, Max (1993), *Adorno's Aesthetics of Music.* Cambridge UK and New York: Cambridge UP.

Plass, Ulrich (2007), *Language and History in Adorno's* Notes to Literature. Routledge: New York and London.

Rose, Gillian (1978), *The Melancholy Science: An Introduction to the Thought of Theodor W. Adorno.* New York: Columbia UP.

— (1993), 'From Speculative to Dialectical Thinking: Hegel and Adorno', in *Judaism and Modernity: Philosophical Essays.* Cambridge, MA and Oxford: Blackwell, 1993, 3–63.

Savage, Roger W. H. (2004), 'Dissonant Conjunctions: On Schönberg, Adorno, and Bloch', *Telos* 127, 79–95.

Sloterdijk, Peter (1987), *Critique of Cynical Reason*, trans. Michael Eldred. Minneapolis: U of Minnesota P.

Spitzer, Michael (2006), *Music as Philosophy: Adorno and Beethoven's Late Style.* Bloomington and Indianapolis: Indiana UP.

Taylor, Ronald, ed. (1977), *Aesthetics and Politics.* London and New York: Verso.

Thomson, Alex (2006), *Adorno: A Guide for the Perplexed.* London and New York: Continuum.

Verene, Donald Philip (1985), *Hegel's Recollection: A Study of Images in the* Phenomenology of Spirit. Albany: SUNY.

Warminski, Andrzej (1987), *Readings in Interpretation: Hölderlin, Hegel, Heidegger.* Minneapolis: U of Minnesota P.

Weber, Max (1958), *The Protestant Ethic and the Spirit of Capitalism*, trans. Talcott Parsons. Charles Scribner's Sons: New York, 1958.

Weber, Samuel (2000), '"As Though the End of the World had Come and Gone": Critical Theory and the Task of Reading', *New German Critique* 81, 83–105.

Wellmer, Albrecht (1991), 'Truth, Semblance, Reconciliation', in *The Persistence of Modernity*, trans. David Midgley. Cambridge, MA: MIT, 1–35.

— (2000), 'The Death of the Sirens and the Origin of the Work of Art', *New German Critique* 81, 5–19.

Whitebook, Joel (1993), 'From Schoenberg to Odysseus: Aesthetic, Psychic, and Social Synthesis in Adorno and Wellmer', *New German Critique* 58, 45–64.

— (1995), *Perversion and Utopia: A Study in Psychoanalysis and Critical Theory*. Cambridge, MA: MIT.

Wiggershaus, Rolf (1994), *The Frankfurt School: Its History, Theories, and Political Significance*, trans. Michael Robertson. Cambridge, MA: MIT.

Wolin, Richard (1992), *The Terms of Cultural Criticism: The Frankfurt School, Existentialism, Poststructuralism*. New York: Columbia UP.

Zizek, Slavoj (1989), *The Sublime Object of Ideology*. London and New York: Verso.

— (2000), 'From *History and Class Consciousness* to *The Dialectic of Enlightenment* and Back Again', *New German Critique* 81 (Fall 2000), 107–23.

Zuidervaart, Lambert (1991), *Adorno's Aesthetic Theory: The Redemption of Illusion*. Cambridge, MA and London: MIT.

Index